Relocating to Los Angeles and Orange County

CONTENTS

ACKNOWLEDGMENTS

For research: Michelle Tang and Mikell Palma.

For the newcomer's view: Debby Dodds, Cheryl Gurin, Cindy Johns, Madison Lewis, Laura Lippstone, and Jacque Watson.

For editing: David Richardson and Andrew Vallas.

For Design: Melanie Haage.

For lawyering: Paul Levine.

For other insights: Deni Loubert and Dennis Mallonee.

Thanks to one and all.

INTRODUCTION

In Southern California—in particular, Los Angeles County and Orange County—you'll find people with silicone-filled bodies and spongy brains, a way of life that venerates cars and sneers at pedestrians, and no culture except for several hundred woozy religious cults. And don't forget the smog that chokes the lungs, earthquakes that shatter the buildings, gangs that are brutally violent, cops who are even worse, and no seasons. At least, that's what the detractors say.

Me, I like it here. As far as I'm concerned, Southern California is like sex: Even when it's bad, it's still pretty good. And when it's good, which is a lot of the time, it's my favorite place in the world.

What about the silicone bodies and car veneration and cults and spongy brains? All of that stuff is here if you want to look for it. But if you don't want it, you don't have to go near it. Even the smog and earthquakes don't go everywhere—at least, not everywhere at once—and you can even find snow and other evidence of distinct seasons not far away.

But if you expect a conventional urban experience, Southern California will startle you. When you stroll midtown Manhattan, for instance, you find an entire city hurtling your way. From the aromas of street-vendor hot dogs to the flashes from animated billboards to the blasts of truck horns to the onrushing hordes of roiling crowds, Manhattan and other cities thrust a million experiences at you at once.

Southern California doesn't work that way. This region has just about everything that other urban areas do, including street vendors and animated billboards, but they're spread out over a vast region, waiting for you to discover them.

That's what this book is about: helping you discover them.

The first thing to understand about the area is its size. Taken together, Los Angeles County and Orange County comprise more than 5,000 square miles. That's more than Delaware, Rhode Island, and the District of Columbia combined. You could take New York City, Chicago, Houston, and Philadelphia, lay them down together like jigsaw-puzzle pieces, and you'd fill only about a fourth of L.A. and Orange counties.

Because the region is so vast, it lives by the automobile. Many people say that you can't live here without a car. That's not true. I spent years here without one. But if you don't have one, you'll spend a lot of time waiting and walking. The public transit system eventually can take you to neighborhoods full of retail stores and other businesses; but to get into less bustling areas, like the southeast parts of Orange County, the high desert near Palmdale, or even the cozy homes of the Hollywood Hills, the nondriver will need a good pair of walking shoes or a sturdy bicycle and lots of free time. Or a friend who has a car.

The area is surprisingly varied. You can stand on a sunny beach and see snowy mountains, then drive to them within a couple of hours. Almost any terrain—desert, forest, hillside, lake shore—is easily accessible to anyone with a car. Not to mention all kinds of neighborhoods: the wealthy enclave of Beverly Hills, the artists' colony of Laguna Beach, the college-filled academic haven in Pasadena, and the halfway foreign districts like Los Angeles's Koreatown and Little Tokyo.

The region's variety and spread make it perfect for the person who wants both diversity and privacy, who likes the variety and amenities of city life but wants more room and space than he or she can get in the tightly cramped, maddeningly crowded neighborhoods typical of some other urban areas.

The difference between Southern California and other places can take some getting used to. Author David Clark, in his book *L.A. on Foot: A Free Afternoon,* put it well: "A person could easily live in Los Angeles for years without ever getting to know anyone, and many have. Yet the city also offers to that same person a variety of experiences and lifestyles of fantastic diversity. Variety, the chance to choose between different paths, is the very definition of freedom. L.A. thrusts freedom upon you, whether you want it or not." Clark was talking not just about the city of Los Angeles but about the whole region, and he was and is right. Few places on Earth give you so much freedom and opportunity to pursue happiness in your own way.

Newcomers sometimes complain that it's hard to make friends here. Fortunately, the area's sheer variety allows it to accommodate all kinds of people, and those people form all kinds of groups. From the ultra-conservatives of Newport Beach to the ultra-liberals of what's sometimes called the People's Republic of Santa Monica, from the Athletic Singles Association to the Silent Society (for fans of silent movies) to the Academy of Magical Arts, the region has enough associations, organizations, street festivals, nightclubs, support groups, and religious communities that a person with almost any interest or hobby can find people who share it.

Why does Southern California offer so many choices? Because the people want it that way. They often come here to escape more tradition-bound communities and to create new lives. It's easy to do, because the place is fairly new—at least as far as the history of Western civilization is concerned.

The region's recorded history began in 1769, when the city of Boston was already nearly 150 years old and Mexico City more than 250. Gaspar de Portola, the Spanish governor of Mexico's Baja California, led a few dozen explorers up the California coast. He found valleys and fields that could easily support agriculture, plus rivers that supplied them with water. He named one of the rivers Santa Ana; one of his men, a priest named Juan Crespi, named another Los Angeles.

Portola and his men also found people: Chumashes, Gabrielinos, and others who would today be called Native Americans. They lived by hunting the abundant wildlife, and they didn't offer Portola's group much resistance.

For the natives' own sake, maybe they should have. The foreigners carried unfamiliar diseases that killed quite a few of the locals, and conquest wiped out even more.

The conquest wasn't much at first: In the wake of Portola's explorations, Spanish missionaries settled in the area. But eventually, the missions—including San Juan Capistrano in what's now Orange

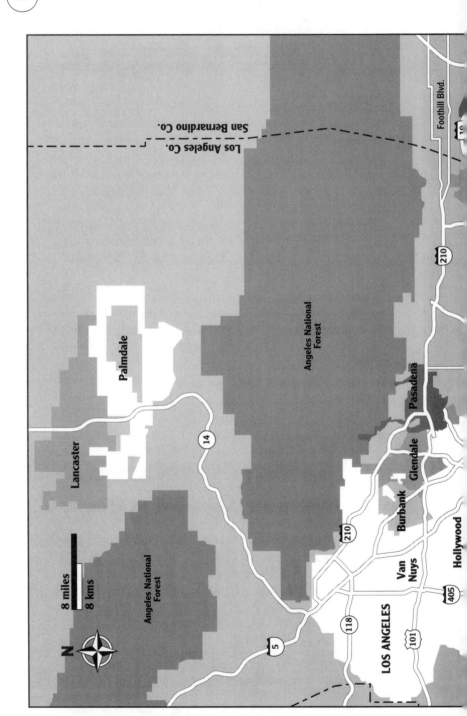

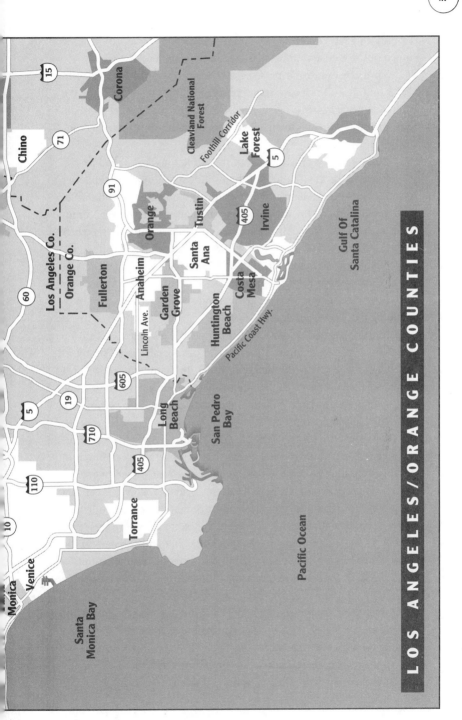

LOS ANGELES/ORANGE COUNTIES

County and San Fernando Rey in L.A. County—ended up controlling much of the land and political power in the region.

Southern California passed from Spanish control to Mexico in 1822, and into the United States' possession in 1848. Then came the railroads—one line from San Francisco in 1876 and another from the East in 1885—which ignited a land boom that in some ways has continued until this day.

Real estate was only the first of the attractions that pulled people to the region. In the first half of the twentieth century, the industries of oil, defense (especially aircraft), and entertainment grew like wild, and people flooded the area to join them. During World War II, millions of soldiers trained in the area and disembarked there after their hitch, and quite a few stayed. After the war, the creation of the interstate highway system built the freeways, which allowed the area's vast labor force to have homes a great distance from their workplaces yet travel between them quickly. The freeways sparked a boom of suburb building that is still going on.

It's not just the freeways that bring people out here. Part of the area's appeal is its famous climate. The place really is as sunny as you've heard. Even in the dead of winter, the temperature in most well-populated areas rarely falls below the 40s and can reach into the 80s. As the screenwriter William Goldman has said, "Unless you're a Hawaiian born and bred, the weather is terrific."

But watch out for its variations. You can find a twenty-degree difference between Canoga Park in L.A. County and Newport Beach in Orange County. The commute from Santa Monica to downtown L.A., which thousands make every day, can mean getting into your car in a neighborhood that's less than seventy degrees and getting out in a place that's over 80. Lancaster, in the high desert at the northwest part of L.A. County, dips below freezing in December and shoots into the high 90s in July, and can rise or fall thirty degrees in a single month.

For all of the area's uniqueness, a surprise that dawns on people once they spend a little time in Southern California is how much it's like other areas. Not everyone here is a surfer, actor, or nutjob. Most people are normal: They raise kids, pay their taxes, fantasize about garrotting the boss—the usual stuff.

But everyone here knows that Southern California is, in many ways, a charmed land. Take a simple walk on the always available beach, and you'll see bodies of a kind that the ancient Greeks imagined for their gods. (According to actor Rob Lowe, no small beauty himself, the entertainment industry has attracted a lot of pretty people who wanted to find stardom but instead found each other and made gorgeous kids.) Drive to work, and you might pass a world-famous film studio or streets lined with the long white moving vans that signal a movie being shot on location. Go outside in December and get a tan. Hop in the car and, within an hour, drive so deep into a thick-forested mountain range that you can forget that civilization exists—or get tired of the mountains and stroll through a small city 30 minutes away.

God knows that the place has its faults. But its openness and diversity allow anyone who comes here to choose a new life or improve on an old one. That's why L.A. County and Orange County have been growing for decades and haven't stopped yet.

And it's why natives and newcomers alike have no plans to leave.

Los Angeles and Orange County Statistics

Climate

Average Temperature by Season
(L.A. County and Orange County)

Winter:	57 degrees
Spring:	60 degrees
Summer:	68 degrees
Autumn:	66 degrees

Source: Oakwood Corporate Housing

Average Rainfall

Winter:	1.5 inches per month
Spring:	1.1 inches per month
Summer:	0 inches per month
Autumn:	1.4 inches per month

Source: Oakwood Corporate Housing

Except for the mountains at the eastern side of the two counties, most of the area gets virtually no snowfall.

Population

Los Angeles County: 9,800,000
Orange County: 2,700,000

Sources: Los Angeles County and Orange County

Population by Ethnicity

Los Angeles County

75.2%	*White*
11.2%	*Black*
12.9%	*Asian/Pacific Islander*
0.6%	*Native American*
43%	*Hispanic (of any race)*
<1%	*Other*

Orange County

84.8%	*White*
1.8%	*Black*
12.8%	*Asian/Pacific Islander*
0.6%	*Native American*
27.9%	*Hispanic (of any race)*

Source: USA Counties (University of Oregon)

Population by Gender

Los Angeles County

49.9%	*Male*
50.1%	*Female*

Orange County

50.4%	*Male*
49.6%	*Female*

Source: USA Counties (University of Oregon)

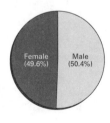

Population by Age

Los Angeles County

8.3%	*Under 5*
13.9%	*5 to 14*
10.8%	*15 to 21*
15.7%	*22 to 29*
17.9%	*30 to 39*
12.1%	*40 to 49*
8.0%	*50 to 59*
6.8%	*60 to 69*
4.3%	*70 to 79*
2.2%	*80 and up*

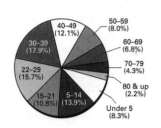

Orange County

7.7%	*Under 5*
12.9%	*5 to 14*
10.7%	*15 to 21*
16.0%	*22 to 29*
18.0%	*30 to 39*
13.3%	*40 to 49*
8.7%	*50 to 59*
6.7%	*60 to 69*
3.9%	*70 to 79*
2.1%	*80 and up*

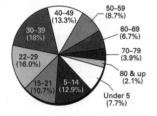

Source: USA Counties (University of Oregon)

Average Annual Income

Los Angeles County

Per capita:	*$21,562*
Per household:	*$32,689*

Orange County

Per capita:	*$25,516*
Per household:	*$45,116*

Source: USA Counties (University of Oregon)

Housing

Average Monthly Rent for a Three-Bedroom Apartment

Los Angeles County: *$995*

Orange County: *$1,193*

Source: Department of Housing and Urban Development

Median Price for a House

Los Angeles County: *$200,000*

Orange County: *$260,000*

Source: Los Angeles Times

Median Price for a Condominium

Los Angeles County: *$160,000*

Orange County: *$160,000*

Source: Los Angeles Times

Books and Resources

Perhaps the first and most important book to buy is a *Thomas Guide*. Since 1915, Thomas Brothers has been publishing maps, and their spiral-bound overviews of Southern California are close to definitive. The company has individual books for Los Angeles and Orange counties, and a combination book that contains both. Without a *Thomas Guide*, getting around the area is terribly confusing and just plain difficult.

For information on settling in the area, *McCormack's Guides* offer information on everything from rental housing to crime rates to how to get a driver's license. The company offers books on both Los Angeles County and Orange County.

Since Southern California isn't a cheap place to live, you should get *Buying Retail is Stupid!* by Trisha King and Deborah Newmark (NMI Publishers). This book is filled with advice, store listings, and coupons for discounts at shops all over the area.

If you have kids, try *Fun with the Family in Southern California* by Laura Kath Fraser and Pamela Price Lechtman (Globe Pequot) as well as *Where Should We Take the Kids?: California* by Clark Norton

(Fodor's). These books cover amusement parks, hotels, restaurants, and other places to take the family for a little fun.

Speaking of restaurants, the *Zagat Survey* is very helpful. It lists hundreds of restaurants in the two counties and beyond, and delivers information about price, type of food, quality of food, quality of service, and many other critical factors.

For excursions and entertaining out-of-town guests (and believe me, you will get them; everyone wants to visit Southern Cal), there are any number of guidebooks, such as *Let's Go: California, Fodor's Up Close: Los Angeles,* Gayot's *The Best of Los Angeles and Southern California, Mobil's Travel Guide: California and the West* and *The California Coast: A Traveler's Companion* by Donald B. Neuwirth and John J. Osborn, Jr. (Countryman).

For guests and for yourself, there are specialized guides such as *Day Hiker's Guide to Southern California* by John McKinney (Olympus), *Museum Companion to Los Angeles* by Borislav Stanic (Museon), and *L.A. Bizarro: The Insider's Guide to the Obscure, the Absurd, and the Perverse in Los Angeles* by Anthony R. Lovett and Matt Maranian (Buzz/St. Martin's).

The region has a nice selection of magazines and newspapers to keep you apprised of attractions and necessities. The *Los Angeles Times* dominates the area, but don't neglect the *Daily News* (for Los Angeles's San Fernando Valley) or the *Orange County Register.* There are also weekly alternative papers, generally free of charge: *New Times, L.A. Weekly,* and its Orange County sister *OC Weekly.* For the upscale among us, there are the slick monthlies *Los Angeles* and *Orange Coast.* And as you might expect in an area this diverse, there are lots of specialty papers, from the Spanish-language daily *La Opinion* to the *Jewish Journal.*

Most if not all SoCal publications have Web sites full of information about their areas. There are also several good general sites unconnected to publications, like these:

- @LA, the Los Angeles and Southern California Guide: *www.at-la.com/*
- InfoOutfitters, Compilers of Decision Enabling Information: *www.infooutfitters.com/*
- Orangecounty.com, Orange County's Search Engine: *www.orangecounty.com.home.html*

For relocation and moving information, try the following.

- American Relocation Center: *www.buyingrealestate.com/*
- Relocation Tools: *www.homefair.com/homefair/newstool.html?NETSCAPE_LIVEWIRE,src=jobbank*
- MoversNet (government information on moving): *www.usps.gov/moversnet/*
- Electronic Relocation Guide: *relo-usa.com/*
- Relo-USA (relocation information): *www.relo-california.com/*

Of course, among the most important fountainheads of information is the government. Here are some useful sources.

Los Angeles County Board of Supervisors
Kenneth Hahn Hall of Administration
500 West Temple Street
Los Angeles, CA 90012
(213) 974-1311

www.co.la.ca.us

Orange County Government Center
10 Civic Center Plaza
Santa Ana, CA 92701-4061
(714) 834-3100

www.oc.ca.gov/

Los Angeles County

ANTELOPE VALLEY

The Antelope Valley is an island surrounded by land. A wide, flat slab of arid soil, the valley lies near the Mojave Desert at the northern edge of Los Angeles County, more than fifty miles from the city of Los Angeles. There's only one way to get to the valley from other parts of the county: take the Antelope Valley Freeway (also known as Highway 14) through the San Gabriel Mountains, the Angeles National Forest, and the famous San Andreas earthquake fault. A sign of the distance comes through on your radio: FM band 88.9 broadcasts the major National Public Radio station in most of L.A. County, but in the Antelope Valley it becomes a source of Christian radio.

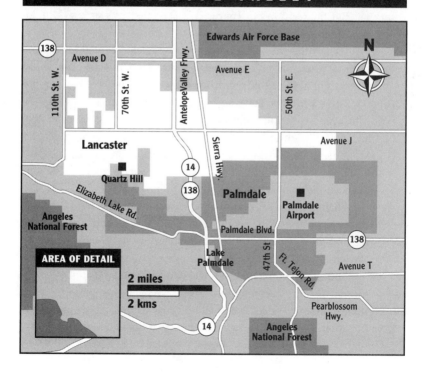

ANTELOPE VALLEY

Because the Antelope Valley is so isolated from the rest of Los Angeles County, it's not exactly a sophisticated, cosmopolitan urban experience. Don't come here looking for the region's hippest jazz club or fanciest restaurant. Nor is it a mecca for intellectual heavyweights; it's nowhere near as thick with colleges as such towns as Claremont or Fullerton.

But the valley has quite a few advantages. It has lots of parks, nature preserves, and other places for outdoor fun. Its air is some of the cleanest in Southern California. It's the home of Edwards Air Force Base, the test-flight mecca that author Tom Wolfe celebrated in his book *The Right Stuff*. And it's one of the fastest-growing places in Southern California, quickly attracting industry and jobs.

LANCASTER

With about 130,000 people on nearly eighty-nine square miles, Lancaster's the biggest town in the Antelope Valley. In a sense, it's the valley's unofficial capital.

But the real story of Lancaster isn't in the city's streets or buildings. It's in the air.

It's not the weather, although the weather is something to consider if you plan to move there. Lancaster tends to have wilder extremes of hot and cold temperature than other parts of L.A. County.

No, it's the sky. Look up in Lancaster, and you'll see a blue sky with white stripes: the contrails of jets. Lancaster is proud of its connection with Edwards Air Force Base and military flight in general. Monuments to pilots line one of the town's main streets, Lancaster Boulevard, and the local baseball field, Lancaster Municipal Stadium, has been nicknamed the Hangar.

Flight isn't the only outdoor activity that the citizens of Lancaster enjoy. The city proudly sponsors an alfalfa festival and a poppy festival, and the city park's softball field advertises itself with the slogan, "Where else 'ya gonna play?"

Lancaster's populace is younger and whiter than that of other Los Angeles County communities. The town's housing prices are low, while household income is high. There's a little bit of cowboy to Lancaster: The town has two museums that celebrate the Old West.

Palmdale, to Lancaster's south, may soon outstrip Lancaster in sheer population. But with its focus on aviation, Lancaster may remain the heart of the Antelope Valley.

Neighborhood Statistical Profile

Population by Ethnicity

4%	Asian
8%	Black
25%	Hispanic
1%	Native American
62%	White
<1%	Other

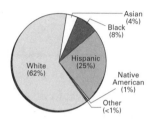

Population by Gender

50%	Female
50%	Male

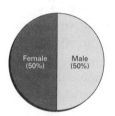

Population by Age

24%	0–13
16%	14–24
15%	25–34
17%	35–44
16%	45–59
3%	60–64
9%	65+

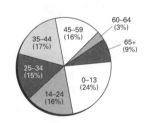

Crime

Arson, 37	Homicide, 8
Assault, 1,021	Petty theft, 2,190
Auto theft, 624	Rape, 57
Burglary, 1,215	Robbery, 253

Housing Costs

Average rent:	*$490*
Average house price:	*$134,934*

Income

Per capita:	*$24,320*
Median household:	*$56,557*

Source: Info Outfitters

PALMDALE

Palmdale doesn't feel like a city of more than seventy square miles that houses more than 120,000 people. You can stand in the middle of the civic center and sense that acres of yellow dirt and scrub brush lie not far away.

The feeling derives only partly from the low, flat buildings (even in the downtown business district) and the clean desert air. It's also a matter of community. Palmdale's a conservative, family-oriented place. Its best-known civic leader is state Senator Pete Knight, who became famous in 1999 for sponsoring a ballot initiative that would make gay marriage unconstitutional in California.

Crime rates are low in Palmdale. The school system's students "consistently score well above average on placement tests," brags the city's Web site.

Palmdale is a haven for skilled technical workers. More than a quarter of the employed citizens work in what the data service Info Outfitters calls "precision production [and] craft," primarily for aerospace companies like Boeing and NASA Dryden Flight Research. The town's largest single employers are in aerospace—the Lockheed Martin "Skunk Works" (5,500 employees) and Northrop Grumman (3,100)—followed by the Palmdale School District (2,500) and Antelope Valley Hospital (1,700).

While other communities in Southern California pursue "slow growth" or "managed growth," Palmdale is not so shy. The city publishes a quarterly brochure called *Growth Factors*; its Winter 2000 issue included headlines like "Palmdale Is Business Friendly!" "New Home Construction on the Rise," and "Retail Development Booming." The city is planning to build its own airport, annex 3,000 acres of nearby land, and improve local roads to prepare for a rise in traffic.

So if Palmdale feels like a small town now, it may not feel that way for long.

Neighborhood Statistical Profile

Population by Ethnicity

5%	Asian
7%	Black
34%	Hispanic
53%	White
1%	Native American
<1%	Other

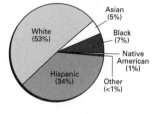

Population by Gender

50%	Female
50%	Male

Population by Age

30%	0–13
15%	14–24
14%	25–34
19%	35–44
15%	45–59
2%	60–64
5%	65+

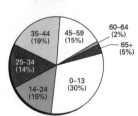

Crime

Arson, 44	Homicide, 7
Assault, 879	Petty theft, 1,028
Auto theft, 581	Rape, 37
Burglary, 1,063	Robbery, 187

Housing Costs

Average rent:	*$419*
Average house price:	*$154,477*

Income

Per capita:	*$19,245*
Median household:	*$53,287*

Source: Info Outfitters

LOS ANGELES VALLEYS

The Conejo Valley, the San Fernando Valley, and the San Gabriel Valley (from west to east) are Los Angeles's bedroom. The area has quite a few businesses, from the Walt Disney Company to Anheuser-Busch,

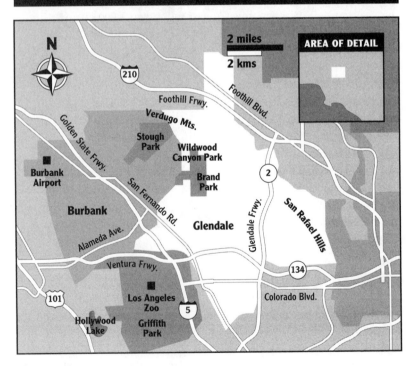

but it's best known as the set of suburbs where workers go to sleep at night.

For a long time, the rap on the valleys was that they rolled up their streets after 7 P.M. Night life was indeed scarce for a long time—even around colleges like California State University Northridge—but areas like Pasadena's Old Town and parts of Ventura Boulevard (the San Fernando Valley's main drag) have livened up in recent years.

Another ongoing trend is the move toward cityhood for the San Fernando Valley. Many citizens, tired of paying Los Angeles City Hall more in taxes than they receive in city services, have pushed for secession. Whether the movement will amount to anything is up in the air.

BURBANK

Hollywood isn't Hollywood; Burbank is Hollywood. That is, Burbank is the home of Warner Bros., the Walt Disney Company, NBC Studios, and other makers of entertainment. (What's more, Universal Studios and DreamWorks aren't far away.) According to the business magazine *Inc.*, Burbank's 17.3 square miles "boast more than 1,000 entertainment businesses and more sound-stage space than New York City." No wonder the town calls itself the media capital of t' world. Even its major shopping mall complex is named the Media Center.

Those who don't work directly in the entertainment business aren't on assembly lines or plowing fields. The lion's share of the work force—about 40 percent—works as administrative personnel, from support staffers to executives.

Nevertheless, Burbank retains something of a blue-collar feeling. Tulsa, Oklahoma, native John Bidasio moved his family there because he wanted a place like Tulsa; he's described Burbank as "a dowdy kind of small town, plain vanilla."

Part of the reason for Burbank's small-town vanilla-ness is age. The town has a higher proportion of people age forty-five or older than many other places in Southern California.

And not everyone spends his life at a studio. One of the most important sites in town is Burbank Airport. On the northeast, the city opens up to the Verdugo Mountains and Wildwood Canyon Park.

So don't get the feeling that Burbank's a village of folk sittin' around the ol' cracker barrel 'n' chewin' the fat. The town's combination of regular folks and the hot, fast surging of its entertainment industry makes Burbank the home of choice for nearly 100,000 people.

Neighborhood Statistical Profile

Population by Ethnicity

8%	Asian
2%	Black
31%	Hispanic
<1%	Native American
59%	White
<1%	Other

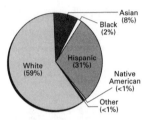

Population by Gender

51%	Female
49%	Male

Population by Age

17%	0–13
11%	14–24
15%	25–34
18%	35–44
20%	45–59
4%	60–64
15%	65+

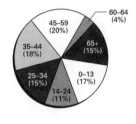

Crime

Arson, 4	Homicide, 4
Assault, 179	Petty theft, 1,853
Burglary, 421	Rape, 8
Auto theft, 601	Robbery, 94

Housing Costs

Average rent:	*$649*
Average home price:	*$263,887*

Income

Per capita:	*$25,367*
Median household:	*$45,869*

Source: Info Outfitters

GLENDALE

With nearly 200,000 people in more than thirty square miles, Glendale is Los Angeles County's third largest city. It's a diverse spot. "Over sixty different languages are spoken in the City's schools," says the city's Web site. "Income levels also vary greatly, [and] the city has strong neighborhood identification, with a total of twenty-three active neighborhood associations."

In other words, community matters in Glendale, so make sure that you find a neighborhood that suits you.

When you do, you'll probably settle in an apartment. To quote the Web site again, "Glendale has one of the highest percentages of multi-family dwelling units of any city in California." In other words, more than half of the citizens live in apartment houses and similar dwellings. And with good reason: The purchase price of a house in Glendale ranks among the highest in Southern California.

Glendale's most prominent business complex isn't in entertainment, like Burbank, or an air force base, like Lancaster, but that icon of family-oriented suburban life and public gatherings: a shopping mall, the Glendale Galleria.

The town is surrounded by the media center Burbank on the west and the more genteel community of Pasadena on the east. A few miles to the south is downtown Los Angeles. If you want your kids to meet different kinds of people, the family-oriented Glendale is a good choice.

Neighborhood Statistical Profile

Population by Ethnicity

18%	Asian
1%	Black
25%	Hispanic
<1%	Native American
56%	White
<1%	Other

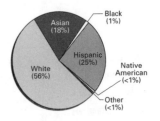

Population by Gender

52%	Female
48%	Male

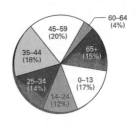

Population by Age

17%	0–13
12%	14–24
14%	25–34
18%	35–44
20%	45–59
4%	60–64
15%	65+

Crime

Arson, 45	Homicide, 2
Assault, 331	Petty theft, 3,178
Auto theft, 873	Rape, 19
Burglary, 737	Robbery, 206

Housing Costs

Average rent:	$675
Average house price:	$349,595

Income

Per capita:	$23,466
Median household:	$41,289

Source: Info Outfitters

PASADENA

"Pasadena is a lush community of 135,000, with quirky bungalows and Spanish-Colonial architecture. The city has an air of Eastern gentility, compared with its crass neighbor, Los Angeles." So wrote travel writer Verne G. Kopytoff in the *New York Times* a few years ago.

One can quibble with the bits about the crass neighbor and the population (it's about 142,000), but for the most part, Kopytoff had it right.

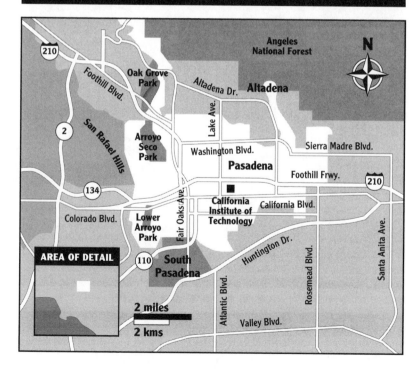

Home of the Rose Bowl football game, the Tournament of Roses parade, the Jet Propulsion Laboratory, and the California Institute of Technology (CalTech), Pasadena's twenty-three square miles combine old money and vibrant youth. Located ten miles northeast of downtown Los Angeles, Pasadena has world-class museums and some of the most venerable mansions in Southern California, and its Old Town section has been transformed into a collection of hip eateries, clubs, and shops.

It's a white-collar place. Its major employers are the Jet Propulsion Lab, CalTech, Huntington Memorial Hospital, Bank of America, Kaiser Permanente Hospital, Pasadena Unified School District, Pasadena City College, Countrywide Credit Industries, the City of Pasadena, and Pacific Bell. The city's Web site reports that the town's population, a fairly diverse mix of young and old, is aging slightly and will lean to the older side in the coming years.

Pasadena has a considerable range of attractions for almost any adult. Even snobs from the East may consider it one of the most civilized cities in all of Southern California.

Neighborhood Statistical Profile

Population by Ethnicity

9%	Asian
18%	Black
35%	Hispanic
<1%	Native American
38%	White
<1%	Other

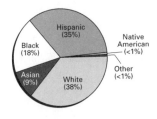

Population by Gender

51%	Female
49%	Male

Population by Age

19%	0–13
12%	14–24
16%	25–34
18%	35–44
17%	45–59
4%	60–64
14%	65+

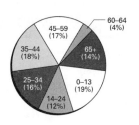

Crime

Arson, 57	Homicide, 10
Assault, 59	Petty theft, 3,432
Auto theft, 548	Rape, 25
Burglary, 1,061	Robbery, 354

Housing Costs

Average rent:	$638
Average house price:	$288,596

Income

Per capita:	$26,096
Median household:	$44,484

Source: Info Outfitters

VAN NUYS (CITY OF LOS ANGELES)

With almost 150,000 people, Van Nuys—or to use the city of Los Angeles government's designation, Van Nuys–North Sherman Oaks— has been one of Los Angeles's fastest-growing neighborhoods (although it has slowed down in recent years).

If you're new to Van Nuys's thirteen square miles, you're not alone. More than half of the people there have lived in the area for five years or less. Nearly 40 percent of the district—bordered on the south by Ventura Boulevard, the west by the 405 Freeway, the east by Coldwater Canyon Avenue, and the north by Southern Pacific railroad tracks—is filled with single-family houses, and most of the residents

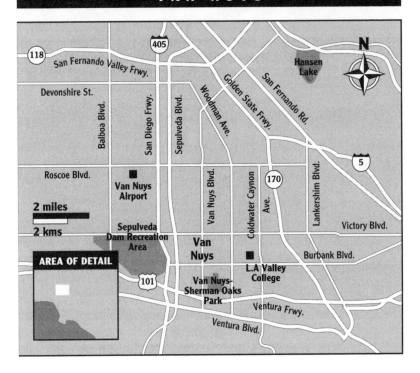

VAN NUYS

118 San Fernando Valley Frwy.

405

Devonshire St.

N

Hansen Lake

San Fernando Rd.

Golden State Frwy.

Balboa Blvd.

San Diego Frwy.

Sepulveda Blvd.

Woodman Ave.

Roscoe Blvd.

■
Van Nuys
Airport

2 miles

2 kms

Sepulveda
Dam Recreation
Area

Van
Nuys

Van Nuys Blvd.

Coldwater Caynon
Ave.

170

Lankershim Blvd.

5

Victory Blvd.

■

L.A Valley
College

Burbank Blvd.

AREA OF DETAIL

101

Van Nuys-
Sherman Oaks
Park

Ventura Frwy.

Ventura Blvd.

rent their homes rather than own. (Most apartments rent for $500 to $750 per month.)

Although more than half of Van Nuys is composed of housing, the neighborhood isn't all homes. It houses the San Fernando Valley's main government center (likely to be City Hall if the valley ever secedes from Los Angeles), plus the Sherman Oaks Fashion Square shopping mall, Los Angeles Valley College, and Van Nuys–Sherman Oaks Park.

Frankly, Van Nuys isn't the most exciting part of town (although sections of Ventura Boulevard, the valley's main street, do get hopping at night). But it's probably one of the most popular places to put down a root or two.

Neighborhood Statistical Profile

Population by Ethnicity

6%	*Asian*
5%	*Black*
35%	*Hispanic*
<1%	*Native American*
54%	*White*

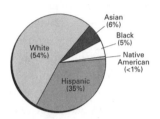

Population by Age

16%	*0–11*
12%	*12–21*
39%	*22–39*
19%	*40–59*
3%	*60–64*
11%	*65+*

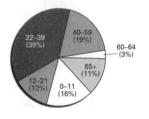

Crime (Crime statistics for Los Angeles neighborhoods include the surrounding areas.)

Arson, NA	*Homicide, 14*
Assault, 2,121	*Petty theft, NA*
Auto theft, 3,069	*Rape, 95*
Burglary, 2,101	*Robbery, 935*

Income

Per capita:	*NA*
Median household:	*$41,612*

Source: City of Los Angeles

EAST LOS ANGELES COUNTY

East L.A. County is a hard thing to define. Some people simply call it the Inland Valleys or an extension of the San Gabriel Valley, and let it go at that.

One of the area's cities, San Dimas, became famous as the site for the teen comedy *Bill and Ted's Excellent Adventure*. Another,

Claremont, is the home of the Claremont Colleges, a complex of some of the most prominent schools in Southern California.

Otherwise, though, the region rarely hosts the riots, fires, or celebrity-stuffed parties that draw attention to other parts of the region. The headlines in a recent issue of the *Los Angeles Times*'s Inland Valley section included "Lawyers Outline Deal on Hospital," "Company Begins Repair of Collapsed Street," and "Ice-Cream Truck Regulations Set"—not exactly the kind of news items that grip the nation's attention.

If you're suited to a life with normal-sized problems and victories—and without big disasters or massively public thrills—East L.A. County may suit you. It certainly suits lots of others.

POMONA

Pomona gives the casual visitor a sense of being lived-in. Stroll through downtown, and you'll soon find yourself near a college, an artists' neighborhood, or an antiques district. The city's twenty-three square miles look comfortable and pleasant, if a bit shabby or run-down here and there.

Located on the border of San Bernardino County, Pomona is best known as the home of the Fairplex, which in turn is best known as the home of the Los Angeles County Fair, which draws more than 1.5 million people per year. It's fairly close to such landmarks as the Claremont Colleges and Ontario International Airport.

Of Pomona's 140,000 people, about two-thirds are married, Hispanic, and/or young (under thirty-five years old; the median age is a touch over twenty-seven). The town has a slightly higher number of African Americans than whites—unusual for Southern California.

Though unemployment is, unfortunately, fairly high and per capita income is low, few households go hungry or homeless. For one thing, houses are fairly inexpensive. What's more, the median household income is over $40,000 a year, nearly three times the individual average. One way or another, most people seem to be getting by, even if they need three incomes per household to do it.

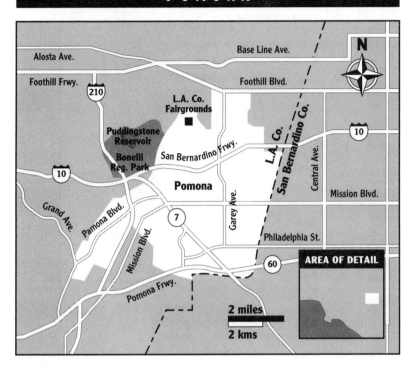

P O M O N A

Neighborhood Statistical Profile

Population by Ethnicity

7%	*Asian*
14%	*Black*
65%	*Hispanic*
<1%	*Native American*
14%	*White*
<1%	*Other*

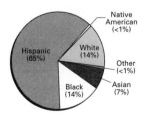

Population by Gender

49%   Female
51%   Male

Population by Age

29%   0–13
17%   14–24
17%   25–34
16%   35–44
13%   45–59
2%   60–64
6%   65+

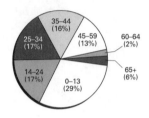

Crime

Arson, 54   Homicide, 16
Assault, 1,223   Petty theft, 2,440
Auto theft, 1,068   Rape, 50
Burglary, 1,167   Robbery, 409

Housing Costs

Average rent: $608
Average house price: $138,669

Income

Per capita: $14,561
Median household: $41,619

Source: Info Outfitters

METROPOLITAN LOS ANGELES

This is it, the Big Taco: the city of Los Angeles. More suburban than most American cities, more urban than most suburbs, the town confuses people accustomed to more conventional cities. It might confuse the locals, too, but most of them don't bother trying to define the place. They just live here.

L.A. is hard to encapsulate because it's a lot of city.

It's nearly ten times the size of Boston and has almost six times the population of Alaska. This sheer size gives the citizens of the Chatsworth district, in the city's northwest corner, little in common with the people of Watts in the southeast. As a destination for immigrants from both Asia and Latin America, L.A. is more ethnically mixed than towns like the primarily white Phoenix or primarily black Detroit.

Perhaps most important, L.A. has lots of other cities. Beverly Hills, Santa Monica, Glendale, Burbank, West Hollywood, San Fernando, Inglewood, and Culver City are surrounded on at least three sides by L.A., while plenty of other towns abut up against the town's borders. Thousands if not millions of people live in L.A. but work or play elsewhere, or at least want to.

Consequently, the city is short on a unifying sense of civic identity or pride. It's possibly the only major metropolis that didn't put together a major celebration for the end of the millennium—not even a sizable street fair—while towns from Sydney to Paris presented epochal displays of fireworks and other excitements. Perhaps the only factor that unites the whole city is the Dodgers, and even they can't do it all the time.

But the locals go on, filling the freeways and enjoying the sunshine. They may not feel like they're a part of L.A. or that the town is a part of them. Los Angeles is something that happens around them, and for the most part, they don't mind at all.

A word about statistics: The data for neighborhoods in the city of Los Angeles aren't exactly analogous to statistics for other cities. The organizations that gather statistics on entire cities don't necessarily gather them for neighborhoods. Further complicating matters, it seems that every organization that does gather neighborhood statistics has a slightly different definition of the boundaries of Van Nuys, Hollywood, or other places. If a neighborhood appeals to you, visit it thoroughly before you commit to live there.

DOWNTOWN LOS ANGELES (CITY OF LOS ANGELES)

Downtown is the home of the big institutions: City Hall for government, the *Los Angeles Times* for journalism, the Music Center for culture. There's history here in Olvera Street, the birthplace of L.A., plus a taste of Japan in the Little Tokyo neighborhood and all varieties of food at the big indoor bazaar called the Grand Central Market. The fashion industry is centered here, from sweatshops to purveyors of fine designer clothing to a university called the Fashion Institute of Design and Merchandising. Here you can also find the Staples Center arena, home to top professional teams and touring rock bands, as well as the Los Angeles Convention Center and some of the region's poshest hotels. You can reach it all by the region's freeways, many of which come together here.

Not bad for only 3.5 square miles.

If you're new to the neighborhood, you're not alone. The area has plenty of newcomers. Of its approximately 25,000 residents, more than two-thirds have lived there for less than six years. If you're a young Latino, you'll have lots of company: Nearly half of the residents are Hispanic and in their twenties or thirties. So you'll probably have something in common with your neighbors—but be careful. The crime rate in the neighborhood is unfortunately high.

Housing occupies only 5 percent of downtown. Almost all of the residential buildings are devoted to multiple-family use—apartment houses and such. That's the highest amount devoted to apartments (rather than single-family homes) in the whole city.

Consider living downtown if you work there. Given the ugly commutes that many Angelenos have to make, there's something appealing about a home that's only a few blocks from your office.

DOWNTOWN/CENTRAL CITY

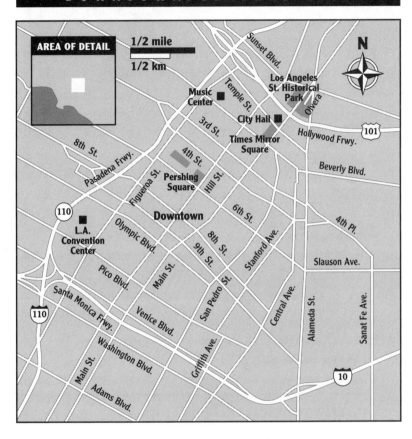

Neighborhood Statistical Profile

Population by Ethnicity

10%	Asian
21%	Black
49%	Hispanic
1%	Native American
19%	White

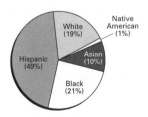

Population by Age

7%	0–11
12%	12–21
41%	22–39
21%	40–59
4%	60–64
15%	65+

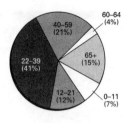

Crime (Crime statistics for Los Angeles neighborhoods include the surrounding areas.)

Arson, NA	Homicide, 16
Assault, 949	Petty theft, NA
Auto theft, 642	Rape, 36
Burglary, 954	Robbery, 1,141

Housing Costs

Average house price: not applicable (there are very few single-family detached houses in downtown Los Angeles)

Income

Per capita:	NA
Median household:	$24,283

Source: City of Los Angeles

HOLLYWOOD (CITY OF LOS ANGELES)

Hollywood is not glamorous.

Maybe it used to be in the 1930s. Back then, movie studios like Columbia and RKO had vast complexes in the neighborhood, and many stars lived fairly close by.

In recent decades, though, Hollywood became a gritty, even sleazy place. Fortunately, that situation seems to be changing.

A huge business development at Highland Avenue and Hollywood Boulevard, in the neighborhood's heart, is under construction at this writing. Another, in the district's southwest section, on La Brea Avenue and Santa Monica Boulevard, is in the planning stages. Prominent, refurbished theaters like the El Capitan (partly owned by the Walt Disney Company) and the Egyptian (home of the

HOLLYWOOD

AREA OF DETAIL

1 mile

1 km

Olive Ave.

134

Ventura Frwy.

5

N

Barham Blvd.

Forest Lawn
Memorial Park

Los Angeles
Zoo

101

Golden State Frwy.

Hollywood Frwy.

Griffith Park

Laurel Canyon Blvd.

Nichols
Canyon

Hollywood
Reservoir

Wattles
Gardens Park

Griffith
Observatory

Franklin Ave.

Los Feliz Ave.

Hollywood Blvd.

Hollywood

Vine St.

Barnsdall
Park

Sunset Blvd.

Sunset Blvd.

Santa Monica Blvd.

2

Vermont Ave.

Melrose Ave.

La Cienega Blvd.

Fairfax Ave.

La Brea Ave.

Highland Ave.

Beverly Blvd.

Western Ave.

Silver Lake

prestigious film-buff institution, the American Cinematheque) attract customers from miles away. So do long-established institutions such as the Hollywood Bowl and Mann's Chinese Theater, nightclubs like the Palace and playhouses like the Pantages. The area also has Griffith Park, America's largest urban park, which includes the Los Angeles Zoo and Griffith Observatory. And, of course, there's Hollywood Boulevard's Hollywood Walk of Fame, with its star-decorated sidewalks.

If Hollywood sounds like a town deeply rooted in L.A. life, its 230,000 citizens are another story. More than half are foreign-born, while almost two-thirds have lived in the area less than six years. It's a young place, where nearly half of the people are in their twenties or thirties.

Hollywood's physical terrain is fairly diverse. There are small apartments in the flatlands near Hollywood Boulevard, spacious single-family homes in the Hollywood Hills, and downright fancy near-mansions on Franklin Avenue and Los Feliz Boulevard.

So what is Hollywood? Varied in almost every way, grungy and polished at once, Hollywood is Los Angeles writ small.

Neighborhood Statistical Profile

Population by Ethnicity

10%	Asian
4%	Black
36%	Hispanic
<1%	Native American
50%	White

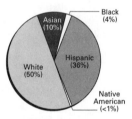

Population by Age

13%	0–11
12%	12–21
41%	22–39
20%	40–59
4%	60–64
10%	65+

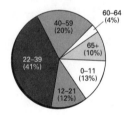

Crime (Crime statistics for Los Angeles neighborhoods include the surrounding areas.)

Arson, NA	Homicide, 19
Assault, 1,692	Petty theft, NA
Auto theft, 2,390	Rape, 86
Burglary, 1,467	Robbery, 1,416

Income

Per capita:	NA
Median household:	$42,008

Source: City of Los Angeles

WESTLAKE (CITY OF LOS ANGELES)

Mention Westlake, and many Angelenos think of Westlake Village, on the western edge of the San Fernando Valley. That's a different community, more upscale and tightly planned than the Westlake in metropolitan Los Angeles.

Metro L.A.'s Westlake lies on downtown's western edge, a few miles southeast of Hollywood. It's not a big area—about three square miles—but it's packed. The area houses more than 110,000 residents. According to city of Los Angeles demographic documents, "Westlake

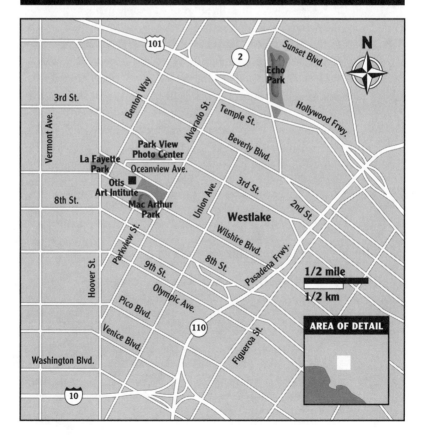

houses the highest number of persons per acre in the entire city. This density, more than fifty persons per acre, exceeds 32,000 persons per square mile. By way of comparison, New York City houses 24,000 persons [per square mile]."

Westlake is one of the neighborhoods of choice for new arrivals from Latin America. Almost two-thirds of the residents have lived there for five years or less, more than three-quarters are Hispanic, and nearly 90 percent are foreign-born.

Almost all of Westlake's residents live in multiple-family buildings; that is, in apartments rather than one-family houses. Nearly two thirds of these buildings are old by L.A. standards—more than fifty years—as opposed to neighborhoods like Van Nuys, where less than a tenth of the housing is that old.

It's a poor area. Westlake's average household income is less than half the L.A. average, while the amount of people living in poverty is twice the average.

On the bright side, rents are fairly low, and the neighborhood puts you in the center of things. It has such business centers as the Pacific Stock Exchange and the Los Angeles Area Chamber of Commerce. Aspiring illustrators, designers, and fine artists flock to its Otis/Parsons art school, L.A.'s oldest art university. There's also the popular MacArthur Park, with the gorgeous lake that gave the neighborhood its name. (Be careful, though; the park's great to visit during the daytime but dangerous at night.) And this Hispanic neighborhood incongruously houses one of L.A.'s best Jewish delis, the venerable Langer's.

Neighborhood Statistical Profile

Population by Ethnicity

11%	*Asian*
3%	*Black*
80%	*Hispanic*
<1%	*Native American*
6%	*White*

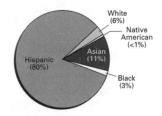

Population by Age

20%	0–11
17%	12–21
39%	22–39
15%	40–59
2%	60–64
7%	65+

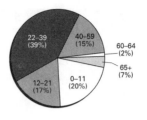

Crime (Crime statistics for Los Angeles neighborhoods include the surrounding areas.)

Arson, NA	Homicide, 51
Assault, 2,801	Petty theft, NA
Auto theft, 1,827	Rape, 97
Burglary, 1,550	Robbery, 1,690

Income

Per capita:	NA
Median household:	$21,179

Source: City of Los Angeles

WESTWOOD (CITY OF LOS ANGELES)

Westwood, lying just west of Beverly Hills, is the home of the University of California Los Angeles. The neighborhood's four square miles contain more than 40,000 residents.

Westwood is one of Los Angeles's least ethnically diverse places. More than three-quarters of the citizens are white, while the average for L.A. as a whole is 30 percent.

Newcomers are common. More than two-thirds of Westwood's citizens have lived there for five years or less, and nearly two-thirds are renters.

Housing isn't cheap, though. Most houses cost more than $500,000, while rental housing can easily run more than $1,000 per month.

With prices like that, you'd expect Westwood residents to be rich. To be sure, average household incomes are nearly twice the city average, but the area also has a higher-than-average poverty rate. This disparity is easy to explain: many people who live permanently in the

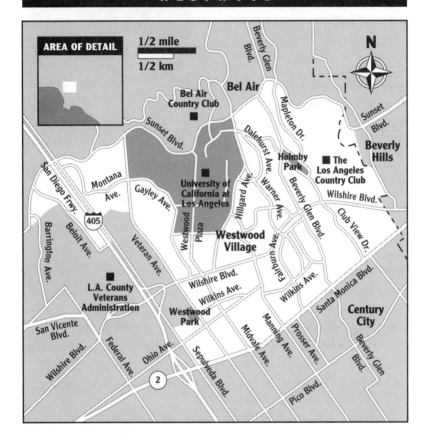

WESTWOOD

neighborhood have a lot of money, but the people in UCLA's dormitories and other student housing are as broke as students anywhere.

As you might imagine, the residents of this college-centered district are well educated. Westwood has the third highest level of education of any neighborhood in Los Angeles.

The pulse of the district is Westwood Village, a strollable section of restaurants, shops, and theaters. Nearby are some of the city's tallest skyscrapers outside of downtown, home of real-estate developers and other powerful industrialists.

For all of its economic activity and educational strength, Westwood does have a contemplative, even somber side. In a small cemetery behind some office buildings, you can find the final resting place of Marilyn Monroe.

Neighborhood Statistical Profile

Population by Ethnicity

14%	Asian
3%	Black
7%	Hispanic
<1%	Native American
76%	White

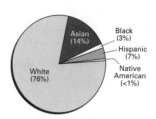

Population by Age

4%	0–11
31%	12–21
33%	22–39
16%	40–59
4%	60–64
12%	65+

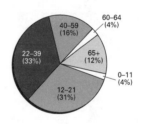

Crime (Crime statistics for Los Angeles neighborhoods include the surrounding areas.)

Arson, NA	Homicide, 6
Assault, 738	Petty theft, NA
Auto theft, 1,635	Rape, 49
Burglary, 1,466	Robbery, 651

Income

Per capita:	NA
Median household:	$81,056

Source: City of Los Angeles

BEACH COMMUNITIES

If the American dream is a house of one's own, the California dream is a house on the beach. The softly lapping ocean, the tanned and toned bodies, the seaside dining and shopping—it seems like paradise.

Because it's so desirable, seaside living is expensive. Houses and apartments by the shore can rank among the costliest in the region.

What's more, the cool ocean breezes can make seaside towns among the coldest in the area. A seaside town like Santa Monica is obviously sunnier than comparable places in Oregon or Maine, but it's

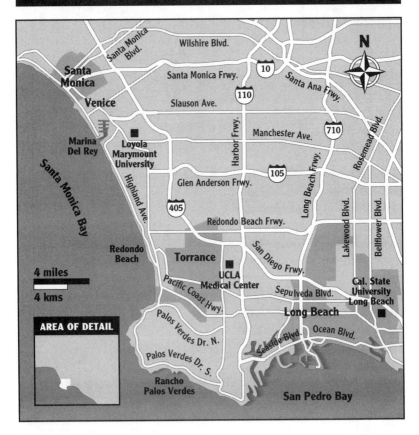

colder than downtown L.A. If you're coming to Southern California for warmth and sunshine, think twice about living by the beach.

But if you don't mind a bit of cool air and high rent, a seaside house is a great choice. If nothing else, it'll make you the envy of others—even other Southern Californians.

LONG BEACH

Located on the Pacific Ocean very close to Orange County and about twenty miles south of downtown Los Angeles, Long Beach's fifty square miles used to be nicknamed Dullsville by the Drink. Even today, its Convention and Visitors Bureau tries to entice travelers by calling the town the Big City Down by the Beach—not exactly the zingiest slogan.

Don't let the poky names fool you. Long Beach has more attractions and opportunities than its lackluster PR indicates.

With nearly 440,000 residents, Long Beach has California's fifth largest population. It has 2,800 oil wells and the west coast's busiest port. During the 1990s, the city broke ground on a $650 million waterfront development, tripled the size of its convention center, opened the much-ballyhooed Long Beach Aquarium of the Pacific, worked on redeveloping the city's downtown, and played host to more than 4 million visitors annually.

The visitors probably had fun. Annually, Long Beach hosts the Catalina Ski Race (for water skiing), the Toyota Grand Prix (street racing), and a Christmas boat parade, plus events on the *Queen Mary* historic cruise ship—a Scottish Festival, Fourth of July fireworks, and a haunted ship for Halloween. In addition, the city offers thirty miles of beaches, nearly sixty parks, and more than 3,000 boat slips.

Despite all of these opportunities for recreation, much of Long Beach is more homey than hedonistic. Long Beach was for years something of a retirement community, and many of its neighborhoods retain that flavor. Thanks to the busy harbor, many of the blue-collar workers have a more comfortable standard of living than people in comparable jobs elsewhere. There's even an artists colony.

Be careful, though. Some neighborhoods can get dangerous. If you shop for a home in Long Beach, watch out for gang activity.

In other words, Long Beach can be a great place to settle or to party—if you choose the appropriate part of town.

Neighborhood Statistical Profile

Population by Ethnicity

14%	*Asian*
14%	*Black*
32%	*Hispanic*
<1%	*Native American*
40%	*White*
<1%	*Other*

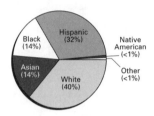

Population by Gender

50%	*Female*
50%	*Male*

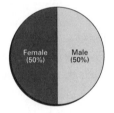

Population by Age

22%	*0–13*
14%	*14–24*
16%	*25–34*
17%	*35–44*
16%	*45–59*
3%	*60–64*
12%	*65+*

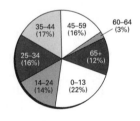

Crime

Arson, 186	*Homicide, 38*
Assault, 1,783	*Petty theft, 7,922*
Auto theft, 3,551	*Rape, 111*
Burglary, 3,908	*Robbery, 1,765*

Housing Costs

Average rent: $631
Average house price: $219,865

Income

Per capita: $20,405
Median household: $40,205

Source: Info Outfitters

SANTA MONICA

You've seen Santa Monica. Its beaches, its pier (complete with Ferris wheel), and its streets show up in television shows and movies over and over again. Its 8.3 square miles, which house just under 100,000 people, comprise one of the world's most famous small cities.

It's a desirable place to live—so much so that houses there are among the costliest in Southern California. It's filled with shopping (four separate shopping districts and malls) and dining (literally hundreds of restaurants). In fact, restaurants, caterers, and eating places comprise the town's single largest source of employment.

Santa Monica is a haven for unmarried people. At least half of the residents are single, a much higher proportion than in the rest of Los Angeles County. (More than two-thirds of the households are composed of only one or two people.) It's an especially good place to be a single man, as the town has thousands more females than males.

If you're a senior citizen, you'll have plenty of company. The town also has a relatively high proportion of people aged sixty-five and up.

Politically, Santa Monica is known as a very liberal town. According to a city-sponsored survey, the citizens are mostly pleased with the municipal government, although they are concerned about the presence of homeless people on the streets. Career-wise, a relatively high proportion of the work force is composed of professional men and women—doctors, lawyers, and such.

Perhaps the main problem of living in Santa Monica is convincing people that you don't spend every weekend at the beach, that you are, in fact, a person of depth and brains rather than surf and tan.

Neighborhood Statistical Profile

Population by Ethnicity

8%	Asian
5%	Black
16%	Hispanic
<1%	Native American
71%	White
<1%	Other

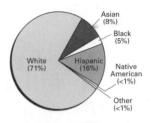

Population by Gender

52%	Female
48%	Male

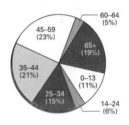

Population by Age

11%	0–13
6%	14–24
15%	25–34
21%	35–44
23%	45–59
5%	60–64
19%	65+

Crime

Arson, 86	Homicide, 12
Assault, 345	Petty theft, 3,300
Auto theft, 730	Rape, 22
Burglary, 703	Robbery, 268

Housing Costs

Average rent:	$571
Average house price:	$500,001

Income

Per capita:	$42,031
Median household:	$50,552

Source: Info Outfitters

TORRANCE

Torrance is the largest city in Los Angeles County's South Bay. More than 130,000 residents (and a daytime population of over 400,000) fill its twenty-one square miles. (Long Beach is bigger, but some people consider Long Beach a region of its own rather than a component of the South Bay.) Torrance is not, strictly speaking, a beach community, since only a few of its blocks run along the shore; but it's close enough, and a good representative of other towns that lie nearby.

Torrance is one of the South Bay's primary bedroom communities. More than two-thirds of the homes are detached single-family houses or duplexes; more than half of the residents own rather than rent their homes. Unfortunately for the newcomer, rents and house prices are high—surprisingly so, as the area isn't usually considered very ritzy or fashionable.

It's a stable community; most of the residents have lived there ten years or longer, and nearly half the population is age forty-five or older. It's mostly white, but it has a higher proportion of Asians than most other parts of Southern California.

Torrance's business community leans toward the mechanical and technological, with companies like AlliedSignal Aerospace, Robinson Helicopter Company, Panasonic, and American Honda. One of the town's most prominent sights is its huge Mobil Oil refinery.

Torrance is the kind of community that the rest of the area doesn't notice all that much. It doesn't have fires, floods, celebrity sightings, or wild controversy. Torrance goes about its own business, letting the flashier communities pull in the headlines—and one gets the feeling that it's happy to do so.

Neighborhood Statistical Profile

Population by Ethnicity

27%	*Asian*
2%	*Black*
12%	*Hispanic*
<1%	*Native American*
59%	*White*
<1%	*Other*

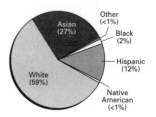

Population by Gender

51%	Female
49%	Male

Population by Age

15%	0–13
11%	14–24
14%	25–34
18%	35–44
22%	45–59
5%	60–64
15%	65+

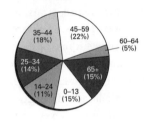

Crime

Arson, 31	Homicide, 3
Assault, 214	Petty theft, 2,953
Auto theft, 812	Rape, 21
Burglary, 901	Robbery, 226

Housing Costs

Average rent:	$791
Average house price:	$347,899

Income

Per capita:	$30,038
Median household:	$61,659

Source: Info Outfitters

VENICE (CITY OF LOS ANGELES)

When people think of Venice, located immediately south of Santa Monica, they think of the famous boardwalk that lines the town's beach. The Venice Boardwalk Association calls the stretch L.A.'s playground, and the title is apt. Street performers juggle or make music, cyclists and skaters roll along their own smooth beachside path, gawkers stare at the hunks on Muscle Beach, artists and vendors and shopkeepers hawk their wares, and the whole place is as pure a Southern California experience as anyone can imagine.

The boardwalk is only part of the story, of course. Located immediately south of Santa Monica, Venice was designed and built to evoke the Italian Venice, complete with canals. The canals still exist, and walking alongside them is a lovely way to pass an afternoon or get a little exercise. There's also the fashionable Abbot Kinney Boulevard, with its artsy shops and chic restaurants.

Since Venice lies only a few miles north of Los Angeles International Airport, you'd expect these amenities to attract plenty of tourists. They do—but they also pull in the locals, and there are a lot of locals to pull. Venice is one of Los Angeles' more densely populated neighborhoods, with more than 40,000 people in its three square miles.

It's a town of people who don't like being tied down. Nearly half of the residents live alone; nearly three-quarters rent rather than own their homes; almost two-thirds have lived in the area for less than six years. If you're single and not interested in putting down roots at the moment, Venice may be the place for you.

If you can afford it, that is. The cost of housing is fairly high. Venice has a higher average household income and a lower poverty level than Los Angeles as a whole. The crime rate runs high as well.

For all the high costs and potential dangers, though, Venice presents the kind of loose, casual life that refugees from more uptight towns crave.

Neighborhood Statistical Profile

Population by Ethnicity

3%	*Asian*
8%	*Black*
24%	*Hispanic*
1%	*Native American*
64%	*White*

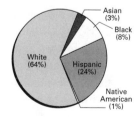

Population by Age

10%	0–11
9%	12–21
46%	22–39
23%	40–59
4%	60–64
8%	65+

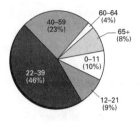

Crime (Crime statistics for Los Angeles neighborhoods include the surrounding areas.)

Arson, NA	Homicide, 14
Assault, 2,121	Petty theft, NA
Auto theft, 3,069	Rape, 95
Burglary, 2,101	Robbery, 935

Income

Per capita:	NA
Median household:	$52,468

Source: City of Los Angeles

Orange County

Many people in Los Angeles consider Orange County to be reactionary, dull, smug, and bland. They're only a little bit right.

Much of Orange County is composed of upscale housing developments and other planned communities. The people—nearly 3 million of them—are mostly white, mostly Republican, mostly family folks rather than single, and mostly living in single-family detached houses that they own rather than rent.

The area's biggest employers are Disneyland, Boeing, the phone company AirTouch Cellular, American Protective Services, and Rockwell Semiconductor Systems, with nearly 27,000 employees among them. These employers and others must pay fairly well; the median household income in the county runs over $60,000.

It sounds almost like a caricature of prosperous, successful suburbia. And in truth, the area isn't as diverse as Los Angeles County.

While L.A. County's Antelope Valley is much different from metropolitan Los Angeles or the beach communities, the northern beach communities in OC are in many ways similar to the county's central inland communities.

But this analysis overlooks the differences among the county's forty-plus cities and unincorporated areas. And those differences are a large part of the descriptions that follow.

NORTH ORANGE COUNTY BEACH COMMUNITIES

HUNTINGTON BEACH

Once "a gritty, blue-collar burg" (in the words of *Sunset* magazine's Catherine Karnow), the fifty-two square miles of Huntington Beach have become a place of high incomes and very high housing prices.

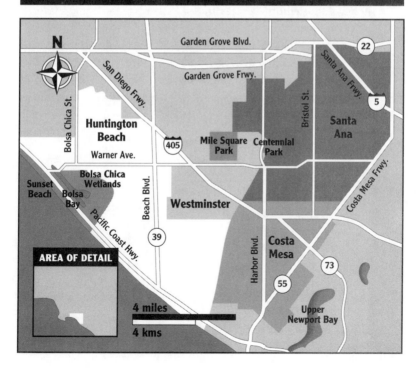

HUNTINGTON BEACH/SANTA ANA/COSTA MESA

The major employers, including Boeing, the utility company GTE California, and the plastics maker Cambro Manufacturing, keep the place prosperous, with an unemployment rate at a remarkably low 2 percent.

Freeways cut through almost all of the other north Orange County cities covered in this chapter—but not Huntington Beach. (The San Diego Freeway, also known as Highway 405, does pass over a little of the town's northeast section.) Nevertheless, it's not hard to reach. The town is fairly close to Long Beach Airport and Orange County's John Wayne Airport. On Huntington Beach's northern border lies the United States Naval Weapons Station, and on its south is the wealthy town of Newport Beach.

Huntington Beach in some ways fits the typical image of an Orange County suburb. Its populace of nearly 200,000 is overwhelmingly white, and most of its adults are married and living in single-family homes.

But there are some unexpected surprises. Even though it's a stronghold of business development, Huntington Beach is also the home of the California coast's biggest wetlands preserve and a favorite of environmentalists: the 1,200-acre Bolsa Chica ecological reserve. What's more, the city's 8 1/2 miles of beaches are a world center for surfers, with a surfing museum, a surfer's church, and a college surfing team. Every year, the town hosts world-class surfing competitions.

It's not for everyone (what place is?), but if you've got the money and enjoy the outdoors, Huntington Beach may be the place for you.

Neighborhood Statistical Profile

Population by Ethnicity

10%	Asian
1%	Black
15%	Hispanic
73%	White
1%	Other

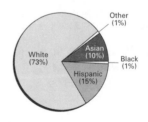

Population by Gender

50%	*Female*
50%	*Male*

Population by Age

15%	*0–13*
13%	*14–24*
18%	*25–34*
18%	*35–44*
21%	*45–59*
4%	*60–64*
11%	*65+*

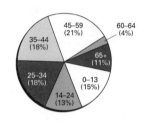

Crime

Arson, 17	*Homicide, 5*
Assault, 493	*Petty theft, 3,636*
Auto theft, 743	*Rape, 34*
Burglary, 1,419	*Robbery, 111*

Housing Costs

Average rent:	*$830*
Average house price:	*$274,500*

Income

Per capita:	*$29,632*
Median household:	*$61,678*

Source: Info Outfitters

NORTH ORANGE COUNTY INLAND COMMUNITIES

ANAHEIM

Anaheim isn't wholly the town that Disney built, but it's close. The Happiest Place on Earth is the largest employer of the town's 300,000 citizens (12,000 employees, with another 1,700 at the Disneyland Hotel), and plenty of additional employers—hotels, restaurants, and other accommodations—have built businesses around the park. Other top Anaheim attractions include two of Orange County's most prominent professional sports teams, baseball's Angels and hockey's Mighty Ducks—both of which are owned by the Walt Disney Company.

    The second largest city in Orange County, Anaheim is surrounded by the cities of Garden Grove, Orange, Buena Park, Fullerton,

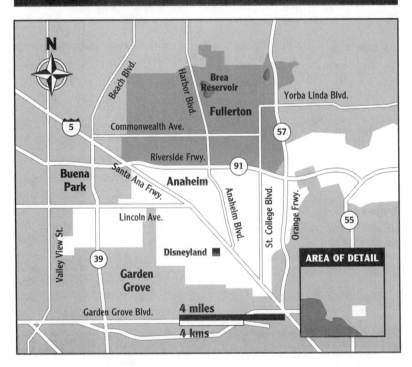

FULLERTON/ANAHEIM

and Placentia—and it's not far from Orange County's other truly big city, Santa Ana. To Anaheim's east lies the Santa Ana River.

Anaheim is a mid-range kind of place. The people living in its sprawling fifty square miles aren't especially rich or poor, and the town's not as overwhelmingly white or conservative as other parts of the county—but they're not terribly liberal or a melting pot of races, either.

Anaheim is undergoing several development or redevelopment projects, building or fixing up places from individual buildings to entire streets. If the town's personality and traditions are any indication, even these upheavals will be done in a moderate manner.

Call it the Long Beach of Orange County—a big place that doesn't make the amount of noise that big places usually make.

Neighborhood Statistical Profile

Population by Ethnicity

12%	*Asian*
2%	*Black*
42%	*Hispanic*
44%	*White*
<1%	*Other*

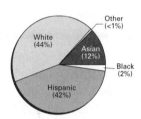

Population by Gender

49%	*Female*
51%	*Male*

Population by Age

23%	*0–13*
15%	*14–24*
18%	*25–34*
17%	*35–44*
15%	*45–59*
3%	*60–64*
9%	*65+*

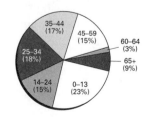

Crime

Arson, 55	*Homicide, 15*
Assault, 1,037	*Petty theft, 5,924*
Auto theft, 1,972	*Rape, 100*
Burglary, 2,270	*Robbery, 812*

Housing Costs

Average rent:	*$676*
Average house price:	*$190,000*

Income

Per capita:	*$18,872*
Median household:	*$44,419*

Source: Info Outfitters

FULLERTON

With 22.3 square miles and more than 120,000 people, Fullerton is one of the biggest cities in Orange County's northern section. It's also one of the oldest towns in the whole county—and seemingly proud of it. "Unlike many Orange County cities," notes the Fullerton Chamber of Commerce's Web site in what seems like a condescending tone, "Fullerton has maintained its historic landmarks." The town is currently upgrading its downtown, which is more than a century old.

Despite its age, Fullerton is not caught in the past. It keeps up with technology. Like many other Orange County cities, it's deeply involved in manufacturing; the town's biggest companies include Hughes Aircraft, Weber Aircraft, and Raytheon aerospace company, not to mention such high-tech mechanical firms as Hewlett-Packard, Johnson Controls, and Beckman Instruments. Fittingly, the town has its own municipal airport.

Additional big employers are St. Jude Medical Center and California State University at Fullerton. The university is one of the centers of Fullerton arts and culture. In fact, Fullerton is something of a college town; it has five colleges and universities.

Fullerton is fairly close to Disneyland. It's bordered by Brea, Buena Park, La Habra, Placentia, Anaheim, and the Los Angeles

County town of La Mirada. The 57 and 91 freeways pass near the town, but they don't spend much time inside it, giving most of the residents access to faraway places without the excess noise and traffic that freeways can sometimes bring.

In a way, that's Fullerton—a place that uses modern techniques but isn't enslaved to them.

Neighborhood Statistical Profile

Population by Ethnicity

15%	Asian
2%	Black
29%	Hispanic
54%	White
<1%	Other

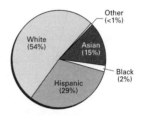

Population by Gender

50%	Female
50%	Male

Population by Age

18%	0–13
16%	14–24
18%	25–34
16%	35–44
17%	45–59
4%	60–64
11%	65+

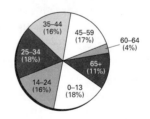

Crime

Arson, 19	Homicide, 2
Assault, 248	Petty theft, 2,989
Auto theft, 587	Rape, 30
Burglary, 738	Robbery, 157

Housing Costs

Average rent:	*$692*
Average house price:	*$263,000*

Income

Per capita:	*$22,938*
Median household:	*$48,130*

Source: Info Outfitters

GARDEN GROVE

Garden Grove is unusual. While most O.C. towns are very white, Garden Grove has no one ethnic group in the majority. Whites are merely the largest minority, and the town has a larger proportion of Asian Americans than most other places in Orange County—or for that matter, all of Southern California.

While towns like Fullerton and Anaheim house large companies that employ thousands of workers, Garden Grove is a town of smaller firms. The biggest employer, Garden Grove Hospital, has 630 workers, while the next biggest firms—Crystal Cathedral, Air Industry Corporation, and Pilkington Aerospace—have less than 450 each.

Still, Garden Grove is an Orange County town. Like the citizens of other O.C. towns, most people in Garden Grove work for manufacturing firms, albeit not huge ones. Like other O.C. communities, it's a family place, where most adults are married with children. (Fortunately for these families, Garden Grove house prices are pretty reasonable.)

The town is fairly small in area—17.8 square miles—but sizable in population at over 156,000 residents. It gives the visitor the feeling of a working-class town that's moving up. Its biggest landmark is a church, the Crystal Cathedral, which doubles as the home for Reverend Robert Schuller's television ministry.

In a sense Garden Grove isn't that unusual after all. It's a pretty typical Orange County town—if it were in the Orange County of forty years ago.

GARDEN GROVE/ORANGE

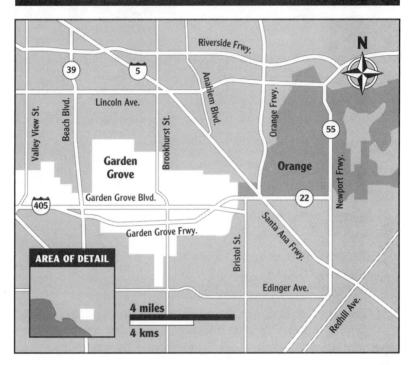

Neighborhood Statistical Profile

Population by Ethnicity

25%	Asian
1%	Black
33%	Hispanic
41%	White
<1%	Other

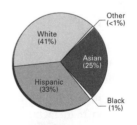

Population by Gender

49%	Female
51%	Male

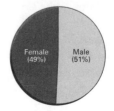

Population by Age

23%	0–13
15%	14–24
17%	25–34
18%	35–44
15%	45–59
3%	60–64
9%	65+

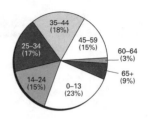

Crime

Arson, 36	Homicide, 3
Assault, 509	Petty theft, 2,895
Auto theft, 1,028	Rape, 22
Burglary, 1,186	Robbery, 276

Housing Costs

Average rent:	$726
Average house price:	$175,000

Income

Per capita:	$15,825
Median household:	$42,273

Source: Info Outfitters

ORANGE

Like other Orange County communities, Orange is a moderate-sized place, with 123,000 people in 23.3 square miles. In other ways, though, it's mighty different.

Employment is one factor. While many towns near Orange concentrate on manufacturing, Orange's biggest employers include St. Joseph's Hospital, the University of California Irvine Medical Center, and the Orange County Transportation Authority. Presumably, Orange's workers spend more time working with (or on) people than with building things.

One of Orange's most prominent features is its charming Old Towne, filled with old-fashioned shops. "Everything about Old Towne Orange, from its large concentration of pre-1940s homes and businesses to its laid-back atmosphere, speaks of a time gone by, which may be why this nostalgic village (including 1,700 of those buildings) was recently listed on the National Register of Historic Places," writes *Sunset* magazine's David Lansing. "Fittingly, Orange is the self-proclaimed antiques capital of Southern California."

Not that the entire town is rooted in the past. Orange has two of the biggest shopping malls in the county—Mall of Orange and The City. It's close to Anaheim's Disneyland and Edison Field (home of the Angels baseball team) and Santa Ana's Mainplace Mall. Within its city limits is Villa Park, a wealthy little independent city. And its southwest corner is the site of a gigantic confluence of freeways: the 57, the 5, and the 22.

With these factors bearing on the town, it should come as no surprise that Orange is the second fastest-growing city in Orange County.

Neighborhood Statistical Profile

Population by Ethnicity

10%	*Asian*
1%	*Black*
32%	*Hispanic*
56%	*White*
1%	*Other*

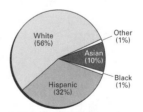

Population by Gender

49%	*Female*
51%	*Male*

Population by Age

20%	0–13
16%	14–24
16%	25–34
17%	35–44
17%	45–59
4%	60–64
10%	65+

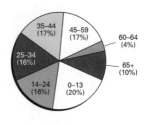

Crime

Arson, 43	Homicide, 12
Assault, 386	Petty theft, 1,725
Auto theft, 537	Rape, 29
Burglary, 701	Robbery, 106

Housing Costs

Average rent:	$713
Average house price:	$209,000

Income

Per capita:	$23,466
Median household:	$54,725

Source: Info Outfitters

CENTRAL ORANGE COUNTY COMMUNITIES

COSTA MESA

Costa Mesa is smaller than many O.C. towns—about 100,000 people in about sixteen square miles. But almost no one in the county can ignore it.

For starters, Costa Mesa is in the middle of things. It's surrounded by prominent cities such as Santa Ana, Huntington Beach, Irvine, and Newport Beach. What's more, Costa Mesa is the home of such Orange County institutions as John Wayne Airport, the Orange County

Fairgrounds, and South Coast Plaza, Orange County's most successful shopping mall. Three major freeways—the 55, 73, and 405—pass through the town. Sooner or later, just about everyone in Orange County comes to Costa Mesa.

Like the city of Orange, Costa Mesa makes its living providing services. The town's biggest employers are the Coast Community College District (1,300 employees), the Automobile Club of Southern California, the health-services company Fairview Development Center (1,200 apiece), AVCO Financial Services (1,000), and the department stores Nordstrom (950) and Macy's (900).

Costa Mesa takes some pride in being a pleasant place to live; it boasts several prominent theaters and (in the mayor's words) "more accessible park land than any other city in Orange County." What's more, it's fairly close to the popular and beautiful shorelines of Huntington Beach and Newport Beach.

If you like recreational activities and can stand the rents—among the highest in Southern California—Costa Mesa may be the town for you.

Neighborhood Statistical Profile

Population by Ethnicity

8%	*Asian*
1%	*Black*
30%	*Hispanic*
61%	*White*
<1%	*Other*

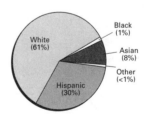

Population by Gender

51%	*Male*
49%	*Female*

Population by Age

18%	0–13
12%	14–24
21%	25–34
20%	35–44
16%	45–59
3%	60–64
10%	65+

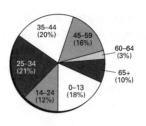

Crime

Arson, 9	Homicide, 3
Assault, 191	Petty theft, 3,106
Auto theft, 545	Rape, 32
Burglary, 613	Robbery, 145

Housing Costs

Average rent:	$773
Average house price:	$217,500

Income

Per capita:	$23,159
Median household:	$47,788

Source: Info Outfitters

IRVINE

Irvine is growing. *The Comparative Guide to American Suburbs* says that the town has had more new housing permits per year than any other city in Orange County or Los Angeles County. In the 1990s, according to the U.S. Census Bureau, Irvine's population grew by nearly 25 percent.

You might expect that a city moving that fast is some sort of Wild West boom town. Not so. Irvine is planned. It's one of the biggest planned communities in the United States, with more than 130,000 people on more than forty-seven square miles. It's largely owned and

IRVINE/TUSTIN/LAKE FOREST

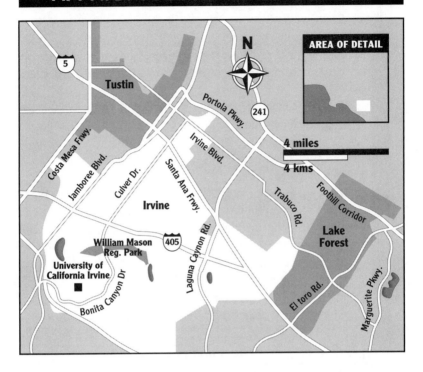

run by the land-developing Irvine Company, which originally intended that the town would surround and serve the University of California Irvine campus. The town grew beyond those boundaries but stayed as closely organized as ever.

At less than 2 percent, its unemployment rate is very low. So is its crime rate. The schools boast some of California's highest SAT scores.

If you want the raw, juicy variety and liveliness that characterize other cities, or the rootsy warmth of small towns, Irvine is not for you. In parts of Irvine, "the planning is so meticulous that it conjures up images of *The Stepford Wives*," the *Economist* magazine has reported. "Anyone who puts up a neon sign bearing his company's name, or paints his building other than white, is reminded of the Irvine Company's 'rules and regulations.'"

Physically, Irvine is a land of big sky. It's a flat place, with low buildings and not much in the way of power lines or telephone poles to block the view.

Economically, the town is a high-tech hub, a home for companies that make medical equipment and computer software and hardware. Its Irvine Spectrum area is one of America's most successful business parks.

Prices in Irvine are high, but so are wages. The town's biggest employers include Fluor Daniel, Inc. (3,100 employees), Allergan (2,000), St. John Knits (1,900), and Parker Hannifin Corp. (1,800)—but nearly two-thirds of the city's workers are employed by companies of five employees or fewer.

Irvine's population runs older than that of nearby cities. While the largest age group in Costa Mesa or Anaheim is aged twenty-five through thirty-four, the biggest age segment in Irvine is forty-five through fifty-nine. Like the people in other parts of Orange County, Irvine's populace is mostly married.

In other words, a young, single person who's hunting for thrills won't find the best pickings in Irvine. But if you're a settling-down type who wants to raise a family, Irvine may be the place.

Neighborhood Statistical Profile

Population by Ethnicity

23%	Asian
2%	Black
6%	Hispanic
69%	White
<1%	Other

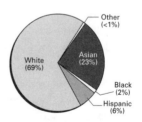

Population by Gender

49%	Male
51%	Female

Population by Age

17%	0–13
17%	14–24
15%	25–34
19%	35–44
21%	45–59
3%	60–64
8%	65+

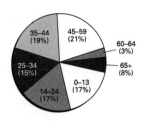

Crime

Arson, 37	Homicide, 1
Assault, 165	Petty theft, 2,264
Auto theft, 346	Rape, 10
Burglary, 860	Robbery, 44

Housing Costs

Average rent:	$787
Average house price:	$244,000

Income

Per capita:	$30,594
Median household:	$66,421

Source: Info Outfitters

LAKE FOREST

It's symbolic: Lake Forest's City Hall is a suite of offices inside an escrow company building. This small city has in many ways been planned as a set of real-estate developments.

Not that it's just another suburb. Lake Forest is more woodsy than other Orange County cities. "The city's neighborhoods are set among parks, lakes, and forests against the backdrop of the Cleveland National Forest and Saddleback Mountains," says the town's Web site.

Racially, the 60,000 citizens who live in Lake Forest's thirteen square miles comprise one of the whitest communities in Orange

County (and that's saying a lot). The town is also one of the county's most prosperous. It's a family-oriented place, where most of the adults are married homeowners, and there are plenty of activities for kids. The town belongs to one of Orange County's best school districts, and it has some of the county's lowest rates of unemployment and crime. (Unlike other communities, Lake Forest can go entire years without seeing a single murder.) And surprisingly for a place where incomes are high, house prices are actually fairly low—more than 20 percent lower than the prices in neighboring towns like Irvine and Mission Viejo.

Most people who live in Lake Forest work elsewhere. As the authoritative data service Info Outfitters puts it, "There are no major employers in the city of Lake Forest, which is primarily a residential community with a combination of retail and small commercial businesses."

So if you have money and kids, and don't mind a fairly lengthy drive to the office, Lake Forest may suit you well.

Neighborhood Statistical Profile

Population by Ethnicity

12%	Asian
2%	Black
13%	Hispanic
73%	White
<1%	Other

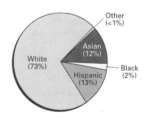

Population by Gender

51%	Female
49%	Male

Population by Age

20%	0–13
14%	14–24
16%	25–34
18%	35–44
21%	45–59
3%	60–64
8%	65+

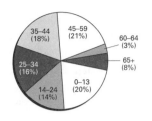

Crime

Arson, 8	*Homicide, 0*
Assault, 99	*Petty theft, 698*
Auto theft, 113	*Rape, 4*
Burglary, 261	*Robbery, 31*

Housing Costs

Average rent:	*$735*
Average house price:	*$174,500*

Income

Per capita:	*$26,577*
Median household:	*$65,193*

Source: Info Outfitters

SANTA ANA

This town of twenty-seven square miles and over 300,000 people, one of the oldest cities in Southern California, is Orange County's downtown. Surrounded by Garden Grove, Costa Mesa, Tustin, Irvine, and other cities, Santa Ana is the seat of the county's government and home to some of its biggest businesses. A diverse lot they are, too: they include Ingram Micro, the *Orange County Register* newspaper, and United Western Medical Centers, followed by Xerox, ISS Service Systems, Nordstrom, Express Manufacturing, the *Los Angeles Times*, Farmers Insurance Group, ITT, and Canon.

When the (primarily white) executives and bureaucrats go home, they leave behind a town that's mostly Hispanic, where the largest age group is under fourteen years old. Despite all of the jobs that the town provides, unemployment in Santa Ana is high, at least by Orange County standards.

Apartment rents are high, but the purchase prices of homes are pretty reasonable. Amid all of its civic and business activity, the town has room for an artists' village, a botanical garden, a zoo, and the kid-oriented museum called the Discovery Science Center, not to mention the Mainplace shopping mall and the stadium where the Orange County Zodiac soccer team plays. Lying close to the town are John Wayne Airport, Disneyland, the Costa Mesa shopping mall South Coast Plaza mall, and the Orange mall The City.

In other words, Santa Ana mixes and matches in ways that would confuse other towns. (One might even call it Orange County's version of Los Angeles, but one suspects that the Santa Anans would take offense.) If variety appeals to you, Santa Ana may appeal as well.

Neighborhood Statistical Profile

Population by Ethnicity

10%	Asian
2%	Black
75%	Hispanic
13%	White
<1%	Other

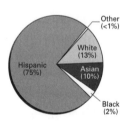

Population by Gender

54%	Male
46%	Female

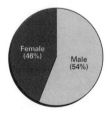

Population by Age

27%	0–13
20%	14–24
21%	25–34
15%	35–44
10%	45–59
2%	60–64
5%	65+

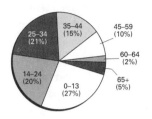

Crime

Arson, 370	Petty theft, 5,748
Assault, 920	Rape, 91
Auto theft, 2,681	Robbery, 978
Burglary, 1,605	Arson, 370
Homicide, 27	

Housing Costs

Average rent:	$729
Average house price:	$155,000

Income

Per capita:	$11,251
Median household:	$37,513

Source: Info Outfitters

TUSTIN

While Santa Ana makes decisions that affect the whole county, and Costa Mesa attracts people from all over the area, Tustin's activities are strictly local.

At this writing, one of the big issues in town is what to do with its prominent Marine base, which is now shuttered. The local paper, the *Tustin News*, features front-page headlines like "Tustin to Keep Water System" and "Police Build Memorial to Fallen Comrade." Compare those lines to the *Irvine Citizen*'s "12-Year-Old Suspected of Sexual

Battery" and pages of coverage on a new and very controversial tax bill, and you'll get a sense of Tustin's down-to-earth way of life.

It's in many ways a working-class manufacturing town (the largest employers are the office-furniture maker Steelcase, the computer-chip maker Silicon Systems, and the electronics firm Ricoh). With more than 65,000 people in 11.3 square miles, it's no near-metropolis like Santa Ana or upscale-rustic suburb like Lake Forest. It has no major colleges, slick shopping malls, or giant theme parks to pull in people from all over.

What it's got is people. Tustin's population grew by about 25 percent in the 1990s. And it's planning to have more. The Tustin Ranch area is "a new, large master-planned community of 1,900 acres with many different types of housing," says the city's Web site.

As for the future: Will Tustin become a fancier place or just a more crowded one? No one knows—but its thousands of citizens seem willing to take on whatever comes.

Neighborhood Statistical Profile

Population by Ethnicity

13%	Asian
5%	Black
32%	Hispanic
50%	White
<1%	Other

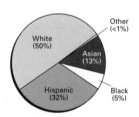

Population by Gender

50%	Female
50%	Male

Population by Age

22%	0–13
14%	14–24
19%	25–34
18%	35–44
16%	45–59
3%	60–64
8%	65+

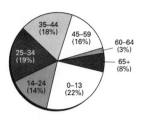

Crime

Arson, 11	Homicide, 3
Assault, 261	Petty theft, 1,442
Auto theft, 255	Rape, 10
Burglary, 470	Robbery, 67

Housing Costs

Average rent:	$614
Average house price:	$245,000

Income

Per capita:	$23,152
Median household:	$49,081

Source: Info Outfitters

SOUTH ORANGE COUNTY COMMUNITIES

You may have noticed that there aren't any listings for Orange County's southern communities. There's a good reason. Newcomers aren't likely to settle there at first.

The southern county towns tend to have smaller populations than the county's other cities, or at least populations that grow more slowly. They're richer, too. Homes in Newport Beach, for example, are almost three times the price of homes in Santa Ana. Even the small town of Dana Point, with about 35,000 people, has about 2,500 yachts, plus perhaps the county's costliest (and best) restaurant, the Ritz-Carlton.

Consequently, unless you're one of the few, the proud, and the rich, you're not likely to make this part of the county your first home in southern Orange County.

But if you are among the lucky ones who can afford to live here, you might like a little information.

South Orange County's communities are among the most politically conservative in the area. While Buena Park, up near Anaheim and Fullerton, is split almost evenly among Republicans and Democrats, Laguna Hills and Laguna Niguel in the southern part of the county are more than two to one Republican.

The cities in this part of the county are also among the most physically beautiful. Places like Corona del Mar are resort towns, with all the luxury facilities that a weekend out of town would require. Laguna Beach is famous for its art galleries—about fifty of them on and near Pacific Coast Highway alone. San Juan Capistrano is pleasantly old-fashioned, with a historic district, a famous Spanish mission, and small shops specializing in antiques, Western wear, and other reminders of the past.

As you might expect in areas so prosperous, the unemployment rate is among the lowest in all of Southern California. The crime rate is low as well; Laguna Niguel and Laguna Hills rank among the ten towns with the fewest crimes of property or violence in the region.

If you're hunting for night life, culture, and entertainment, the beachside towns are your best bet. As you move inland to places like Laguna Hills or the eastern parts of San Juan Capistrano, you're less likely to find theaters, nightclubs, or even universities.

So if you're young, single, and broke, think twice before settling in one of these towns. But if you're well off and looking to settle in someplace safe and conservative, the southwest parts of Orange County may be right for you.

Outside the Area

OUTSIDE LOS ANGELES COUNTY

To the east of Los Angeles County lies San Bernardino County. It's a fairly arbitrary separation. No mountain range or wide river divides the counties; you can drive from one county to the other without noticing.

San Bernardino County is huge, several times the size of Los Angeles County and Orange County combined, bigger than some northeastern states. Consequently, some towns in San Bernardino County are much closer to L.A. County than they are to the center of their own county. Among the most prominent of these towns are Chino and Ontario.

CHINO

Chino feels newly suburbanized. A block from houses that would fit in such upscale towns as Calabasas are stores selling hay and farm supplies—and both the houses and the stores stand on Riverside Drive, one of the town's most important avenues. The streets around the civic center have no traffic signals, just stop signs (unthinkable in the high-traffic civic centers of towns like Santa Ana or Los Angeles). And signs announcing new housing developments pop up like springtime weeds.

The town's seventeen square miles—situated near Pomona, Ontario, and Chino Hills State Park—simply don't feel like the home of approximately 65,000 people. At this writing, Chino is one of the few cities in Southern California that doesn't have a Web site.

Nor does it have much in the way of large-scale private industry. The citizens' largest employers include the California Institute for Men (the local prison) and the Chino Unified School District.

So much for the things that Chino doesn't have. What it does have is youth. More than half of the population is under age thirty-five, and the biggest age group is under fourteen. The city's diverse new real-estate developments provide plenty of affordable housing.

In other words, Chino is a place where young parents are raising young families. It's a town to watch.

Neighborhood Statistical Profile

Population by Ethnicity

4%	Asian
6%	Black
45%	Hispanic
<1%	Native American
45%	White
<1%	Other

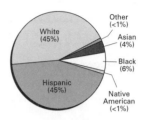

Population by Gender

44%	Female
56%	Male

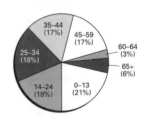

Population by Age

21%	0–13
18%	14–24
18%	25–34
17%	35–44
17%	45–59
3%	60–64
6%	65+

Crime

Arson, 68	Homicide, 2
Assault, 178	Petty theft, 1,375
Auto theft, 379	Rape, 7
Burglary, 512	Robbery, 94

Housing Costs

Average rent:	$624
Average house price:	$172,920

Income

Per capita:	$15,568
Median household:	$46,590

Source: Info Outfitters

ONTARIO

With almost 150,000 people in about thirty-seven square miles, Ontario is big—bigger than either of its neighbors Chino or Pomona. Its citizens are mostly young, Hispanic, and male. The price of housing, both for rent and for sale, is relatively low. Unfortunately, the crime rates are pretty high.

Wages aren't, though. As economist John Husing wrote in a report for the city, "Ontario offers companies concerned with labor costs access to workers who will generally work for less to avoid long commutes to Los Angeles and Orange Counties."

K-Mart, the city government of Ontario, and United Parcel Service are Ontario's biggest employers. There's also Ontario Mills, which bills itself as Southern California's largest entertainment and outlet mall, and Ontario Airport, one of the busiest air fields for many miles around.

Ontario also attracts manufacturing and engineering firms. Those firms tend to offer the city's highest salaries.

Although it sits near the foot of a wall of mountains, Ontario has room to grow. "It is the closest area to Los Angeles County that still has major tracts of inexpensive, undeveloped industrial and commercial land," Husing points out.

The bottom line for Ontario seems to be that, though the citizens may not get rich, they'll have the opportunity to make a living and raise families.

Neighborhood Statistical Profile

Population by Ethnicity

4%   Asian

7%   Black

52%   Hispanic

<1%   Native American

37%   White

<1%   Other

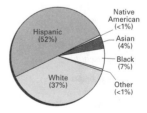

Population by Gender

50%	Female
50%	Male

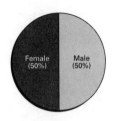

Population by Age

27%	0–13
15%	14–24
16%	25–34
17%	35–44
15%	45–59
3%	60–64
7%	65+

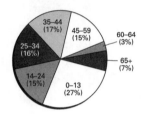

Crime

Arson, 92	Homicide, 18
Assault, 652	Petty theft, 4,337
Auto theft, 1,562	Rape, 43
Burglary, 1,354	Robbery, 362

Housing Costs

Average rent:	$589
Average house price:	$140,293

Income

Per capita:	$14,290
Median household:	$39,394

Source: Info Outfitters

OUTSIDE ORANGE COUNTY

Chino Hills State Park and the Cleveland National Forest stand on the eastern side of Orange County—and on the eastern side of the park and forest stands Riverside County. With such a divide in place, many citizens of Orange County towns like Huntington Beach or Costa Mesa don't spend a lot of time in Riverside County.

Too bad. The county offers a number of attractions. Stretching all the way to the Arizona border, Riverside County contains some of California's most striking sights, including the San Bernardino National Forest and vast stretches of desert. Among the best of the county's attractions is the city of Corona, the Riverside County town that's physically closest to Orange County.

CORONA

Corona is on the move. The U.S. Census Bureau reports that the town grew in population by nearly 50 percent in the 1990s, rising to over 110,000 people and making it one of the ten fastest-growing cities in the United States.

The city has been busy making places to put its new populace. According to *The Comparative Guide to American Suburbs*, Corona's 28.5 square miles have by far the greatest number of new housing permits in the Los Angeles area—which includes Los Angeles County, Orange County, and much of Riverside, San Bernardino, and Ventura counties. Corona has issued more than twice as many new home permits per year as the second-ranked town, Irvine. Possibly because of this abundance of housing, Corona has some of the lowest rents in Southern California.

It also has some of the highest incomes. According to the city's Web site, "The city's 1996 median income of $53,000 is well above that for Riverside, San Bernardino, or Los Angeles Counties, and nearly equal to Orange County. The largest percentage of its families make $45,000–$74,999." The biggest employers include the Corona-Norco Unified School District, the Naval Weapons Research Center, and the Corona Regional Medical Center.

For all of its growth, Corona has not gone all high-falutin'. Suburban-style houses stand on the same street as the city hall. And the town is no hotbed of fancy entertainment or night life (though one suspects that musical and dramatic organizations will spring up to serve the growing population).

No doubt Corona will change as it continues to grow. Exactly what direction the growth will take is anyone's guess.

Neighborhood Statistical Profile

Population by Ethnicity

9%	Asian
3%	Black
34%	Hispanic
<1%	Native American
54%	White
<1%	Other

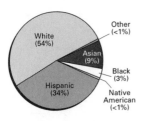

Population by Gender

50%	Female
50%	Male

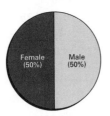

Population by Age

26%	0–13
15%	14–24
15%	25–34
18%	35–44
17%	45–59
3%	60–64
6%	65+

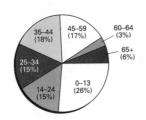

Crime

Arson, 19	Homicide, 1
Assault, 206	Petty theft, 2,198
Auto theft, 674	Rape, 40
Burglary, 816	Robbery, 141

Housing Costs

Average rent: $473
Average house price: $189,047

Income

Per capita: $18,195
Median household: $50,265

Source: Info Outfitters

CHAPTER 2

Advice on Finding an Apartment

A partment life in Los Angeles is much like apartment life elsewhere: You make the best of a limited amount of space, try to keep the neighbors quiet, and hope that they don't hear you making love.

But there are differences. If you're used to high-rise life, you won't find much of it here. Through most of the region's history, few people wanted to build anything taller than a dozen stories, for fear that an earthquake would knock it over. Besides, the region had so much land that developers didn't have to build upward. If they wanted more units, they could put up another building on a neighboring street or a neighboring town.

And they have. As film critic Pauline Kael has said, Los Angeles is "the only great city that is purely modern, that hasn't even an architectural past in the nineteenth century." If L.A.'s buildings are newer than those of other cities (and they pretty much are), the buildings of Orange County or Antelope Valley are newer still. If you want an apartment house with old-fashioned Art Nouveau flourishes or Gothic Revival touches, you'll be out of luck. But you can expect plumbing and elevators that were installed within your own lifetime, which can be an advantage.

Finally, Southern California apartment life can be quite a temporary thing. While a New Yorker may settle into apartment living for a long stretch of time, the American dream of a house for every family is very strong in Southern California, where real-estate development has been a way of life. Even for childless couples and single adults, it's not unusual to move from apartment to house in fairly short order.

If apartment life is for you, at least for your first few years in the region, you'll need to be armed with information. Some useful facts follow.

Percentage of Population Renting

Los Angeles County	*51.8 percent*
Orange County	*39.9 percent*

These data are derived from information on the number of housing units occupied by renters versus those occupied by owners (Source: University of Virginia).

Availability of Rental Housing

The housing market in Southern California is tight. In both Los Angeles County and Orange County, only 5.5 percent of all housing units (both for sale and for rent) tend to be vacant at any given moment. This figure is lower than that of San Francisco County (7.0 percent) and San Diego County (6.2 percent), not to mention New York County (8.8 percent), Chicago's Cook County (7.0 percent), and Houston's Harris County (12.6 percent) (Source: University of Virginia).

Pros and Cons of Renting an Apartment

Maintenance is a crucial factor when deciding whether to buy a home or to rent an apartment. The climate in Southern California is pretty mild, but some areas are less mild than others, with weather that can harm a house. The humid, salty air of coastal communities, for instance, can quickly warp wood and do other damage. If you own your home, you're the one responsible for repairs; but if you rent, you can yell at the landlord. (Whether the landlord will actually make repairs is another matter.)

A major advantage of an apartment in Southern California is protection against crime. A house, after all, is flat on the ground, with lots of doors and windows for criminals to enter, while an apartment may be several stories up and thus less accessible. If you're in a high-crime area, you may want to consider renting a place several stories above the ground.

Cost is important, of course. Cities such as West Hollywood and Santa Monica are fairly expensive places to buy a home, but their strong tenants' rights laws make them a magnet for renters. Before you decide to rent in a community, call its City Hall and ask if the area has rent control and other safeguards.

Many apartment houses and complexes have laundry rooms, pools, saunas, and other facilities that single-family houses may lack. The fancier complexes can offer spas, saunas, beauty salons, maid service, park-style grounds, tennis courts, and other amenities. If you're in a neighborhood that's densely packed with such

CITY FACT

Long Beach Arena's mural *Planet Ocean*, by an artist named Wyland, was for years the world's largest mural. Completed in 1992 and covering more than 120,000 square feet, the painting offers views of dolphins and gray whales. It was the champ of its field until 1995, when Colorado's Pueblo Levee Project produced a mural of nearly 180,000 square feet.

services, like Newport Beach, you may not need these extras inside your gates. But if you're in a region where the nearest laundromat is a fairly long car ride away, as in parts of the San Fernando Valley, having everything close at hand can be very useful.

Summary: Pros and Cons of Renting an Apartment

- Maintenance: The effects of weather
- Crime: Accessibility to break-ins
- Cost: Rent control
- On-site facilities: Laundry room, pool, others

Things to Consider
While Looking for an Apartment

Location, location, and location are the three most important things in real estate, say the professionals. It makes sense: If you don't like the place where you live, you can change it in ways from repainting to tearing down entire walls, but the site is always the same.

The amount of the rent, of course, is also important, as are extras like security deposits. Always find out, in advance, all of the costs that the landlord asks you to bear. Los Angeles has some mighty high prices, and you may have to hunt for a long time to get a place that's both livable and affordable.

MOVING TIP

Orange County's Pacific Bell Yellow Pages include Local Talk, a set of phone numbers that you can call twenty-four hours a day to get recorded information about important matters, including such crucial topics as family law, eye care, Social Security, real estate ... and cosmetic surgery. Just call (714) 741-2999, extension 3843.

The best source of information about an apartment house is the people who live there. Once you find a place that you like, ask the landlord if you can visit the tenants in their apartments. This way, you'll not only get to meet your prospective neighbors but also find out how well the landlord maintains the building.

See if you find the tenants compatible with you and your lifestyle. If you're young and single, you may not want to live in a building filled with large families or senior citizens. If you speak only English, you may not want to live where everyone else speaks only Spanish or Korean.

Pay attention to sounds. Are the walls so thin that you can hear the neighbors breathe? Is the building located so close to a freeway or main street that you'll constantly be buffeted by traffic noises?

Look for safe and sanitary conditions. A hairline crack on a wall may result from a poorly applied swath of paint, or it may hint at earthquake-related structural damage. A stray insect may simply wander in from outdoors, or it may be one of a multitude nesting and breeding in the building. Ask the tenants if the management is responsive to tenant needs and complaints, how well the management maintains the building, and how much the tenants can modify or redecorate their apartments.

Find out if the building's facilities suit your needs. If you have a German shepherd, you'll have to rule out buildings that refuse pets. If your family has two cars, but the building's garage has only one parking space for each apartment, it may not be the right place for you. If you want a laundry room, a pool, a backyard, or other amenities, find out if the place has them.

Keep crime in mind.

- Have any tenants been robbed in the past year?
- Does the building have security locks on the exterior doors?
- Can anyone open the property's gates, or do the gates require a special device that only tenants can get?
- Are the walls of nearby buildings tagged with graffiti and other evidence of vandalism?
- Has someone smashed the windows of buildings or cars?
- Do you feel safe in the neighborhood at night?

The street where the building stands is obviously important. If you like to entertain guests, see if the streets and curbs have unoccupied spaces in which guests can park their cars, or if they're so crowded that a guest would have to park blocks away. Some towns and neighborhoods require permits for parking. Ask the landlord if the city issues guest permits, how many you can get, and how much they cost.

In the main streets around your prospective neighborhood, look at the businesses. Are they doing well, or are there lots of boarded-up storefronts? Do the businesses and other parts of the neighborhood suit your way of life? If you're a parent of small children, you'd

CITY
FACT

The local cities with the lowest property crime rates, according to *The Comparative Guide to American Suburbs*, are Rancho Palos Verdes, Palos Verdes Estates, Sierra Madre, Laguna Niguel, and Yorba Linda. The cities with the highest property crime rates are Commerce, Santa Fe Springs, West Hollywood, Lake Elsinore, and Santa Monica.

obviously want streets with plenty of daycare centers, schools, and other facilities for kids, not a place full of adult book shops and strip clubs. If you like outdoor sports, you'll naturally keep an eye out for parks, recreation centers, and other opportunities to sweat in the sun.

Consider your commute to work. If possible, try a test run: drive during morning rush hour from the apartment house to your workplace, and drive from your workplace to the apartment in the evening.

Keep alternate routes in mind. If you live in Laguna Beach and work in Irvine, and Laguna Canyon Road is closed or traffic-jammed, you'll probably be late for work; Laguna Canyon is virtually the only main street between the two. But if you live in Garden Grove, you can reach Irvine via the Golden State Freeway, the San Diego Freeway, or a variety of surface streets.

The decision about an apartment ends where it begins: location, location, location. Fortunately, in Southern California, there are a lot of locations to choose.

Summary: Things to Consider
- Location: The neighborhood and the commute
- Price: Rent, security deposits, and other costs
- Other tenants: Compatible or incompatible
- The building: Safe and sanitary, or a dangerous hellhole?

Looking on Your Own
Versus with an Apartment Finder

The most basic way to find an apartment is to pick a neighborhood and drive around, seeking out For Rent signs. In that way, quite a few newcomers have found a home in a weekend.

But if you want to get a place before you move out here, you may need an apartment finder. Some of them charge for their services; some don't. Some specialize in particular cities, while others blanket the entire region (if sometimes thinly).

Investigate the apartment finder before you use it. Ask what they charge, which areas they cover, and what kind of information they supply beyond rental rates and number of rooms.

Resources for Finding an Apartment

The following resources include newspapers and other publications, apartment-finder services, Web sites, and other organizations.

Ad Quest
www.adquest3d.com

Apartment Guides
www.apartmentguides.com

Apartment Hunters
451 Altamonte Avenue
Altamonte Springs, FL 32701
(888) 707-HUNT;
(407) 834-4490

www.apartmenthunters.com/

Apartment Links
P.O. Box 13514
Pittsburgh, PA 15243
(800) 477-2282 (fax)

www.apartmentlinks.net

Apartment Search
(800) 691-2000

www.apartmentsearch.com

Apartment Selector
P.O. Box 600355
Dallas, TX 75360-0355
(214) 361-4420; (800) 324-3733

www.aptselector.com

Apartment World
909 Northeast Loop 410, #818
San Antonio, TX 78217
(800) 410-4545; (210) 826-4644

www.apartmentworld.com

Apartments.com
www.apartments.com

Apartments for Rent

www.aptsforrent.com

Apartments Online

www.aptline.com

Apartments USA

601 East 66th Street, #108
Savannah, GA 31405
(912) 356-9920

www.aptusa.com

Classifieds 2000

www.classifieds2000.com

Cort Business Services

(800) 448-5595

For Rent Magazine

(800) 882-2830;
(800) 835-6668

www.aptsforrent.com

This biweekly publication, distributed free in many parts of Southern California, is one of the most prominent sources of information on housing.

Los Angeles Times

www.latimes.com/class/rentals/

National Apartment Locator

www.aptloc.com

Netscape Classifieds

classifiedplus.netscape.com/

Relocation Links

www.relolinks.com

Relocation Mall

www.relomall.com/

Rentcheck

www.rentcheck.com

Rentlocation.com

www.rentlocation.com

Rent.net

www.rent.net

Springstreet

www.springstreet.com/n.nd/
ss/pgHome

Switchboard.com

(508) 836-1814

www.switchboard.com

Yahoo Classifieds

classifieds.yahoo.com

LOS ANGELES COUNTY RESOURCES

General

Apartment Hunters
201 North Robertson Boulevard
Beverly Hills
(877) 947-7368;
(310) 276-4663

Daily News Rentals
sar.classifiedwarehouse.com/
search.cw1?t=2&lc=news&cat=
rrt&spm=ro&cp=
atv2__&news=news__lad

Homehunters
1038 North Fairfax Avenue
Los Angeles
(800) 987-2682;
(323) 848-3490

www.bestrents.com

Rentimes
7901 Melrose Avenue
Hollywood
(323) 653-7368; (310) 260-9985

www.rentimes.com

Southern California for Rent
www.socal4rent.com/
LosAngeles.htm

Agoura Hills

Rent Line
26901 Agoura Road, #150
(818) 774-2177

Burbank

Burbank Leader
220 North Glenoaks Boulevard
(818) 843-8700

www.latimes.com/tcn/Burbank

Burbank Times
3917 West Riverside Drive
(818) 841-6397

Encino (City of Los Angeles)

Rent Line
16400 Ventura Boulevard
(818) 382-7360

www.789-rent.com

Glendale

Foothill Leader
3527 North Verdugo Road, #A
(818) 249-8090

Glendale News Press
425 West Broadway, #300
(818) 241-4141

www.latimes.com/gnp

Rental World
1412 West Glenoaks Boulevard, #A
(818) 507-1137

Hermosa Beach

South Bay Rental Connection
524 Pacific Coast Highway
(310) 395-7368

www.southbayliving.com

Lancaster

Antelope Valley Press
Lancaster Office
44939 North 10th Street
(661) 948-0921

www.avpress.com

North Hollywood
(City of Los Angeles)

Leasing Referral Service
6260 Laurel Canyon Boulevard, #205
(818) 509-7925

Ontario

Apartment Guide—Inland Empire
3401 Centre Lake Drive
(909) 390-9966

Inland Valley Daily Bulletin
2041 East 4th Street
(909) 987-9200

Pacific Palisades

Pacific Palisades For Rent
www.ca90272.com/rental.htm

Palmdale

Antelope Valley Press
37404 North Sierra Highway
(661) 273-2700

www.avpress.com

Renter Center
200 East Avenue R
(661) 272-1624

Panorama City
(City of Los Angeles)

San Fernando Valley Gazette
14621 Titus Street
(818) 782-8695

Pasadena

Pasadena Star News
911 East Colorado Boulevard
(626) 578-6300

www.pasadenastarnews.com

Pasadena Weekly
50 South De Lacey Avenue
(626) 584-1500

www.pasadenaweekly.com

Pomona

Inland Valley News
2249 North Garey Avenue
(909) 392-6907

Santa Monica

L.A. Property Connection
(310) 392-6049

Santa Monica Rental Guide
www.places4rent.com

Westside Rental Connection
630 Santa Monica Boulevard
(310) 395-7368

www.westsiderentals.com

Van Nuys
(City of Los Angeles)

*Apartment Guide—L.A.
and San Fernando Valley*
16360 Roscoe Boulevard, #100
(213) 893-1249

www.ApartmentGuide.com

Pennysaver
15350 Sherman Way, #290
(818) 908-0600

www.penny-saver.com

West L.A.
(City of Los Angeles)

Pets & People Home Finders
11611 Washington Place
(310) 268-1148

www.pets-people.com

Westwood
(City of Los Angeles)

UCLA *Daily Bruin*
www.dailybruin.ucla.edu/db/
advertising/classifieds/

ORANGE COUNTY RESOURCES

General

**Orange County
Apartments & Places**
members.aol.com/amppts/
index.htm

Orange County Register
Real Estate Guide
re.zip2.com/ocregister

Brea

Apartment Locators
1033 East Imperial Highway #9
(714) 257-7368

Costa Mesa

Orange County Weekly
Classified Department
P.O. Box 10788
(714) 708-8408

www.ocweekly.com/classifieds/
rentals/?friend=
21c0fd6d75d8c644

Renter Express
2706 Harbor Boulevard
(714) 535-3733

Newport Beach

Apartment Guide
1300 Dove Street, #105
(949) 221-0525
www.newhomesguides.com

Santa Ana

**Apartment Magazine of
Southern California**
130 East Dyer Road
(714) 545-3040

Living Alone Versus with a Roommate

In her book *Depression Is Fun!*, cartoonist Nina Paley described activities that she called "Housemate Games." They include Eat the Food ("Eat everything in the house that isn't yours!"), Breaking & Entering ("Enter your housemate's room while s/he isn't around. Take anything you want!"), and Dictator & Slaves ("A fun role-playing game in which one housemate plays dictator in order to 'finally get something done around here, goddammit,' while the other housemates play rebellious slaves").

These games may be jokes, but they're examples of the troubles that can arise when living with other people. There's also the pain of scheduling the chores, the stress of incompatible styles of neatness and sloppiness, and the strain of dealing with a roommate's tormented love life, stalled career, and meathead friends—or even worse, a love life, career, and friends that are much, much better than yours.

But the presence of a roommate has genuine advantages. A good one keeps you company when your lover has left you, congratulates you when you're successful, and commiserates with you when you lose a job. When you have no time to buy groceries, when you need a back rub, when you want to borrow a shirt, or when you're short on cash, a supportive roommate is a gem.

Besides, having roommates prevents the problems that arise from *not* having roommates. The loneliness of facing an empty apartment day after day can bore holes into the heart of even the toughest urbanite. Having no one to help during illness or natural disaster can weigh down the most independent soul. Doing every chore and errand alone can wear out the most rugged individualist.

But if you're temperamentally suited to being alone, the freedom of solitude is powerful. Doing what you want when you want, without having to think of how anyone else will react to it, can be a rare and valuable gift.

Moving to Southern California throws its own twists into the roommates-versus-solitude argument. If you're new in town and feel lonely, a roommate can keep you company and even pull you into her social circle. If you don't know L.A. and your roommate does, you have a live-in source of advice on the town's pleasures and dangers. If you have no car at first, a roommate who's willing to play chauffeur is a blessing.

Beware, though: A bad roommate can turn a newcomer's life into a flaming pit. Moving to a new town is hard enough; a roommate who's noisy, filthy, and inconsiderate can make you want to leave Southern California and never look back. And a roommate who's painfully needy or inept at living with others can keep you so busy with his problems that you'll rarely leave the apartment long enough to discover the region.

So what's right for you: roommates or solitude? It all depends on your personality. If you're a loner, the stresses of living alone are more bearable than the friction of dealing with other people. If you can't stand solitude, even the most annoying roommate is preferable.

Summary: Roommates or Solitude

- Roommates can interfere with your life.
- Roommates can interfere with your enjoying Southern California.
- Roommates can eliminate the loneliness of moving to a new town.
- Roommates can support you in times of need and cheer you on in times of victory.

Roommate Finder Services

E-Roommate

www.e-roommate.com

Roommate Service

www.roommateservice.com

Roommate Locator Inc.

P.O. Box 10252
Alexandria, VA 22310-0252

www.roommatelocator.com

LOS ANGELES COUNTY RESOURCES

Burbank

Roommate Express
859 North Hollywood Way
(818) 842-5010
www.roommateexpress.com

Hollywood
(City of Los Angeles)

Roommate Matchers
7901 Melrose Avenue, #205
(323) 653-7666; (310) 260-9985
www.roommatematchers.com

Long Beach

Roommate Express
5595 East 7th Street
(562) 595-0750
www.roommateexpress.com

Manhattan Beach

Beach Cities Roommates
820 Manhattan Avenue, #104
(310) 374-3077

Roommate Specialists
3713 Highland Avenue
(310) 546-2563

Pasadena

Roommate Express
2245 East Colorado Boulevard
(626) 574-0340
www.roommateexpress.com

West L.A.
(City of Los Angeles)

Roommate Express
1800 South Robertson Boulevard
(213) 250-1095
www.roommateexpress.com

Roommate Express
3765 Motor Avenue
(310) 330-3910
www.roommateexpress.com

Westwood
(City of Los Angeles)

***Daily Bruin* Roommates ads**
www.dailybruin.ucla.edu/db/ad
vertising/classifieds/

ORANGE COUNTY RESOURCES

Costa Mesa

Roommate Express
2706 Harbor Boulevard, #212
(714) 557-4045
www.roommateexpress.com

Temporary Housing

When you first come out to Southern California, you may have no place to stay. You'll need to find one fast—but you may not find what you expect.

Southern California is thin on residence hotels, apartment hotels, or whatever else you might want to call hotels that you can live in as you do apartments (or apartments that offer the services of hotels). True, celebrities like Warren Beatty have turned the Beverly Hills Hotel and similar lodgings into their West Coast homes, but they're the affluent exceptions.

If you're being transferred out here by a deep-pocketed corporation, you may find yourself staying at one of the companies that specialize in lodging executives on their transition from out-of-town to a permanent dwelling. The Marriott hotel chain offers ExecuStay and Marriott Residence Inns, which you can find on the Internet at *www.marriott.com* or by phoning (800) 228-9290.

Be careful, though. If your company pays your moving expenses, including the cost of temporary lodgings, you may face a nasty tax bite. The Internal Revenue Service has been known to count these costly perks as income, even though no money entered your hands.

If you're not a movie star or a hot-shot corporate kingpin, you may have to stay at less fancy places. Hostels, YMCAs, and boarding houses are among the most common.

HOSTELS

A good place to start with hostels is with the Web site of Hostelling International. The URL is *www.iyhf.org/*.

For local hostels, try these.

LOS ANGELES COUNTY

Avalon

Hostel La Vista
145 Marilla Avenue
(310) 510-0603

Hermosa Beach

Surf City Hostel
26 Pier Avenue
(310) 798-2323

Hollywood
(City of Los Angeles)

Banana Bungalow Hollywood
2775 Cahuenga Boulevard West
(323) 851-1129

Hollywood Hills Hostel
6772 Hawthorn Avenue
(323) 462-3777

Orange Drive Manor Hollywood
1764 North Orange Drive
(323) 850-0350

Inglewood

Backpackers Paradise
4200 West Century Boulevard
(310) 672-3090

San Pedro
(City of Los Angeles)

Hostelling International Los Angeles
3601 South Gaffey Street, Building 613
(310) 831-8109

Santa Monica

American Youth Hostels Inc.
1434 2nd Street
(310) 393-3413

Venice

Airport Hostel
2221 Lincoln Boulevard
(310) 305-0250

Share-Tel Apartments
20 Brooks Avenue
(310) 392-0325

ORANGE COUNTY

Fullerton

Fullerton-Hostelling International
1700 North Harbor Boulevard
(714) 738-3721

Huntington Beach

Colonial Inn Youth Hostel
421 8th Street
(714) 536-3315

San Clemente

San Clemente Beach Hostel
233 Avenida Granada
(949) 492-2848

YMCAS

"Young man," says the Village People song, "there's a place you can go." The YMCA has long been the first stop for people coming to a new town. Following is a list of Southern California YMCAs, but call ahead before you show up on the doorstep with your duffel bag. Not all of them will have rooms available. And be sure to check out the Y's Web site, *www.ymca.com*.

LOS ANGELES COUNTY

Alhambra

YMCA of West San Gabriel Valley
401 Corto Street
(818) 576-0226

Altadena

North Lake Family YMCA
2325 Lake Avenue
(626) 798-5040

Bellflower

Los Cerritos Branch YMCA
15530 Woodruff Avenue
(562) 925-1292

Beverly Hills

YMCA of Beverly Hills
9930 Santa Monica Boulevard
(310) 553-0731

Burbank

YMCA of Burbank
321 East Magnolia Boulevard
(818) 845-8551

Chino

Chino Valley YMCA
5665 Edison Avenue
(909) 597-7445

Covina

San Gabriel Valley YMCA
412 East Rowland Street
(818) 339-6221

**Crenshaw District
(City of Los Angeles)**

Crenshaw Family YMCA
3820 Santa Rosalia Drive
(323) 292-9195

Culver City

Culver-Palms Family YMCA
4500 Sepulveda Boulevard
(310) 390-3604

Diamond Bar

Diamond Bar/Walnut YMCA
22600 Sunset Crossing Road
(909) 860-9622

Downey

Downey Family YMCA
11531 Downey Avenue
(562) 862-4201

Downtown/Central City
(City of Los Angeles)

Stuart M. Ketchum-Downtown YMCA
401 South Hope Street
(213) 624-2348

East Los Angeles
(City of Los Angeles)

28th Street/Crenshaw YMCA
1006 East 28th Street
(213) 232-7193

Gardena

Gardena-Carson Family YMCA
1000 West Artesia Boulevard
(310) 523-3470

Glendale

YMCA of Glendale
140 North Louise Street
(818) 240-4130

Hawthorne

Centinela Valley YMCA
4081 West El Segundo Boulevard
(310) 644-7600

Hollywood
(City of Los Angeles)

Hollywood Wilshire YMCA
1553 Schrader Boulevard
(213) 467-4161

Huntington Park

Southeast-Rio Vista Family YMCA
6208 Seville Avenue
(213) 588-2256

Inglewood

Inglewood Family YMCA
319 East Kelso Street
(310) 671-7615

La Canada Flintridge

Crescenta-Canada YMCA
1930 Foothill Boulevard
(818) 790-0123

Lakewood

Weingart-Lakewood Family Branch YMCA
5835 Carson Street
(562) 425-7431

Long Beach

Buffum-Downtown Branch YMCA
600 North Long Beach Boulevard
(562) 436-9622

Camping Services Branch YMCA
P.O. Box 90995
(562) 496-2756

Fairfield Family Branch YMCA
4949 Atlantic Avenue
(562) 423-0491

Los Altos Family Branch YMCA
1720 North Bellflower Boulevard
(562) 596-3394

YMCA of Greater Long Beach
P.O. Box 90995
(562) 425-9986

Mission Hills (City of Los Angeles)

North Valley Family YMCA
10925 Columbus Avenue
(818) 365-3231

Monrovia

Santa Anita Family YMCA
501 South Mountain Avenue
(626) 359-9240

Montebello

Montebello Family YMCA
2000 West Beverly Boulevard
(213) 887-9622

North Hollywood

East Valley YMCA
5142 Tujunga Avenue
(818) 763-5126

Ontario

Ontario-Montclair YMCA
215 West C Street
(909) 986-5847

Pacific Palisades (City of Los Angeles)

Palisades-Malibu YMCA
821 Via De La Paz
(310) 454-5591

Palmdale

Antelope Valley Family YMCA
39251 10th Street West
(661) 273-1525

Pasadena

Pasadena Family YMCA
2750 New York Drive
(626) 798-0862

Pasadena Metropolitan YMCA
1010 East Union Street
(818) 432-5880

Pomona

YMCA of Pomona Valley
350 North Garey Avenue
(909) 623-6433

Reseda (City of Los Angeles)

West Valley Family YMCA
18810 Vanowen Street
(818) 345-7393

**San Pedro
(City of Los Angeles)**

San Pedro & Peninsula YMCA
301 South Bandini Street
(310) 832-4211

Santa Monica

Santa Monica Family YMCA
1332 6th Street
(310) 393-2721

**South Central Los Angeles
(City of Los Angeles)**

Weingart Urban Center YMCA
9900 South Vermont Avenue
(213) 754-3191

South Pasadena

**South Pasadena-San Marino
YMCA**
1605 Garfield Avenue
(818) 799-9119

Torrance

**Torrance-South Bay Family
YMCA**
2900 Sepulveda Boulevard
(310) 325-5885

**Tujunga
(City of Los Angeles)**

Verdugo Hills Branch YMCA
6840 Foothill Boulevard
(818) 352-3255

Van Nuys

Mid Valley Family YMCA
6901 Lennox Avenue
(818) 989-3800

**Weingart-East Los Angeles
YMCA**
2900 Whittier Boulevard
(213) 260-7005

**Westchester
(City of Los Angeles)**

Westchester Family YMCA
8015 South Sepulveda Boulevard
(310) 670-4316

**West L.A.
(City of Los Angeles)**

Westside Family YMCA
11311 La Grange Avenue
(310) 477-1511

Whittier

East Whittier Branch YMCA
15740 Starbuck Street
(562) 943-7241

YMCA of Greater Whittier
12510 Hadley Street
(562) 907-2727

Wilshire District
(City of Los Angeles)

YMCA of Metropolitan Los Angeles
625 South New Hampshire Avenue
(213) 380-6448

ORANGE COUNTY

Anaheim

YMCA of Anaheim
1209 West Lincoln Avenue
(714) 635-9622

Corona

Corona-Norco Family YMCA
1331 River Road
(909) 736-9622

Fullerton

North Orange County Family Branch YMCA
2000 Youth Way
(714) 879-9622

Huntington Beach

West County Family Branch YMCA
7262 Garfield Avenue
(714) 847-9622

Laguna Niguel

South Coast Branch YMCA
29831 Crown Valley Parkway
(949) 495-0453

Mission Viejo

Saddleback Valley YMCA
27341 Trabuco Circle
(949) 859-9622

Newport Beach

Newport-Costa Mesa-Irvine Branch YMCA
2300 University Drive
(714) 642-9990

Orange

YMCA of Orange
2241 East Palmyra Avenue
(714) 633-9622

San Juan Capistrano

Capistrano Beach Cities YMCA
32242 Paseo De Adelanto
(949) 496-1609

Tustin

YMCA of Orange County
13821 Newport Avenue
(714) 549-9622

Yorba Linda

Yorba Linda-Placentia Branch YMCA
18333 Lemon Drive
(714) 777-9622

BOARDINGHOUSES

Boardinghouses are among the oldest kinds of temporary housing. Residents get a room (often furnished) and meals, which provide not just sustenance but a chance to meet other residents.

Always call ahead before you drop in on a boardinghouse, and not just because they may not have a room available. Some of them, like retirement homes, specialize in the kind of people whom they lodge and the services that they offer. A traveler just out of college probably won't fit in among people in their seventies.

LOS ANGELES COUNTY

Glendale

Magnolia Retirement Villa
326 Magnolia Avenue
(818) 548-1586

Hollywood
(City of Los Angeles)

Bethany House
850 North Hobart Boulevard
(323) 665-6937

Cleo's Guest Home
1416 North New Hampshire Avenue
(323) 661-1683

Littlerock

Tony's Board & Care
10654 East Avenue R
(661) 944-9162

Long Beach

Lilly's Guest Home
2340 East 15th Street
(562) 433-7314

Tiangco's Guest Home
2451 Oregon Avenue
(562) 424-3210

Pasadena

Bella Vista
1760 North Fair Oaks Avenue
(626) 794-4103

Fairoaks Manor
1753 North Fair Oaks Avenue
(323) 684-8807

Mountain View Manor
1811 North Raymond Avenue
(626) 798-6811

Pasa Alta Manor
1790 North Fair Oaks Avenue
(626) 798-6986

Raymond Hamilton's House
872 North Raymond Avenue
(626) 792-8814

Santa Monica

The Manor
1905 Pico Boulevard
(310) 450-1748

Ocean View Manor
1044 3rd Street
(310) 393-0737

Van Nuys

La Jolla Manor
15929 Vanowen Street
(818) 908-0822

Venice

Ivy On Rose Home
410 Rose Avenue
(310) 399-2088

Westlake

Kolping House
1225 South Union Avenue
(213) 480-8154

ORANGE COUNTY

Anaheim

R P Guest Home
501 North Hanover Street
(714) 527-6353

Fullerton

Balcom Park Apartments
110 South Balcom Avenue
(714) 879-0931

Garden Grove

Gary Guest Home
11892 Gary Street
(714) 636-3675

M C K's Room & Board
12101 Nutwood Street
(714) 537-8742

Rose Garden Chalet
9552 Lambert Circle
(714) 638-1432

Huntington Beach

Abegail Guest Home
9932 Bon Circle
(714) 963-6861

Helen Buhrow's Group Home
5151 Heil Avenue
(714) 846-2791

Laguna Hills

Hendon Home
24985 Hendon Street
(949) 699-0877

Lake Forest

Grace Manor
25001 Pine Flat Circle
(949) 855-3175

Orange

California Guest Home
2840 East Quincy Avenue
(714) 289-0827

Leisure Tower Guest Home
1305 East Chapman Avenue
(714) 771-4723

San Clemente

Tessie's Place
2716 Via Montezuma
(949) 369-7304

Santa Ana

Espiritu Guest Home
2602 North Grand Avenue
(714) 997-9453

Stocker's Guest Home
629 South Townsend Street
(714) 558-9651

Tustin

Casa De Amigos
202 Fashion Lane
(714) 544-8804

Lestonnac Residence
16791 East Main Street
(714) 558-9872

A Final Word

If you arrive in town and have absolutely no place to stay, call the City Hall of wherever you've landed. Most cities have information for newcomers—a visitor's bureau, a tourist commission, even shelters for the homeless. When in doubt, don't hesitate; yell for help!

CHAPTER 3

Advice on Finding a House

In a classic installment of the comic strip *Peanuts*, the crabby fuss-budget Lucy is angrily surveying the multitude of gifts that she's received for Christmas. Her brother Linus asks why she's so unhappy, and Lucy says that she didn't get the gift that she really wanted. When Linus asks what gift she could be missing, Lucy answers (with the frustration of someone having to explain the obvious), "Real estate!"

Lucy is a Californian at heart.

Pros and Cons of Buying a House

As Lucy learned, it's hard to acquire real estate. Buying a house in Southern California is not cheap. Even a condominium can easily run to $100,000, while houses in decent neighborhoods rarely run under $200,000—and a surprisingly high number are priced well into the seven figures. Taxes are important, too; a homeowner can face an annual bite in the thousands of dollars.

Buying a house isn't just costly; it's complicated. The real estate laws of Southern California are as complex as those of any other area. Anyone contemplating the purchase of property should have a good lawyer examine the contracts.

And, of course, there are the chores. It's been said that the definition of a homeowner is someone going into or out of a hardware store. Mowing, painting, cleaning, repairing—these are the things that fill the homeowner's weekend.

So why, if the homeowner's burdens are so heavy, are so many thousands and even millions of people eager to shoulder them?

For one thing, a house in Southern California has long been considered a trustworthy investment. For decades, land and houses have risen in value. In recent years, home prices have fluctuated, moving down as well as up—but real estate remains one of the area's busiest businesses. Since other forms of investment shift even more wildly than Southern California real estate, a house in the sun can seem like a pretty sane bet.

There are emotional rewards, too. A homeowner has considerable pride of ownership, plus the freedom and power to make her home over in her own image. She can revel in privacy, completely assured that no one on the other side of her walls can know what she's doing within. (Unlike parts of the Northeast and other regions, Southern California doesn't have a lot of row houses. Most SoCal homes are detached from each other, ensuring maximum privacy.)

The climate is another reason to get a house. Southern California's sunny weather is a year-round invitation to go outside. For many a homeowner, that means gardening or simply luxuriating in one's own backyard—or, for that matter, one's own front yard. Children in particular want to play outside, and parents want their kids to play someplace that's safe and within earshot. In other words, a kid wants a backyard, and so does a parent.

So should you buy a home? If you're a single person on a tightly fixed income, probably not. But if you make a good living, want to control your life, and have kids (or are expecting a kid or two), a house may be just right for you.

Summary: Pros and Cons of Buying a House

- Costs: Substantial purchase price and taxes
- Maintenance: Housework, yard work, and repairs
- Complications: Contracts and other paperwork
- Investment value: California home prices have tended to rise

- Emotional rewards: Privacy and pride of ownership
- Climate: The call of the weather to enjoy one's own backyard

Things to Consider While Looking for a House

A lot of the factors that go into renting an apartment apply to buying a house. In both renting and buying, location is the most important factor. After all, it's the one thing about your home that you can't change except by moving away entirely, and there's little point of moving into a house if you're just going to move out of it.

Find out what it's like to live in the area you are considering. Drive and walk through the neighborhood—not just once, but several times, and at different times of day and night. If possible, ask your prospective neighbors about the neighborhood's best and worst features. Study the local newspaper to get a sense of the place.

Find out about crime rates. The advice in the section on renting an apartment applies here as well: See if the walls of nearby buildings are tagged with graffiti or if the windows of houses and cars show evidence of break-ins. Visit the nearest police station and ask about crime statistics.

As mentioned earlier in this chapter, price is crucial. When buying a house, find out all of the costs—not just the cost of the house, but the mortgage's interest rate, the points (a percentage of the price of the house that your lender may charge as a fee for lending money), the cost of moving, utility rates, and the expenses of maintaining the house.

Try test runs of trips that you expect to make regularly to see if the neighborhood fits your schedules. The commute to work and back is key, of course, but look also for grocery stores, restaurants, government offices, hardware stores, bed-and-bath shops, and so on.

Check the amount of parking space available near your prospective home. Is there enough space for you and your guests? This is another situation to examine at different times of day.

While you're doing it, keep your eyes and ears open. Is the neighborhood full of screaming children, barking dogs, or other noises? Can you stand them, or do you prefer quiet?

If you have kids of your own, ask another smattering of questions. Are there children in the neighborhood for your kids to befriend—and if so, are they the kind of children that you want your kids to know? Is the street low on automotive traffic, or will reckless, speeding cars endanger your child's life? Are the schools any good? Visit any schools that your children might attend; talk to the principals and sit in on some classes.

Inspect your prospective house and grounds carefully. Hire a building inspector—a home builder or contractor is usually a good choice—to examine the place for everything from structural flaws to termites.

Once you've done all of this questioning and analyzing, add in one more factor: your gut feeling. If the home and neighborhood seem perfect, but something in you is disquieted, maybe you should check the area one more time.

Summary: Things to Consider

- Location: What is the neighborhood like, and where is the house relative to places that you need to visit?
- Crime: What are the dangers?
- Price: What are the obvious costs and the hidden ones?
- Neighborhood: Is there enough parking, and are the sights and sounds suited to your way of life?
- Children: Is the neighborhood fit for your kids?
- Condition: Does the house have any major flaws?

Looking on Your Own Versus with an Agent

If you're new to Southern California, the area's immense size and its variety of neighborhoods can bewilder you. You may want a real estate agent to help you understand the area.

An agent knows (or can easily find out) about houses that are new on the market and houses that have been waiting for a buyer so long that the owners will slash the price. Usually, she's familiar with the neighborhoods that she's selling. And she understands the legal and financial sides of home buying.

But never forget that she's a saleswoman. The desire to close a deal might encourage an agent to describe a rundown street in terms more glowing than the facts indicate, or to concentrate on a house's potential rather than its troubled reality.

If you shop for a home without an agent, be extra vigilant. Go to open houses to get a sense of what's on the market. Talk to the agent who's showing each house. Ask him why the owners are selling and always get a set-up (a sheet of paper that describes the house's price, lot size, number of bedrooms, neighborhood, and other crucial data).

Whether or not you have your own agent to help you find a house, the person selling will likely have his own agent. If your agent is not necessarily your pal, the seller's agent is even less so. Bring in your own agent, your own lawyer, or another expert to help you negotiate the deal.

Good luck!

CITY FACT

"If Los Angeles County were an independent nation," says the Web site Los Angeles Almanac, "it would have the nineteenth largest economy in the world, larger than that of either Switzerland, Belgium, Sweden, or Austria."

Summary: To Agent or Not to Agent?

- Pro: An agent supplies information, negotiating skills, and advice that are useful to any home buyer, especially a newcomer.
- Con: An agent is essentially a salesperson, and buyers should take the agent's words with a whole Dead Sea of salt.

Resources for Finding a Home

Southern California's newspapers are filled with real estate ads. They'll give you an idea of local prices, architectural styles, and other basics.

For a region that has been more or less built on land speculation, the area has relatively few magazines with objective information on homes. There are publications like *Los Angeles Homes & Open Houses*, which are filled with ads from real estate agencies—they're not long on dispassionate, trustworthy description and analysis.

A number of Web sites provide information on housing. Many are simply collections of ads, but some are more useful. Check out as many as possible.

HOMES FOR SALE BY THEIR OWNERS

By Owner Sales

www.byownersales.com/

For Sale by Owner Connection

www.fsboconnection.com

For Sale by Owner Registry

(888) 290-9637

www.888byowner.com

OTHER RESOURCES

Citibank Owned Homes

mortgages.citicorp.com

Homebuilder.com

A Subsidiary of HomeStore.com, Inc.
17120 North Dallas Parkway, Suite 175
Dallas, TX 75248
(972) 732-0090; (800) 252-9001

Homes.com

800 Menlo Avenue, Suite 210
Menlo Park, CA 94025
(650) 470-1450
(650) 470-1458 (fax)

www.homes.com

Homespace.com

(877) 466-3772

www.homespace.com

iOwn.com

333 Bryant Street, Lower Level
San Francisco, CA 94107
(415) 618-3600;
(877) 669-4696

www.iown.com

MSN home advisor

homeadvisor.msn.com

Newhomesearch

homebuilder.com/

Owners.com

Attn: Customer Support
164 Townsend Street, Suite #3
San Francisco, CA 94107
(800) 273-0732

owners.com/

Realtor.com

(800) 874-6500

www.realtor.com

www.new.realtor.com/CALIFORNIA

Real Estate Companies

Southern California has literally thousands of real estate agents. To find a suitable one, call a bunch of them and interview them as you'd interview a prospective employee. Ask about their experience, how they work with their clients, how they'd take care of your needs, and so on.

The following list isn't by any means complete—a complete list would fill this entire book—but it's a start.

LOS ANGELES COUNTY

Agoura Hills

Fred Sands Realtors
5875 Kanan Road
(818) 879-9100
(818) 879-9191 (fax)
KMehringer
@fsrcorporationcom

Alhambra

Coldwell Banker George Realty
1611 South Garfield Avenue
(626) 457-2388
(626) 308-4768 (fax)
coldwellbankergeorgerealty
@realtor.com

Morgan Realty
233 South Fremont Avenue
(626) 289-3504
MorganRealty@realtor.com

Altadena

Jim Dickson Realtors
1471 East Altadena Drive
(626) 791-1000
contact@jimdickson.com
www.jimdickson.com

Arcadia

Art Del Rey Realty, Inc.
733 West Naomi Avenue
(626) 445-8760
pdelrey405@aol.com

Baldwin Real Estate Services
901 South First Avenue
(626) 447-0858;
(626) 445-0136
gordonm@baldwinrealty.com

Dilbeck Realtors—Better Homes & Gardens
8 East Foothill Boulevard
(626) 445-6701
(626) 445-8330 (fax)
slindsey@earthlink.net
www.dilbeck.com

Artesia

Ace Realty Company
18012 Pioneer Boulevard
(562) 924-1411
(562) 924-2608 (fax)
acerealty@realtor.com

Bell

Western Realty
5200 East Gage Avenue
(323) 562-4204
(323) 562-6079 (fax)
westernrealty@realtor.com

Beverly Hills

Celebrity Properties
9328 Civic Center Drive
(310) 657-6000
(310) 657-6009 (fax)
celebrity
properties@realtor.com

Coldwell Banker
166 North Canon Drive
(310) 273-3113
(310) 278-4934 (fax)
srichman@coldwellbanker.com
or homes@jademills.com

Dalton Brown & Long
9411 Santa Monica Boulevard
(310) 275-8686
(310) 724-5708 (fax)

Fred Sands Beverly Hills
9388 Santa Monica
(310) 278-4100
(310) 273-0690 (fax)

Hilton Hyland Real Estate
270 North Canon Drive
(310) 278-3311
(310) 278-4998 (fax)
hiltonhyland@realtor.com

Mossler Deasy & Doe
345 North Maple Drive
(310) 275-2222
(310) 275-3817 (fax)
info@md-d.com

Nelson Shelton & Associates
355 North Canon Drive
(310) 271-2229
(310) 271-0879 (fax)
canon355@aol.com

Nourmand & Associates
210 North Canon Boulevard
(310) 274-4000
(310) 278-9900 (fax)
nourmand@nourmand.com

Prudential John Aaroe & Associates
250 North Canon Drive
(310) 777-7800
(310) 858-1295 (fax)

Re/Max Beverly Hills
9454 Wilshire Boulevard
(310) 205-0050
(310) 205-0070 (fax)

info@realestatelosangeles.com

Sotheby's International Realty
9665 Wilshire Boulevard
(310) 724-7000
(310) 724-7010 (fax)

frank.symons@sothebys.com

Brentwood
(City of Los Angeles)

Coldwell Banker
11990 San Vincente Boulevard
(310) 207-3711
(310) 207-2691 (fax)

ellenbergeron@realtor.com

Nourmand & Associates
11828 San Vicente Boulevard
(310) 300-3333
(310) 300-2000 (fax)

nourmand@nourmand.com

Prudential John Aaroe & Associates
11677 San Vincente Boulevard
(310) 207-7080
(310) 207-5477 (fax)

info@realestatelosangeles.com

Re/Max Westside Properties
11466 San Vicente Boulevard
(310) 979-4000; (310) 826-5528
(310) 979-4001 (fax)

info@realestatelosangeles.com

Sotheby's International Realty
11812 San Vicente Boulevard
(310) 820-4040
(310) 207-7555 (fax)

frank.symons@sothebys.com

MOVING TIP

If you're coming to Southern California by car, remember that it's legal to turn right on a red light in California. The people behind you will remember that fact, and they may honk at you if you don't make the turn.

Burbank

Century 21 Larson Realty
2300 West Magnolia Boulevard
(818) 841-0330
(818) 843-7049 (fax)

C21LARSON@AOL.com

www.century21.com

Coldwell Banker Burbank
303 North Glenoaks Boulevard
(818) 848-6671
(818) 842-3678 (fax)

bmann@realtor.com

First—Better Homes & Gardens
3601 West Magnolia Boulevard
(818) 845-5111;
(818) 766-8800

CITY FACT

Perhaps the quintessential Hollywood novel is Nathanael West's 1939 classic, *The Day of the Locust*. The book is striking for its sharply accurate portraits of the local environment and the people who strive for success in the movies. One of the major characters is described as "the kind of person who comes to California to die, perfect in every detail down to fever eyes and unruly hands." The character's name is Homer Simpson.

Fred Sands First Class Real Estate
1033 North Hollywood Way
(877) 569-7653
(818) 848-9976 (fax)

sales@fsfc.com

Calabasas

Dilbeck Realtors—Better Homes & Gardens
23548 Calabasas Road
(818) 591-8800

www.dilbeck.com

Prudential California Realty
23528 Calabasas Road
(818) 223-9100

sdrock@prusd.com

www.prudentialcal.com

Re/Max Calabasas
23586 Calabasas Road
(818) 888-7362; (818) 703-7400
(818) 591-3181 (fax)

info@calabasashomes.com
or dmtennen@flash.net

Cerritos

Century 21 Astro Realty
11305 183rd Street
(562) 924-3381
(562) 925-5951 (fax)

carolrayburn@aol.com
or Century21Astro@realtor.com

www.century21.com

Coldwell Banker Towne Center
17410 Bloomfield Avenue
(562) 865-9669
(562) 865-9654 (fax)
coldwellbankercerritos
@realtor.com

Presidential Real Estate
11900 South Street
(562) 809-8989
(562) 809-8979 (fax)

Re/Max Select
20220 State Road
(562) 924-4421
(562) 562 924-4530
re-maxselect@realtor.com

Tiffany Mulhearn Realtors
11306 East 183rd Street
(562) 860-2443
(562) 924-4060 (fax)
tiffanymulhearn@realtor.com

Chatsworth
(City of Los Angeles)

Century 21 All Properties
21049 Devonshire Street
(818) 882-2821
(818) 882-1839 (fax)
goldteam@c21allproperties.com
www.century21.com

Coldwell Banker Quality Properties
20521 Devonshire Street
(818) 725-2500
(818) 725-4363 (fax)
sampson@realtor.com

Chino

Diamond Ridge Properties
3811 Shaeffer Avenue
(909) 902-9656; (909) 627-5950

Crenshaw District
(City of Los Angeles)

Century 21 Broman Realty
3681 Crenshaw Boulevard
(800) 569-8264; (323) 290-5013
(323) 290-5010 (fax)
c21broman@aol.com
www.century21.com
or www.c21broman.com

Smith Moore Estates—Better Homes & Gardens
3860 Crenshaw Boulevard
(323) 290-4086
www.smebetterhomes.com

Culver City

Cavanaugh Realtors
9352 Venice Boulevard
(310) 837-7161
(310) 202-9035 (fax)
cavanaughrealtors@realtor.com
www.cavanaughrealtors.com

Realty Executives Westside
*11295 West Washington
Boulevard*
(310) 737-1992
(310) 737-1052 (fax)
mjohnson
@realtyexecutivesws.com

Downey

**Century 21 Jervis &
Associates**
10209 La Reina Avenue
(323) 562-2100; (562) 862-2226
(562) 862-9744 (fax)
c21jervis@realtor.com
www.century21.com

Eagle Rock
(City of Los Angeles)

**Dilbeck Realtors—Better
Homes & Gardens**
2251 Colorado Boulevard
(323) 255-8100
(323) 257-1525 (fax)
annanet@aol.com
www.dilbeck.com

Encino
(City of Los Angeles)

Re/Max Centre Encino
17327 Ventura Boulevard
(818) 501-7362
(818) 994-3232 (fax)
info@encinohomes.com
www.encinohomes.com

El Segundo

Shorewood Realtors
315 West Grand Avenue
(310) 322-4900
info@shorewood.com

Glendale

Coldwell Banker Glendale
914 North Glendale Avenue
(818) 240-1111
(818) 240-1732 (fax)
jrudell@coldwellbanker.com

**Dilbeck Realtors—Better
Homes & Gardens**
1000 North Central Avenue
(818) 240-8100
(818) 240-6018 (fax)
luiselsla@classic.msn.com
www.dilbeck.com

Fred Sands Professionals
1155 North Central Avenue
(818) 241-3000
(818) 243-4200 (fax)
vstepanian@yahoo.com

Home Life-Five City Realty
330 North Glendale Avenue
(818) 548-5050
(818) 548-7535 (fax)
homelifefivecityrealty
@realtor.com

MacGregor Realty
200 West Glenoaks Boulevard
(818) 244-4449

macgregorrealtyglendale
@realtor.com

Prudential California Realty
138 North Brand Boulevard
(818) 247-2121;
(818) 243-4600

sdrock@prusd.com
www.prudentialcal.com

Re/Max of Glendale
333 East Glenoaks Boulevard
(818) 240-6065
(818) 547-6322 (fax)

remaxofglendale@realtor.com

Granada Hills

Century 21 Prechtl & Associates
11011 Balboa Boulevard
(818) 363-1717
(818) 360-5676 (fax)

info@sfvhomes.com
www.sfvhomes.com
or www.century21.com

Hacienda Heights

Mulhearn T. P. A. Realty
17170 East Colima Road
(626) 913-2808

CITY FACT

According to *Curbside L.A.* by Cecilia Rasmussen, the bar-band classic "Louie, Louie" was written on West 54th Street in Los Angeles, within a few miles of the University of Southern California. Songwriter Richard Berry grew up in the area.

Presidential Real Estate
1617 South Azusa Avenue
(626) 839-7168; (626) 839-8899
(626) 964-6996 (fax)

Hawthorne

Century 21 Western Homes
14005 Hawthorne Boulevard
(310) 978-2121; (800) 982-2100

C21WesternHomes@realtor.com
www.century21.com

Hermosa Beach

Shorewood Realtors
950 Artesia Boulevard
(310) 376-8871
info@shorewood.com

Highland Park
(City of Los Angeles)

Century 21 Arroyo Seco
5810 York Boulevard
(323) 254-3966
(323) 258-1299 (fax)
c21randman@aol.com
www.century21.com

Hollywood
(City of Los Angeles)

Century 21 P&S Realty
4844 Hollywood Boulevard
(323) 663-3922
(323) 663-6411 (fax)
www.century21.com

Coldwell Banker Real Estate
2150 Hillhurst Avenue
(323) 906-2400; (323) 665-5841;
(323) 666-4955
(323) 664-2614 (fax)

Dalton Brown & Long
1929 North Hillhurst Avenue
(323) 665-1700
(323) 665-1780 (fax)

Hyde Park
(City of Los Angeles)

United Realtors
6515 Crenshaw Boulevard
(323) 753-5542
(323) 753-5572 (fax)
UnitedRealtors@realtor.com

Industry

Re/Max 2000 Realty
1500 Stoner Creek
(626) 964-8999
(626) 810-1777 (fax)
kuansung@earthlink.net

Inglewood

Coldwell Banker Gene Armstrong
416 West Manchester Boulevard
(310) 412-4049; (310) 330-4688
(310) 412-0384 (fax)

La Canada Flintridge

Coldwell Banker
711 Foothill Boulevard
(818) 790-3334
(818) 790-8583 (fax)
jrudell@coldwellbanker.com

Dilbeck Realtors
1030 Foothill Boulevard
(818) 790-6774
(818) 790-8967 (fax)
lynn.beckenhauer@dilbeck.com
www.dilbeck.com

Ellis Realty
1115 Foothill Boulevard
(818) 790-3554
(818) 790-8997 (fax)
www.ellisrealty.com

Keilholtz Realtors Inc.
727 Foothill Boulevard
(818) 790-5534
(818) 790-7011 (fax)
Keilholtzrealtors@realtor.com
www.keilholtz.com

MacGregor Realty
845 Foothill Boulevard
(818) 790-8300
(818) 790-8971 (fax)
macgregorrealtylacanada
@realtor.com
or jmacgregor@earthlink.net
wwwmacgregor-reality.com

**La Crescenta
(City of Los Angeles)**

Century 21 Crest
4005 Foothill Boulevard
(818) 248-9100; (818) 236-3600
(818) 248-9190 (fax)
cen21crest@aol.com
www.century21.com

**Dilbeck Realtors—Better
Homes & Gardens**
2943 Foothill Boulevard
(818) 248-2248
(818) 957-4517 (fax)
bobboz@ix.netcom.com
www.dilbeck.com

Ellis Realty
3156 Foothill Boulevard
(818) 248-3669
(818) 248-4510 (fax)
ellisrealty@realtor.com
www.ellisrealty.com

Sundance Realty
3248 Foothill Boulevard
(818) 248-6710

Lakewood

Coldwell Banker Star Realty
4916 Palo Verde Avenue
(562) 804-1385
(562) 920-7101 (fax)
dave4cb@aol.com
www.coldwellbankerstar.com

Mulhearn Realtors
11409 East Carson Street
(562) 809-1331

Re/Max Investments Unlimited
5572 South Street
(562) 804-1993; (888) 520-1444
(562) 804-3063 (fax)
remaxiu@realtor.com

Lancaster

Century 21 Doug Anderson & Associates

1727 West Avenue K
(661) 945-4521
(661) 948-4307 (fax)

rstickney@ptw.com
or c21and@ptw.com

www.century21douganderson
.com
or www.century21.com

Re/Max All-Pro

43997 15th Street
(800) 945-9461;
(661) 945-9461
(661) 942-0696 (fax)

peter@remaxallpro.com
www.lasterrealetate.com
or www.palmdalerealestate.com

Long Beach

Century 21 Hunter Associates

3826 Atlantic Avenue
(562) 426-6577

www.century21.com

Century 21 Shoreline Properties, Inc.

6272-B East Pacific Coast Highway
(562) 430-0574
(562) 594-9988 (fax)

century21shoreline@realtor.com
www.century21.com

Century 21 Sparow Realty

6615 East Pacific Coast Highway
(562) 493-6555

c21sparow@realtor.com
www.century21.com
or www.c21sparow.com

Fred Sands Preferred Real Estate

5353 East Second Street
(562) 433-7476
(562) 562 433-4482 (fax)

fredsandspreferred@realtor.com

Mulhearn Dolphin Realtors

5150 East Pacific Coast Highway
(562) 494-8424
(562) 498-4315 (fax)

mulhearndolphin@realtor.com

Prudential California Realty

1650 Ximeno Avenue
(562) 494-4600
(562) 597-2968 (fax)

prudentialcalifornia@realtor.com
or sdrock@prusd.com
www.prudentialcal.com

Re/Max College Park

2610 Los Coyotes Diagonal

(562) 982-0300

remaxcollegeparklongbeach
@realtor.com

Re/Max Real Estate Specialists

6695 East Pacific Coast Highway

(562) 493-3004

(562) 493-0010 (fax)

bobstall@aol.com
or mikeys@gte.net

Robert Weil Associates

5220 East Los Altos Plaza

(562) 494-7000

(562) 431-4364;

(562) 494-4154 (fax)

robertweilassociates
@realtor.com

Woody Financial Realty Corporation

5580 East 2nd Street

(562) 439-3344

(562) 433-0648 (fax)

Manhattan Beach

Real Estate West

905 Manhattan Beach Boulevard

(310) 546-3441

(310) 376-0783 (fax)

rewest@realtor.com

Re/Max Beach Cities

225 South Sepulveda Boulevard

(310) 318-1090; (310) 376-2225

(310) 376-6522 (fax)

info@realestatelosangeles.com

Shorewood Realtors

3300 Highland Avenue

(310) 546-7561

(310) 322-6227 (fax)

info@shorewood.com

MOVING TIP

The California Public Utilities Commission regulates household-goods movers operating in California. For information on movers, call the commission at (800) 366-4782.

Shorewood Realtors

917 Manhattan Beach Boulevard

(310) 545-8401

info@shorewood.com

City Fact

As you might expect, quite a few show-business celebrities are buried in Hollywood. But in an otherwise unassuming cemetery in the north San Fernando Valley neighborhood of Mission Hills lies Richie Valens, the Latino rocker famous for "La Bamba." A marker at his grave site carries a bar of notes from his first hit, "Come On, Let's Go."

Marina del Rey
(City of Los Angeles)

Re/Max Beach Cities/Westside Properties
13400 West Washington Boulevard
(310) 306-4245
(310) 306-0609 (fax)
info@realestatelosangeles.com
or drivas@pacbell.net

Mar Vista
(City of Los Angeles)

George Chung Realtors
3487 Beethoven Street
(310) 391-6346
(310) 390-6713 (fax)
gcr@gte.net

Monrovia

Century 21 Adams & Barnes
433 West Foothill Boulevard
(626) 358-1858; (626) 303-8733
century21adamsandbarnes @realtor.com
www.century21.com

South Bay Brokers
2501 North Sepulveda Boulevard
(310) 546-7611
(310) 545-0515 (fax)
southbaybrokers@realtor.com

Vintage Real Estate Group
920 Manhattan Beach Boulevard
(310) 545-9595

Monterey Park

Century 21 George Michael Realty
2360 South Garfield Avenue
(626) 289-2121; (626) 799-2121

C21GM@realtor.com
www.century21.com

North Hollywood

Century 21 Exclusive Realtors
4640 Lankersheim Boulevard
(818) 760-0897; (818) 860-1313

www.century21.com

Northridge
(City of Los Angeles)

Century 21 All Properties, Inc.
10180 Reseda Boulevard
(818) 886-9121; (800) 346-9118

tjm3m@aol.com

www.century21.com

Paramount Properties—Northridge
9338 Reseda Boulevard
(818) 349-9997
(818) 349-0212 (fax)

paramountproperties
@realtor.com

Pinnacle Estate Properties
9137 Reseda Boulevard
(818) 993-7370
(818) 772-6764 (fax)

pinpropinc@aol.com

Re/Max Ltd.—Select
9110 Tampa Avenue
(818) 993-4606; (800) 407-4606

info@ltdselect.com

Todd C. Olson & Associates
9535 Reseda Boulevard
(818) 349-3330
(818) 949-3404 (fax)

info@toddcolson.com

Todd C. Olson Estate Brokerage
11201 Tampa Avenue
(818) 366-3300
(818) 366-4945 (fax)

info@toddcolson.com
or tsmith@toddcolson.com

Ontario

ERA Preferred Properties
720 North Archibald Avenue
(909) 944-7566
(909) 944-0661 (fax)

erapreferred@realtor.com

www.netcom.com/~eraont

Mulhearn Realtors Gallery of Homes
1063 West 6th Street
(909) 983-9933

**Pacific Palisades
(City of Los Angeles)**

AM Realty
15113 Sunset Boulevard
(800) 769-3332;
(310) 573-4245

amrealty@ix.netcom.com

Fred Sands
15240 Sunset Boulevard
(310) 459-2766

nancymorandi@earthlink.net

Palmdale

Ana Verde Realty
2025 East Palmdale Boulevard
(661) 273-8600

Renaissance Realty
4654 East Avenue S
(661) 533-6700

email@rrpi.net

www.rrpi.net

**Palos Verdes
(City of Los Angeles)**

Coldwell Banker Palos Verdes
430 Silver Spur Road
(310) 541-2421
(310) 541-5865 (fax)

info@coldwellbankerpv.com

Fred Sands Palos Verdes
16 Malaga Cove Plaza
(310) 378-1907
(310) 378-2158 (fax)

realestate@fredsandspv.com

600 Deep Valley Drive
(310) 544-0303
(310) 544-6353 (fax)

realestate@fredsandspv.com

Pasadena

Century 21 Golden Realty
1725 East Washington Boulevard
(626) 797-7622
(626) 797-3865 (fax)

golden21@aol.com

www.century21.com

Dilbeck Realtors—Better Homes & Gardens
132 East Colorado Boulevard
(800) 877-7356;
(626) 584-0101
(626) 584-3889 (fax)

mcgeagh@ix.netcom.com

www.dilbeck.com

Jim Dickson Realtors
336 South Lake Avenue
(626) 795-9571
(626) 795-4688 (fax)

contact@jimdickson.com

www.jimdickson.com

MacGregor Realty—Pasadena
123 North Lake Avenue
(626) 795-8300

macgregorrealtypasadena
@realtor.com

Westlyn Realtors
1199 North Lake Avenue
(626) 398-3500;
(626) 398-0055
(626) 296-0839 (fax)

westlyn@earthlink.net

The William Wilson Company
146 South Lake Avenue
(626) 793-8111
(626) 577-7634 (fax)

thewilliamwilsoncopasadena
@realtor.com
www.williamwilsonco.com

Rancho Palos Verdes

Century 21 Bill Pike Realty
28924 South Western Avenue
(310) 831-0125
(310) 831-4034 (fax)

georgeleonard@realtor.com
www.century21.com

Re/Max Seapoint Realty
29050 South Western Avenue
(310) 514-1364
(310) 514-1420 (fax)

bobbradarich@realtor.com

CITY FACT

The area's costliest homes are in Beverly Hills, La Canada Flintridge, Malibu, Manhattan Beach, Newport Beach, Palos Verdes Estates, Rancho Palos Verdes, San Marino, and Santa Monica. The cheapest are in Twentynine Palms, Coachella, Barstow, Desert Hot Springs, Yucca Valley, Indio, Banning, Beaumont, San Jacinto, and Hemet. None of these low-cost communities are in L.A. County or Orange County proper.

Redondo Beach

Coldwell Banker
2502 Artesia Boulevard
(310) 798-8700
(310) 374-0445 (fax)

source1@realtor.com

Re/Max Execs—Redondo Beach
1720 South Elena Avenue
(310) 378-7747
(310) 378-1997 (fax)

remaxexecsredondobeach
@realtor.com

Shorewood Realtors
1009 Torrance Boulevard
(310) 316-8464

info@shorewood.com

South Bay Brokers
1717 South Catalina Avenue
(310) 375-0583
(310) 375-9616 (fax)

southbaybrokers@realtor.com

Rolling Hills Estates

Prudential California Realty
501 Deep Valley Drive
(310) 544-5091

sdrock@prusd.com
www.prudentialcal.com

San Dimas

Century 21 Citrus Realty
1100 Via Verde
(909) 592-8500

www.century21.com

San Fernando

ERA Rocking Horse Realty Inc.
832 North MacLay Avenue
(818) 361-1235
(818) 361-0242 (fax)

erarockinghorse@realtor.com

San Marino

Dilbeck Realtors—Better Homes & Gardens
2486 Huntington Drive
(626) 287-9625
(626) 309-0171 (fax)

rwells4re@aol.com
www.dilbeck.com

Prudential California Realty
2111 Huntington Drive
(626) 568-8876

sdrock@prusd.com
www.prudentialcal.com

Re/Max Premier Properties
2375 Huntington Drive
(626) 449-6414;
(626) 660-1100
(626) 449-4162 (fax)

remaxsanmarino@realtor.com

The William Wilson Company
2130 Huntington Drive
(626) 576-7889
(626) 576-7887 (fax)

thewilliamwilsoncosanmarino
@realtor.com

San Pedro
(City of Los Angeles)

All American Mulhearn Realtors
823 West 9th Street
(310) 831-0301
(310) 548-8601 (fax)
allamerican@mulhearn.com

Di Bernardo Realty
577 West 9th Street
(310) 832-4572
(310) 832-4575 (fax)
dibernardorealty@realtor.com

Santa Monica

Celebrity Properties
1505 4th Street
(310) 393-8491
(310) 260-3104 (fax)
jasusser@aol.com

Fred Sands Santa Monica
1423 Wilshire Boulevard
(310) 395-7090;
(310) 395-2818
(310) 395-5395 (fax)

Re/Max Westside Properties
2010 Wilshire Boulevard
(310) 264-2225
(310) 264-2200 (fax)
info@realestatelosangeles.com

Sherman Oaks
(City of Los Angeles)

Re/Max on the Boulevard
14242 Ventura Boulevard
(818) 789-7117; (818) 981-9558
(818) 789-0382 (fax)
remaxotbshermanoaks@realtor.com

Sierra Madre

Webb-Martin Realtors
30 North Baldwin Avenue
(626) 355-2384
(626) 355-2388 (fax)
info@webb-martin.com

CITY FACT

Is Orange County the new Detroit? Ford Motor Company is moving its luxury models' headquarters to Irvine. Lincoln and Mercury have been based there for years, and soon Ford's Jaguar, Volvo, and Aston Martin divisions will join them.

South Gate

Mulhearn Realtors
9849 South Atlantic
(323) 563-8813

Western Realty
4453 Tweedy Boulevard
(323) 567-7744

South Pasadena

Dilbeck Realtors—Better Homes & Gardens
1499 Huntington Drive
(626) 799-3020
(626) 799-5073 (fax)
annanet@aol.com
www.dilbeck.com

Huntington Group
301 Pasadena Avenue
(626) 403-8230
(626) 403-8238 (fax)
thldepot@earthlink.net

Studio City
(City of Los Angeles)

Gibson & Associates
13103 Ventura Boulevard
(818) 728-2200
(818) 728-2345 (fax)
gibsonrealtors@realtor.com

Prudential John Aaroe & Associates
4061 Laurel Canyon Boulevard
(818) 755-1000
(818) 985-1690 (fax)

Tarzana
(City of Los Angeles)

Re/Max Grand Central
18946 Ventura Boulevard
(818) 708-6300; (818) 708-6301
(818) 776-9386 (fax)
transactions@realtor.com

Temple City

Coldwell Banker Pacific Dynasty
9228 Las Tunas Drive
(626) 287-9636
(626) 287-9043 (fax)
cbpacificdynasty@realtor.com

Pyramid Realty
5849 Temple City Boulevard
(800) 833-7972; (626) 309-2790
(626) 287-4756 (fax)
pyramidrealty@realtor.com

Toluca Lake
(City of Los Angeles)

Ramsey-Shilling & Associates
10205 Riverside Drive
(818) 763-5162
(818) 980-0052 (fax)
agents@ramseyshilling.com

Torrance

Century 21 All Realty
3620 Pacific Coast Highway
(310) 791-2100
(310) 791-3330 (fax)
info@c21allrealty.com
www.century21.com

Century 21 Amber Realty
23705 Crenshaw Boulevard
(310) 326-8100
(310) 534-0325 (fax)
c21amberrealty@realtor.com
www.century21.com

Century 21 Union Realty
3440 West Carson Street
(310) 793-3309; (310) 371-6330
(310) 370-7265 (fax)
c21unionrealty@realtor.com
www.century21.com

First Realty—Better Homes & Gardens
4433 West Sepulveda Boulevard
(310) 316-9997

Re/Max Beach Cities
3611 Torrance Boulevard
(310) 540-6060
(310) 543-0399 (fax)
info@realestatelosangeles.com

Venice (City of Los Angeles)

Re/Max Beach Cities Realty
155 Washington Boulevard
(310) 577-5300
(310) 577-5301 (fax)
info@realestatelosangeles.com

Venice Properties
610 Hampton Drive
(310) 399-1123
(310) 399-7411 (fax)
venprop@att.net

CITY FACT

The local cities with the lowest violent crime rates, according to *The Comparative Guide to American Suburbs*, are Yorba Linda, Palos Verdes Estates, Sierra Madre, Laguna Hills, and Laguna Niguel. The cities with the highest violent crime rates are Hawthorne, Commerce, West Hollywood, Lynwood, and Compton.

West Hollywood

Dalton Brown & Long
9000 Sunset Boulevard
(310) 205-0305
(310) 205-0809 (fax)

CITY FACT

Southern California has long been the home of weird buildings, including at least two shaped like giant doughnuts: Randy's Donuts near Los Angeles International Airport and Donut Hole in the east Los Angeles County city of La Puente. "Donut Lane actually leads through the holes of giant fiberglass doughnuts that form each end of this little shed-roofed stand," architecture critic Charles Moore has written of Donut Hole. "This is drive-in drama at its best."

Prudential John Aaroe & Associates
8687 Melrose Avenue
(310) 855-0100
(310) 855-0160 (fax)

Westlake Village

Century 21 Westlake Village
2801 Townsgate Road
(805) 495-2181
(805) 371-0121 (fax)
donnam@c21westlake.com
www.century21.com
www.c21.westlake.com

Dilbeck Realtors—Better Homes & Gardens
850 Hampshire Road
(805) 379-1880
(805) 379-3680 (fax)
BradBrook1@aol.com
www.dilbeck.com

Fred Sands Realtors
883 South Westlake Boulevard
(805) 495-1048,
(818) 991-9191
(805) 495-2218 (fax)
aaaastarr@aol.com

Diamond Bar Century 21 E-N Realty
1081 South Grand Avenue
(800) 800-5364; (800) 800-6450;
(909) 861-2100; (909) 964-3497

info@century21en.com
or dianah.c21@iname.com

www.century21.com

Westwood
(City of Los Angeles)

Century 21 Exclusive Realtors—Westwood
2945 Westwood Boulevard
(310) 474-5020
(310) 474-5566 (fax)

c21exclsve@aol.com

www.century21.com

Fred Sands Residential Real Estate
(310) 442-1387
(310) 496-3032 (fax)

bobrosene@aircor.net

Wilshire District
(City of Los Angeles)

Ivy Realty
611 South Wilton Place
(213) 386-8888
(213) 386-8183 (fax)

info@ivyrealty.com

Re/Max 100
4311 Wilshire Boulevard
(323) 933-4567
(323) 933-7050 (fax)

remax100la@aol.com

ORANGE COUNTY

Anaheim

Ashley & Associates
4506 East La Palma Avenue
(714) 693-0777

Century 21 All Pro
1203 South Euclid
(714) 635-4011
(714) 635-5639 (fax)

www.century21.com

Anaheim Hills
(City of Anaheim)

Prudential California Realty— Anaheim Hills
160 South Old Springs Road
(714) 998-7250
(714) 998-0425 (fax)

therock@prusd.com
or sdrock@prusd.com

www.sburt.com
or www.prudentialcal.com

Seven Gables Real Estate
5481 East Santa Ana Canyon Road
(714) 974-7000

Brea

Century 21 Chuck Stevens
200 West Imperial Highway
(714) 990-0140; (888) 273-2777
(714) 990-1525 (fax)
century 21stevens@realtor.com
www.century21.com

Evergreen Realty
860 West Imperial Highway
(714) 990-0770

1 Percent Homeseller
558 East Lambert Road
(714) 990-3914

Corona

Re/Max All Stars Realty-Corona/Norco
765 North Main Street
(909) 739-4000
(909) 739-4060 (fax)
elizabethb@remaxallstars.net

**Corona del Mar
(City of Newport Beach)**

First Team Real Estate
2600 East Coast Highway
(949) 759-5747
(949) 660-4925 (fax)
jonorri@home.com
or tedana1@aol.com

Costa Mesa

Ditech Real Estate
3200 Park Center Drive
(714) 800-6181
(714) 800-5801 (fax)

Cypress

Coldwell Banker Star Realty
9917 Walker Street
(714) 527-9011
coldwellbankerstarrealty
@realtor.com

**New West Real Estate—
Better Homes & Gardens**
5003 Ball Road
(714) 527-9000

Re/Max Tiffany Real Estate
5925 Ball Road
(714) 763-2100; (714) 761-2080
remaxtiffany@realtor.com

Dana Point

Link Realty Center
34213 Pacific Coast Highway
(949) 661-4798;
(949) 597-5287
ashleyhandal@realtor.com

Fountain Valley

Star Real Estate
10055 Slater Avenue
(714) 754-6262
(714) 965-0257 (fax)
starrealestate3@realtor.com

Fullerton

Century 21 Discovery
100 West Valencia Mesa Drive
(800) 221-8085; (714) 738-5444;
(562) 690-7706
(714) 578-1799 (fax)
c21discovery@realtor.com
www.century21.com
or www.c21discovery.com

First Team Real Estate
1400 North Harbor Boulevard
(714) 278-0808

Fred Sands First Choice Realty
3261 North Harbor Boulevard
(714) 871-8840;
(800) 986-4687
(714) 871-8843 (fax)
fredsandsfirstchoice
@realtor.com

Winkelmann Realty
114 North Harbor Boulevard
(714) 879-9610
(714) 879-1638 (fax)
relo@winkrealty.com

Garden Grove

Orange County Realtors
12921 Chapman Avenue
(714) 750-1684
(714) 312-8038 (fax)
orangecountyrealtors
@realtor.com

Huntington Beach

Century 21 Beachside
19671 Beach Boulevard
(714) 969-6100
r-tmchugh@worldnet.att.net
www.century21.com

Fred Sands Paradise Realty
6100 Warner Avenue
(714) 843-0123
(714) 375-6120 (fax)
fredsandsparadiserealty
@realtor.com

**Harbour Homes &
Investments, Inc.**
16875 Algonquin Street
(714) 840-1031
(714) 846-5249 (fax)
info@harbourhome.com

Huntington Beach Realty
322 Main Street
(714) 960-8541
huntbchrlty@earthlink.net

Re/Max Real Estate Services
19720 Beach Boulevard
(714) 536-8000
(714) 378-0358 (fax)

remaxhb@homesoc.com

Star Real Estate
16872 Bolsa Chica Road
(714) 377-2011
(714) 377-2007 (fax)

starrealestate2@realtor.com

Star Real Estate
20951 Brookhurst Street
(714) 968-4456
(714) 968-2979 (fax)

starrealestate1@realtor.com

Welmark & Associates
20422 Beach Boulevard
(714) 969-9400
(714) 960-9055 (fax)

welmark@msn.com

Irvine

Century 21 Professionals
4000 Barranca Parkway
(949) 551-7000;
(800) 654-1457

c21prof@aol.com
www.century21.com

Coldwell Banker
4010 Barranca Parkway
(949) 552-1714

cbirvine@realtor.com

Hanu Reddy Realty
15435 Jeffrey Road
(949) 559-5555
(949) 559-4812 (fax)

hanureddy@realtor.com
or hanureddy
@hanureddyrealty.com
www.hanureddyrealty.com

Prudential California Realty—Irvine
3333 Michelson Drive
(949) 794-5700
(949) 794-5701 (fax)

therock@prusd.com
or sdrock@prusd.com
www.prudentialcal.com

Re/Max Premier Realty
5299 Alton Parkway
(949) 559-9400
(949) 857-2847 (fax)

remaxpremierrealty
@realtor.com
www.remax.com

Tarbell Realtors
4000 Barranca Parkway
(949) 559-8451
(949) 559-1841 (fax)

homes@tarbellirvine.com

Laguna Beach

Coast Newport Properties
31601 South Coast Highway
(888) 644-5600;
(949) 499-6110
(949) 499-7660 (fax)
info@coastnewport.com
or realtor@eni.net

Coldwell Banker
32356 Coast Highway
(949) 499-1320

First Team Nolan Real Estate
900 Glenneyre Street
(949) 497-5454
(949) 497-2154 (fax)
firstteamnolan@realtor.com

Prudential California Realty
1110 Glenneyre Street
(949) 497-3331
(949) 494-2152 (fax)
therock@prusd.com
or sdrock@prusd.com
www.prudentialcal.com

Laguna Hills

Barker & Associates
25431 Cabot Road
(949) 470-4001;
(949) 472-1120
(949) 472-4824 (fax)

Evergreen Realty
25401 Alicia Parkway
(949) 465-0449

First Team Real Estate
26534 Moulton Parkway
(949) 643-1124
(949) 643-3575 (fax)
randyhutchinson@mail.com

Fred Sands Laguna Hills Properties
24031 El Toro Road
(949) 837-3870
(949) 837-4669 (fax)
fredsandslhp@realtor.com

CITY FACT

In northwest Los Angeles County stands the community of Val Verde, which "began in the mid 1920s as a kind of black Palm Springs," says Cecilia Rasmussen in *Curbside L.A.* "Entertainers such as Count Basie, Duke Ellington, Della Reese, and Billy Eckstine visited the rural summer retreat and occasionally gave impromptu concerts at Val Verde Park."

Relocation Center of Southern California
23272 Mill Creek Drive
(949) 452-0730
(949) 452-0730 (fax)
relocationcenter@realtor.com

Laguna Niguel

Ocean Ranch Realty
28202 Cabot Road
(800) 219-1468;
(949) 365-5780

Professional Real Estate Enterprises
28281 Crown Valley Parkway
(949) 348-8828

Prudential California Realty— Laguna Niguel
30012 Ivy Glenn Drive
(949) 495-1800
(949) 249-9064 (fax)
therock@prusd.com
or sdrock@prusd.com
www.prudentialcal.com

The Summit Real Estate Group
23811 Aliso Creek Road
(949) 425-9600
(949) 425-9631 (fax)
hjosepher@eleganthomes.com

La Habra

Century 21 Chuck Stevens
800 North Harbor Boulevard
(800) 524-2272;
(562) 697-1745
(562) 691-8131 (fax)
century 21stevens@realtor.com
or eileenc21s@aol.com
www.century21.com

Today Realty & Investments
2021 East La Habra Boulevard
(714) 529-2212;
(562) 690-5801
(562)-694-6306 (fax)

Lake Forest

Professional Real Estate Enterprises
23002 Lake Center Drive
(949) 454-9980;
(949) 788-0055

La Palma

Century 21 Castle
540 La Palma Avenue
(714) 995-6999
(714) 826-1142 (fax)
century21castle@realtor.com
www.century21.com

Los Alamitos

Century 21 Duncan & Associates
3401 Katella Avenue
(714) 952-1422
(562) 799-8358 (fax)
www.century21.com

Century 21 Unlimited
11292 Los Alamitos Boulevard
(888) 446-4654;
(562) 493-5491

darlac21@earthlink.net

www.century21.com

Re/Max College Park Realty
10791 Los Alamitos Boulevard
(562) 594-6753

remaxcollegeparklosalamitos
@realtor.com

Westways Realtors, Inc.
3532 Katella Avenue
(562) 594-8654
(562) 596-2419 (fax)

westwaysrealtors@realtor.com

Mission Viejo

Associated Realtors
25350 Marguerite Parkway
(949) 581-1100
(949) 837-7974 (fax)

ar@realtor.com

Century 21 Automated Real Estate Center
27785 Santa Margarita Parkway
(800) 854-9341;
(949) 859-2100
(949) 598-2221 (fax)

homes21@realtor.com

www.century21.com

Century 21 Beachside
27802 Vista del Lago
(949) 597-4000
(949) 597-4015;
(949) 597-0143;
(949) 859-8019 (fax)

c21beachsidemv@realtor.com
or barrteam@earthlink.net

www.century21.com

Landmark Realtors
26030 Acero Street
(949) 470-7810;
(949) 470-3600
(949) 768-3788 (fax)

landmarkrealtors@realtor.com

Prudential California Realty— Mission Viejo
25909 Pala Drive
(949) 768-1000
(949) 587-0915 (fax)

therock@prusd.com
or sdrock@prusd.com

www.prudentialcal.com

Re/Max Real Estate Services
23120 Alicia Parkway
(949) 454-8220; (949) 582-0222
(949) 454-0211 (fax)

remaxmv@realtor.com

Regency Real Estate Brokers
25950 Acero Street
(949) 707-4400

regency@realtor.com

Monarch Beach
(City of Dana Point)

Prudential California Realty
2 Ritz Carlton Drive
(949) 443-2000;
(949) 661-7900
(949) 443-2209 (fax)

sdrock@prusd.com
www.prudentialcal.com

Re/Max Real Estate Services
33522 Niguel Road
(949) 661-1400;
(949) 661-0579;
(949) 489-1583
(949) 489-9696 (fax)

remaxmb@homesoc.com
or susiehop@deltanet.com
www.shannonferguson.com

The Summit Real Estate Group
28 Monarch Bay Plaza
(949) 489-7555

hjosepher@eleganthomes.com

Newport Beach

Larry O'Rourke & Company
2244 West Coast Highway
(949) 650-7000;
(800) 682-2121

ljor@earthlink.net

Prudential California Realty—
Newport Beach
23 Corporate Plaza
(949) 644-6200
(949) 640-7429 (fax)

therock@prusd.com
or sdrock@prusd.com
www.prudentialcal.com

Re/Max Real Estate Services
23 Corporate Plaza
(949) 760-5000

Star Real Estate
110 Newport Center Drive
(949) 644-8700

The Summit Real Estate Group
17 Corporate Plaza
(949) 640-7888

hjosepher@eleganthomes.com

Orange

Prudential California Realty
2249 North Tustin Avenue
(714) 283-8300
(714) 283-8333 (fax)

prudentialcalrealty@realtor.com
or sdrock@prusd.com
www.prudentialcal.com

Realty World Lifestyles
311 North Tustin Avenue
(714) 639-3855; (800) 760-7653

realtyworldlifestyles
@realtor.com

Ricci Realty
616 East Chapman Avenue
(714) 633-3600
(714) 633-5500 (fax)

riccirealty@realtor.com

Placentia

Main Street Properties
201 South Lakeview Avenue
(714) 572-8090
(714) 572-8085 (fax)
mainstreetproperties
@realtor.com

Rancho Santa Margarita

The Summit Real Estate Group
29911 Aventura
(949) 589-1100
(949) 589-1102 (fax)
hjosepher@eleganthomes.com

San Clemente

Century 21 O.M.A. Realtors
229 Avenida Del Mar
(949) 492-5413
(949) 492-7850 (fax)
cjeanette@aol.com
or callcaroll@earthlink.net
www.century21.com

Conrad & Associates Realtors
1000 South El Camino Real
(877) 492-9400;
(949) 492-9400
conradrealestate
@email.msn.com

First Team San Clemente
407 North El Camino Real
(949) 498-0300

Re/Max Real Estate Services
501 North El Camino Real
(949) 369-0444
remaxsc@homesoc.com

White Water Realty
608 Avenida Victoria
(888) 788-7873; (949) 498-7873
whitewaterrealty@home.com

San Juan Capistrano

HomeLife Pacific Rim Realty
31897 Del Obispo
(949) 240-7477
homelifepacrim@realtor.com
ww.homeseekers.com

Professional Real Estate Enterprises
32332 Camino Capistrano
(949) 248-9493

Prudential California Realty
32382 Del Obispo
(949) 443-0095
(949) 443-5459 (fax)
therock@prusd.com
or sdrock@prusd.com
www.prudentialcal.com

Santa Ana

Re/Max Metro
3951 South Plaza Drive
(714) 435-0402;
(714) 437-7149; (714) 531-0777
remaxmetro@realtor.com

Santa Ana Realty Company
921 West 17th Street
(714) 542-6721

Tustin

Coldwell Banker
12681 Newport Avenue
(714) 832-0020

First Team Real Estate
17240 East 17th Street
(714) 544-5456
(714) 544-4490 (fax)
firstteamrealestate@realtor.com

CITY FACT

According to *Fodor's '99 Los Angeles*, the boysenberry was created by a Buena Park farmer who mixed loganberries, red raspberries, and blackberries. Today, Knott's Berry Farm stands on his site.

North Hills Realty
17771 17th Street
(800) 833-0285; (714) 731-5900
(714) 731-5829 (fax)
northhills@realtor.com

Properties by Jane Hutchinson
(714) 730-1200

Seven Gables Real Estate
12651 Newport Avenue
(714) 731-3777;
(714) 665-7100
(714) 731-4906 (fax)
sevengables@realtor.com

Tarbell Realtors
12841 Newport Avenue
(714) 832-8800
(714) 731-0661 (fax)
tarb034@realtor.com

Villa Park

Re/Max Villa Park Realty
17767 Santiago Boulevard
(714) 637-3700
casey4re@aol.com
or BartSmith@realtor.com

Yorba Linda

Century 21 Yorba Station
18152 Imperial Highway
(714) 993-9440
www.century21.com
or www.c21yorbastation.com

Re/Max Realty Centre
20459 Yorba Linda Boulevard
(714) 777-5112
remax1@earthlink.net

Packing Up and Moving Out

By Monstermoving.com

CHAPTER 4

Getting Organized and Planning Your Move

Written for both the beginner and the veteran, this chapter contains information and resources that will help you get ready for your move. If money is foremost on your mind, you'll find a section on budgeting for the move and tips on how to save money throughout the move—as well as a move budget-planning guide. If time is also precious, you'll find time-saving tips and even suggestions for how to get out of town in a hurry. You'll find help with preliminary decisions, the planning process, and packing, as well as tips and advice on uprooting and resettling your family (and your animal companions). A budget worksheet, a set of helpful checklists, and a moving task time line complete the chapter.

Paying for Your Move

Moving can certainly tap your bank account. How much depends on a number of factors: whether your employer is helping with the cost, how much stuff you have, and how far you are moving.

To get an idea of how much your move will cost, start calling service providers for estimates and begin listing these expenses on the move budget-planning guide provided at the end of this chapter.

If you don't have the money saved, start saving as soon as you can. You should also check out other potential sources of money:

- Income from the sale of your spare car, furniture, or other belongings (hold a garage or yard sale).

- The cleaning and damage deposit on your current rental and any utility deposits. You probably won't be reimbursed until *after* your move, though, so you'll need to pay moving expenses up front in some other way.

- Your employer, who may owe you a payout for vacation time not taken.

Taxes and Your Move

Did you know that your move may affect your taxes? As you prepare to move, here are some things to consider:

- Next year's taxes. Some of your moving expenses may be tax-deductible. Save your receipts and contact your accountant and the IRS for more information. Visit *www.irs.gov* or call the IRS at (800) 829-3676 for information and to obtain the publication and forms you need.

- State income tax. If your new state collects income tax, you'll want to figure that into your salary and overall cost-of-living calculations. Of course, if your old state collects income tax and your new one doesn't, that's a factor, too, but a happier one—but remember to find out how much, if any, of the current year's income will be taxable in the old state.

- Other income sources. You'll want to consider any other sources of income and whether your new state will tax you on this income. For example, if you are paying federal income tax on an IRA that you rolled over into a Roth IRA, if you move into a state that collects income tax, you may also have to pay state income tax on your rollover IRA.

• After you move or when filing time draws near, consider collecting your receipts and visiting an accountant.

The Budget Move (Money-Saving Tips)

Here you'll find some suggestions for saving money on your move.

Saving on Moving Supplies

• Obtain boxes in the cheapest way possible.

> Ask a friend or colleague who has recently moved to give or sell you their boxes.

> Check the classified ads; people sometimes sell all their moving boxes for a flat rate.

> Ask your local grocery or department store for their empty boxes.

• Borrow a tape dispenser instead of buying one.

• Instead of buying bubble wrap, crumple newspaper, plain unused newsprint, or tissue paper to pad breakables.

• Shop around for the cheapest deal on packing tape and other supplies.

• Instead of renting padding blankets from the truck rental company, use your own blankets, linens, and area rugs for padding. (But bear in mind that you may have to launder them when you arrive, which is an expense in itself.)

MOVING TIP

Save the TV, VCR, kids' videos, and a box of toys to be loaded on the truck last. On arriving at your destination, if you can't find someone to baby-sit, set aside a room in your home where your young children can safely play. Set up the TV and VCR and unpack the kids' videos along with some toys and snacks.

Saving on Labor

- If you use professional movers, consider a "you pack, we drive" arrangement, in which you pack boxes, and the moving company loads, moves, and unloads your belongings.
- Call around and compare estimates.
- If you move yourself, round up volunteers to help you load and clean on moving day. It's still customary to reward them with moving-day food and beverages (and maybe a small cash gift). You may also have to volunteer to help them move some day. But you may still save some money compared to hiring professionals.
- Save on child and pet care. Ask family or friends to watch your young children and pets on moving day.

Saving on Trip Expenses

Overnight the Night Before You Depart

- Where will you stay the night before you depart? A hotel or motel might be most comfortable and convenient, but you could save a little money if you stay the night with a friend or relative.
- If you have the gear, maybe you'd enjoy unrolling your sleeping bag and "roughing it" on your own floor the night before you leave town. If you do this, try to get hold of a camping sleeping pad or air mattress, which will help you get a good night's sleep and start your move rested and refreshed.

Overnight on the Road

- Look into hotel and motel discounts along your route. Your automobile club membership may qualify you for a better rate. Check out other possibilities, too—associations such as AARP often line up discounts for their members, as do some credit cards.
- When you call about rates, ask if the hotel or motel includes a light breakfast with your stay.
- If your move travel involves an overnight stay and you're game for camping, check into campgrounds and RV parks along your route. Be sure to ask whether a moving truck is allowed. Some

parks have size restrictions; some RV parks may not welcome moving trucks; and some limit the number of vehicles allowed in a campsite.

Food While Traveling

Food is one of those comfort factors that can help make the upsetting aspects of moving and traveling more acceptable. Eating also gives you a reason to stop and rest, which may be exactly what you or your family needs if you're rushing to get there. Here are a few pointers to consider:

- Try to balance your need to save money with your (and your family's) health and comfort needs.

- Try to have at least one solid, nutritious sit-down meal each day.

- Breakfast can be a budget- and schedule-friendly meal purchased at a grocery or convenience store and eaten on the road: fruit, muffins, and juice, for example.

- Lunch prices at sit-down restaurants are typically cheaper than dinner prices. Consider having a hot lunch and then picnicking in your hotel or motel on supplies from a grocery store.

MOVING TIP

If you are renting a truck, you'll need to know what size to rent. Here is a general guideline. Because equipment varies, though, ask for advice from the company renting the truck to you.

10-foot truck: one to two furnished rooms

14- to 15-foot truck:

two to three furnished rooms

18- to 20-foot truck:

four to five furnished rooms

22- to 24-foot truck:

six to eight furnished rooms

Scheduling Your Move

Try to allow yourself at least three months to plan and prepare. This long lead time is especially important if you plan to sell or buy a home or if you are moving during peak moving season (May through September). If you plan to move during peak season, it's vital to reserve two to three months in advance with a professional moving company or truck rental company. The earlier you reserve, the more likely you are to get the dates you want. This is especially important if you're timing your move with a job start date or a house closing date, or are moving yourself and want to load and move on a weekend when your volunteers are off work.

WHEN IS THE RIGHT TIME TO MOVE?

If your circumstances allow you to decide your move date, you'll want to make it as easy as possible on everyone who is moving:

- Children adjust better if they move between school terms (entering an established class in the middle of a school year can be very difficult).
- Elders have special needs you'll want to consider.
- Pets fare best when temperatures aren't too extreme, hot *or* cold.

THE "GET-OUT-OF-TOWN-IN-A-HURRY" PLAN

First the bad news: Very little about the move process can be shortened. Now the good news: The choices you make might make it possible to move in less time. The three primary resources in a successful move are time, money, and planning. If you're short on time, be prepared to spend more money or become more organized.

Immediately check into the availability of a rental truck or professional moving service. Next, give your landlord notice or arrange for an agent to sell your home. (If you own your home, you may find it harder to leave town in a hurry.) If your employer is paying for your move, ask if it offers corporate-sponsored financing options that will let you buy a new home before you sell your old one. Then consider the following potentially timesaving choices:

- *Move less stuff.* Of all the moving tasks, packing and unpacking consume the most time. The less you have to deal with, the quicker your move will go. Consider drastically lightening the load by selling or giving away most of your belongings and starting over in your new location. Although buying replacement stuff may drain your pocketbook, you can save some money by picking up some items secondhand at thrift stores and garage sales. (And after all, everything you have *now* is used, isn't it?)

MOVING TIP

Before buying anything for your new apartment or home, stop and consider what you'll need immediately and what you might be able to do without for a while. You'll spend a lot less if you can afford to wait and look for it on sale or secondhand.

- *Make a quick-move plan.* Quickly scan through chapters 4 and 5, highlighting helpful information. Use the checklists and the task time line at the end of this chapter to help you.

- *Get someone else to do the cleaning.* Before you vacate, you'll need to clean. You can be out the door sooner if you hire a professional cleaning company to come and clean everything, top to bottom, including the carpets. Again, the time you save will cost you money—but it may well be worth trading money for time.

Planning and Organizing

Start a move notebook. This could be as simple as a spiral-bound notepad or as elaborate as a categorized, tabbed binder. Keep track of this notebook. You'll find it invaluable later when the chaos hits. In your notebook, write notes and tape receipts. Of course, keep *this* book with your notebook! You may find the checklists and moving task time lines at the end of this chapter helpful. You may also find it helpful to assign a "do-by" date to each task on the checklist. To help you gauge what you face in the coming weeks, perhaps you will find it useful at this point to scan through the task time lines before reading further.

The section of the Moving Task Time Line that will help you the most at this point is "Decision Making: Weeks 12 to 9," which you'll find at the end of this chapter.

Preliminary Decisions

Before you even begin to plan your move, there are a number of decisions you'll need to make regarding your current residence, how you will move (do it yourself or hire a professional), and your new area.

LEAVING YOUR CURRENT HOME (RENTED PROPERTY)

Leaving a rental unit involves notifying your landlord and fulfilling your contractual obligations. This won't be a problem unless you have a lease agreement that lasts beyond your desired move date.

Your rights and options are dictated by state and local landlord/tenant laws and by your lease agreement. Exit fees can be expensive, depending on the terms of your lease. Here are some tips that may help you get out of a lease gracefully and save a few bucks at the same time.

- Know your rights. Laws governing landlord/tenant agreements and rights vary by state and municipality. Consult state and local law and call and obtain a pamphlet on renter's rights for your state and municipality.

- Review your lease agreement. There's no point in worrying until you know whether you have anything to worry about—and no use finding out too late that there were things you could have done.

- Look for a way out. Ask your landlord to consider letting you find a replacement tenant to fulfill your lease term (in some areas, this is a right dictated by law). If your move is due to a corporate relocation, your landlord or the property management company *may* be more willing to be flexible with exit fees—especially if you provide a letter from your employer. (And you may be able to get your employer to pick up the cost if you can't get the fees waived.)

- Adjust the timing. If you need to stay a month or two longer than your current lease allows and you don't want to sign for another six months or longer, ask your landlord for a month-to-month agreement lasting until your move date.

LEAVING YOUR CURRENT HOME (OWNED PROPERTY)

If you own your home, you'll either sell it or rent it out. If you sell, you'll either hire a real estate agent or sell it yourself. If you rent it out, you'll either serve as your own landlord or hire a property management agency to manage the property for you. Here are a few quick pros and cons to help you with the decisions you face.

Hiring a Selling Agent: Pros

- Your home gets exposure to a wide market audience, especially if the agent you choose participates in a multiple listing service.
- Homes listed with a real estate agent typically sell more quickly.
- Your agent will market your home (prepare and place ads and so on), and will also schedule and manage open houses and showings.
- Your agent will advise you and represent your interest in the business deal of selling, including offers, negotiation, and closing, guiding you through the stacks of paperwork.

Hiring a Selling Agent: Cons

- Hiring an agent requires signing a contract. If, for whatever reason, you want out, you may find it difficult to break the contract (it's wise to read carefully and sign only a short-term contract. Typical real estate agent contracts are ninety to 120 days in length).
- You pay your agent a fee for the service, typically a percentage of the selling price.

Selling Your Home Yourself: Pros

- You don't pay an agent's fee.
- You retain more control over showings, open houses, walk-throughs, and so on.

Selling Your Home Yourself: Cons

• Selling a home takes time. You must arrange your own showings and schedule and conduct your own open houses. Combined with everything else that happens during move preparation (working, interviewing for jobs, finding a new home, planning your move, packing, and so on), you will probably be swamped already. Add home showings (which are based around the buyer's schedule, not yours), and you may find yourself looking for an agent to help you after all.

• You pay for marketing costs, which can add up. Consider the cost of flyers, newspaper ads, or listing your home on a "homes for sale by owner" Web site.

• Since you don't have a real estate agent to represent you in the sale, you may need to hire an attorney at that point, which could take up some of the savings.

RENTING OUT YOUR PROPERTY

If you prefer to rent out your home, you can turn it over to a property management agency or be your own landlord. The services an agency will perform depend on the agency and your agreement with them. The following table details some of the rental issues you'll need to consider. As you review these, ask yourself how far away you're moving and whether or not you can handle these issues from your new home. Remember that every piece of work you must hire out cuts into the money in your pocket at the end of the month.

MOVING TIP

Take a tape measure and your notebook with you. Measure rooms; sketch your new home and write room measurements on your sketch. Before you move, you'll know whether your current furniture will fit and will have a good idea of how it should be arranged.

Rental Issue	You As Landlord	Hired Property Manager
Vacancy	You interview candidates, show the property, and choose tenants	The agency finds and selects tenants
Cleaning	You clean or arrange for cleaning services between tenants	The agency arranges for cleaning services between tenants
Late Rent	You collect rent and pursue late rent	The agency collects rent and pursues late rent
Rental Income	The rent you collect is all yours	The agency charges a fee, usually a percentage of the monthly rent
Repairs	You handle repairs and emergencies or find and hire a contractor to do the work	The agency handles repairs and emergencies

Strategic Financial Issues Related to Renting Out Your Old Home

If your property is located in a desirable neighborhood that is appreciating in value 3 percent or more annually, keeping it may in the long run defray or overcome the cost of management fees. If you rent out your property, it ceases being your primary residence. Find out from your accountant if this will affect your federal or state income taxes or local property taxes (some counties/municipalities give owner-occupied credits that reduce the tax burden). If there is an impact, you'll want to figure the difference into your decision of whether or not to sell and into the total you charge for rent.

Deciding How to Move:
Hiring Professionals or Moving Yourself

At first, you may be inclined to handle your own move to save money. But there are other factors to consider, and, depending on your situation, you may actually *save* money if you use professional services.

MOVING TIP

Start packing as soon as you get boxes. Some things you can pack long before the move. For example, off-season holiday decorations and off-season clothes can be boxed right away. The more you do early on, the less there is to do closer to move day, when things are hectic anyway.

Consider the range of service options some professional companies offer. The right combination could save you some of the headache but still compete with the cost of a do-it-yourself move. For example, some professional moving companies offer a "you pack, we drive" arrangement, in which you pack boxes and the moving company loads, moves, and unloads your belongings. Call around and inquire about rates. Also consider the following list of pros and cons to help you decide what's best for you.

The section of the Moving Task Time Line that will help you the most at this point is "Decision Making: Weeks 12 to 9," which you'll find at the end of this chapter.

The Pros of Using Pros

- *Time.* You may not have the hours it will take to pack, move, and unpack, but professional movers do—that's their day job.
- *Materials.* The moving company provides boxes and packing materials.*
- *Packing.* The movers pack all boxes (unless your contract states that you will pack).*
- *Loading and Unloading.* The movers load your belongings onto the moving van and unload your belongings at your destination.*
- *Unpacking.* The movers remove packed items from boxes and place items on flat surfaces.*
- *Debris.* The movers dispose of packing debris such as boxes, used tape, and padding.*
- *Experience.* The movers will know just what to do to transport your precious belongings in good condition.

- *Safety.* The movers do the lifting, which could save you a real injury.

Professional moving contracts typically include the services marked with an asterisk (*). Don't count on something unless you know for sure that the contract covers it, though—it's a good idea to ask your mover a lot of questions and read the contract carefully.

The Cons of Using Pros

- *Administrative chores.* Using professionals requires you to do some up-front work: obtaining estimates, comparing and negotiating prices and move dates, reviewing contracts, and comparing insurance options.
- *Loss of control.* The movers typically take charge of much of the packing and loading process, and you need to adapt to their schedule and procedures.

The Pros of a Self-Move

- *Control.* You pack, so you decide what items get packed together, how they get packed, and in which box they reside.
- *Cost-cutting.* You may save some money. But as you compare costs, be sure to factor in *all* self-move-related moving and travel costs. These include fuel, tolls, mileage charge on the rented truck, food, and lodging. All these costs increase the longer your trip is.

The Cons of a Self-Move

- *Risk to your belongings.* Because of inexperience with packing, loading, and padding heavy and unwieldy boxes and furniture, you or your volunteers may inadvertently damage your property.
- *Risk to yourself and your friends.* You or your volunteers may injure yourselves or someone else.

MOVING TIP

A few weeks before you move, start eating the food in your freezer. Also use up canned food, which is bulky and heavy to move.

- *Responsibility.* Loading and moving day are especially hectic, and you're in charge.
- *Reciprocal obligations.* If you use volunteers, you may be in debt to return the favor.

OTHER THINGS TO KNOW ABOUT PROFESSIONAL MOVING SERVICES

Your moving company may or may not provide the following services, or may charge extra for performing them. Be sure to ask.

- Disassembling beds or other furniture
- Removing window covering hardware (drapery rods, mini-blinds) or other items from the walls or ceiling
- Disconnecting and installing appliances (dryer, washer, automatic ice maker)
- Disconnecting and installing outside fixtures such as a satellite dish, a hose reel, and so on
- Moving furniture or boxes from one room to another

MOVING INSURANCE IN A PROFESSIONAL MOVE

By U.S. law, the mover must cover your possessions at $0.60 per pound. This coverage is free. Consider taking out additional coverage, though, because under this minimal coverage, your three-pound antique Tiffany lamp worth hundreds of dollars at auction fetches exactly $1.80 if the moving company breaks it.

Your homeowner's or renter's insurance provider may be willing to advise you on moving insurance options, and the moving company will offer you a number of insurance options. Be sure you understand each option—what it covers and what it costs you. Ask a lot of questions and read everything carefully. No one wishes for mishaps, but it's best to be prepared and well informed should something break or show up missing.

STORAGE

If you want your moving company to store some or all of your possessions temporarily, inquire about cost and the quality of their facilities:

- Are the facilities heated (or air-conditioned, depending on the time of year that applies to you)?
- Does the moving company own the storage facility or subcontract storage to someone else? If they subcontract, does your contract with the moving company extend to the storage facility company?

Storage Companies in the Area

There are literally dozens of storage firms in Southern California. The following three are among the biggest and best established. They have locations all over Los Angeles and Orange counties. Call or check their Web sites for locations.

Bekins Self Storage
(800) 251-8879

www.bekins.com

Public Storage
(800) 447-8673

www.publicstorage.com

Door to Door Storage
(888) 366-7222

www.doortodoor.com

CHOOSING A MOVER

- Start by asking around. Chances are your friends, family, or colleagues will have a personal recommendation.
- Take their recommendations and list them in a notebook, each on a separate sheet. Call these companies to request a no-obligation, free written estimate—and take notes on your conversation.
- Find out if the company you're talking to offers the services you need. For example, if you want to ship your car, boat, or powered recreational craft in the van along with your household goods, ask if this service is available.
- Do a little investigating. Ask the company to show you its operating license, and call the Better Business Bureau to ask about complaints and outstanding claims.

GETTING AN ESTIMATE

You need to know what kind of estimate the moving company is giving you. The two most common are "non-binding" and "binding." A *non-binding estimate* (usually free, but potentially less accurate) is one in which the moving company charges you by the hour per worker per truck and quotes you an approximate figure to use in your planning. Depending on circumstances, your final cost could be significantly greater than what shows up in the estimate.

The second type is a *binding estimate*, which you typically pay for. In this type, the professional mover performs a detailed on-site inspection of your belongings and quotes a flat price based on the following:

- The amount of stuff you're moving, whether it is fragile or bulky, and how complicated it is to pack
- Final weight
- Services provided
- Total length of travel

Once you choose a mover, it's a good idea to have a representative visit your home, look at your belongings, and give you a written (binding) estimate. Getting a written estimate may cost you money, but it helps prevent surprises when it comes time to pay the final bill.

You play a big role in making sure that the estimate you receive is accurate. Be sure you show the moving company representative everything you plan to move.

- Remember to take the representative through every closet, out to the garage, into the shed, down to the basement, up into the attic, and to your rented storage facility if you have one.
- Tell the representative about any item you *don't* plan to move (because you plan to get rid of it before you move). Then be sure to follow through and get rid of it so there are no surprises on moving day.
- Point out any vehicles you want to ship in the van along with your household goods, and ask your representative to include the cost in your estimate.

WHAT MIGHT INCREASE YOUR FINAL BILL

It is reasonable to expect that certain circumstances will unexpectedly increase your final bill, including:

- You do the packing and it's incomplete or done improperly.
- Circumstances unexpectedly increase the time and labor involved in your move. For example:

  You're moving out of or into a high-rise and movers don't have access to an elevator (perhaps it's broken).

  Access at either location is restricted (for example, there is no truck parking close by or the movers have to wait for someone to unlock).

- You change your move destination after you receive your written estimate.
- You require delivery of your belongings to more than one destination.

Researching Your New Area

The section of the Moving Task Time Line that will help you the most at this point is "Decision Making: Weeks 12 to 9," which you'll find at the end of this chapter. Other chapters of this book discuss the details of your destination city. Here are some additional move-related tips and resources.

GENERAL CITY INFORMATION

- Visit your local library and read up on your new area.
- Go online and look for the local newspaper.
- Have a friend or family member mail you a week's worth of newspapers or have a subscription delivered via postal mail.
- Visit *www.monstermoving.com* for easy-to-find city information and links to local services, information, and Web sites.

JOBS, HOUSING, AND COST OF LIVING

Visit *www.monster.com* for career assistance, and visit *www .monstermoving.com* for links to apartments for rent, and real estate and other services, as well as free cost-of-living information.

CHOOSING SCHOOLS

Selecting schools is of supreme importance for family members who will attend public or private schools.

Do Your Homework

- Ask your real estate agent to help you find school information and statistics or a list of contacts for home school associations.
- Search the Web.

    Visit *www.2001beyond.com*. There you can compare up to four districts at once. Information on both public and private schools is provided. The extensive twelve-page report provides information on class size, curriculum, interscholastic sports, extracurricular activities, awards, merits, and SAT scores. It also provides the principal's name and phone number for each school in the district. You may need to pay a nominal fee for the twelve-page report (or the cost may be covered by a sponsoring real estate professional, if you don't mind receiving a phone call from an agent).

    Visit *www.monstermoving.com*, which provides links to school information.

Visit Schools

Arrange to visit schools your children might attend, and bring them along. Your children will pick up on subtleties that you will miss. As you talk with your children about changing schools, try to help them differentiate between their feelings about moving to a new school and area and their feelings about that particular school by asking direct but open-ended questions. (An *open-ended* question is one that invites dialogue because it can't be answered with a simple "yes" or "no"— "What was the best or worst thing you saw there?" for example, or "Which electives looked the most interesting?")

PLANNING AND TAKING
A HOUSE- OR APARTMENT-HUNTING TRIP

Preparing and planning in advance will help you make the most of your trip. Ideally, by this point, you will have narrowed your search to two or three neighborhoods or areas.

- Gather documents and information required for completing a rental application:

  Rental history: Landlord's name, contact information, dates occupied

  Personal references: Name and contact information for one or two personal references

  Employment information: Current or anticipated employer name and contact info

  Bank account number

- Consider compiling all this information into a "Rental Résumé." Even though most landlords won't accept a rental résumé in lieu of a completed application, spending the time up front could be helpful in a market where rentals are scarce. Handing the landlord a rental résumé lets them know you're serious about finding the right place and are professional and organized in how you conduct your affairs.

- Go prepared to pay an application fee and deposits. Deposit the funds in your account and bring your checkbook. Typically, landlords require first and last month's rent and a flat damage and cleaning deposit.

- Take your Move Planning Notebook. List properties you want to visit, one per notebook page. Clip the classified ad and tape it onto the page. Write notes about the property, rent rate, deposit amount, and terms you discuss with the landlord or property manager.

Planning

Now that you've made pre-move decisions, it's time to plan for the physical move. First, you'll need to organize your moving day. Next, you'll need to prepare to pack.

These are the sections of the Moving Task Time Line that will help you the most at this point:

- "Organizing, Sorting, and Notifying: Weeks 9 to 8"
- "Finalizing Housing Arrangements and Establishing Yourself in Your New Community: Weeks 8 to 6"
- "Making and Confirming Transportation and Travel Plans: Week 6"
- "Uprooting: Weeks 5 to 4"
- "Making and Confirming Moving-Day Plans: Week 3"

You'll find the Moving Task Time Line at the end of this chapter.

PLANNING FOR MOVING DAY

The Professional Move: Some Planning Considerations

- Confirm your move dates and finalize any last contract issues.
- Ask what form of payment movers will accept (check, money order, certified check, traveler's checks) and make necessary arrangements.

The Self-Move: Organizing Volunteers

- Ask friends and relatives to "volunteer" to help you load the truck on moving day.
- Set up shifts, and tactfully let your volunteers know that you are counting on them to arrive on time and stay through their "shift."
- A week or two before moving day, call everyone to remind them.
- Plan on supplying soft drinks and munchies to keep your crew going.

PLANNING CARE FOR YOUR CHILDREN AND PETS

Moving day will be hectic for you and everyone, and possibly dangerous for your young children. Make plans to take younger children and your pets to someone's home or to a care facility.

PLANNING YOUR MOVING-DAY TRAVEL

Driving

- If you will be renting a truck, be prepared to put down a sizable deposit the day you pick up the truck. Some truck rental companies only accept a credit card for this deposit, so go prepared.
- If you belong to an automobile club such as AAA, contact them to obtain maps, suggested routes, alternate routes, rest-stop information, and a trip packet, if they provide this service.
- Visit an online map site such as *www.mapblast.com*, where you'll find not only a map but also door-to-door driving directions and estimated travel times.
- Find out in advance where you should turn in the truck in your new hometown.

Traveling by Air, Train, or Bus

- Arrange for tickets and boarding passes.
- Speak with the airline to request meals that match dietary restrictions.
- Speak with the airline or the train or bus company to make any special arrangements such as wheelchair accessibility and assistance.
- Plan to dress comfortably.
- If you will be traveling with young children, plan to dress them in bright, distinctive clothing so you can easily identify them in a crowded airport, train station, or bus terminal.

PREPARING TO PACK:
WHAT TO DO WITH THE STUFF YOU HAVE

Moves are complicated, time-consuming, and exhausting. But the process has at least one benefit. A move forces us to consider simplifying our lives by reducing the amount of our personal belongings. If we plan to keep it, we also must pack it, load it, move it, unload it, and unpack it. Here are some suggestions for sifting through your belongings as you prepare for packing.

- Start in one area of your home and go through everything before moving to the next area.
- Ask yourself three questions about each item (sentimental value aside):

    Have we used this in the last year?

    Will we use it in the coming year? For example, if you're moving to a more temperate climate, you might not need all your wool socks and sweaters.

    Is there a place for it in the new home? For instance, if your new home has a smaller living room, you might not have room for your big couch or need all your wall decorations.

If you answer "no" to any or all of these questions, you might want to consider selling the item, giving it away, or throwing it out.

Packing

Here are some tips to help you with one of the most difficult stages of your move—packing.

- Follow a plan. Pack one room at a time. You may find yourself leaving one or two boxes in each room open to receive those items you use right up until the last minute.
- On the outside of each box, describe the contents and room destination. Be as specific as you can, to make unpacking easier. However, if you are using a professional moving service but doing the packing yourself, consider numbering boxes and creating a separate list of box contents and destinations.
- Put heavy items such as books in small boxes to make them easier to carry.
- Don't put tape on furniture because it may pull off some finish when you remove it.
- As you pack, mark and set aside the items that should go in the truck last (see checklist at the end of this chapter). Mark and set aside your "necessary box" (for a list of items to include in this box, see the checklist at the end of this chapter).

PACKING FRAGILE ITEMS

- When packing breakable dishes and glasses, use boxes and padding made for these items. You may have to pay a little to buy these boxes, but you're apt to save money in the long run because your dishes are more likely to arrive unbroken. Dishes and plates are best packed on edge (not stacked flat atop each other).
- Pad mirrors, pictures, and larger delicate pieces with sheets and blankets.
- Computers fare best if they are packed in their original boxes. If you don't have these, pack your hardware in a large, sturdy box and surround it with plenty of padding such as plastic bubble pack.
- Use plenty of padding around fragile items.
- *Mark "FRAGILE" *on the top and all sides* of boxes of breakables so it's easily seen no matter how a box is stacked.

WHAT *NOT* TO PACK

- Don't pack hazardous, flammable, combustible, or explosive materials. Empty your gas grill tank and any kerosene heater fuel as well as gasoline in your power yard tools. These materials are not safe in transit.
- Don't pack valuables such as jewelry, collections, important financial and legal documents, and records for the moving van. Keep these with you in your car trunk or your suitcase.

PACKING AND UNPACKING SAFELY WITH YOUNG CHILDREN

No matter how well you've kid-proofed your home, that only lasts until the moment you start packing. Then things are in disarray and within reach of youngsters. Here are some tips to keep your toddlers and children safe.

- Items your youngsters have seldom or never seen will pique their curiosity, presenting a potential hazard, so consider what you are packing or unpacking. If you stop packing or unpacking and leave the room even for a moment, take your youngsters with you and close the door or put up a child gate.

- Keep box knives and other tools out of a child's reach.

- As you disassemble or reassemble furniture, keep track of screws, bolts, nuts, and small parts.

- Beware of how and where you temporarily place furniture and other items. (That heavy mirror you just took down off the wall—do you lean it up against the wall until you go get the padding material, inviting a curious youngster to pull or climb on it?) For the same reason, consider how high you stack boxes.

- On arriving at your destination, if you can't find someone to baby-sit, set aside a room in your home where your young children can safely play. Set up the TV and VCR and unpack the kids' videos, books, coloring books and crayons or markers, and some toys and snacks.

- Walk through your new home with children and talk about any potential dangers such as a swimming pool or stairs, establishing your safety rules and boundaries.

- If you have young children who are unaccustomed to having stairs in the home, place a gate at the top and one at the bottom. If your child is walking and over toddler age, walk up and down the stairs together a few times holding the railing until they become accustomed to using the stairs.

Handle with Special Care: Uprooting and Settling the People and Pets in Your Life

The most important advice you can hear is this: Involving children as much as possible will help transform this anxiety-causing, uncertain experience into an exciting adventure. It would take a book to cover this topic comprehensively, but here are some suggestions for making the transition easier:

- *Involve children early.* Ask for their input on decisions and give them age-appropriate tasks such as packing their own belongings and assembling an activity bag to keep them busy while traveling.

- *Don't make empty promises.* Kids can hear the hollow ring when you say, "It'll be just like here. Just give it time," or "You can stay friends with your friends here." That's true, but you know it's not true in the same way, if you're moving a long distance.

- *Deal with fear of the unknown.* If possible, take children with you to look at potential neighborhoods, homes or apartments, and schools. It may be more expensive and require extra effort, but it will ease the transition and help children begin to make the adjustment.

- *Provide as much information as you can.* If it's not possible to take children with you when you visit new neighborhoods, homes or apartments, and schools, take a camera or video recorder. Your children will appreciate the pictures, and the preview will help them begin the transition. You can also use a map to help them understand the new area and the route you will take to get there.

- *Make time to talk with your children about the move.* Especially listen for—and talk about—the anxieties your children feel. By doing so, you will help them through the move (your primary goal)—and you'll deepen your relationship at the same time, which may be more important in the long run.

- *Share your own anxieties with your children—but be sure to keep an overall positive outlook about the move.* Because most aspects of a move are downers, a negative outlook on your part may shed gloom over the whole experience—including its good aspects. On the

MOVING TIP

Before you leave, measure your current home and draw a sketch plan, showing room measurements and furniture placement. Take the plan with you, along with a tape measure and notebook, and draw up similar plans for the house or rental unit you're thinking of choosing. Sketches needn't be very detailed at this stage to help you avoid unpleasant surprises— no point in dragging that California King bed across country if it won't fit in the bedroom.

other hand, a positive outlook on your part may counteract some of your child's emotional turmoil, uncertainty, and fear.

- *Make it fun.* Give older children a disposable camera and ask them to photograph your move. Once you arrive and are settled in, make time together to create the "moving" chapter of your family photo album.

HELPING FAMILY MEMBERS MAINTAIN FRIENDSHIPS

Moving doesn't have to end a friendship.

- Give each child a personal address book and have them write the e-mail address, phone number, and postal mail address for each of their friends.
- Stay in touch. E-mail is an easy way. Establish an e-mail address for every family member (if they don't already have one) before you move so they can give it out to friends. Many Web mail services are free and can be accessed from anywhere you can access the Internet. Examples include www.msn.com, www.usa.net, and www.yahoo.com.
- Make (and follow through with) plans to visit your old hometown within the first year following your move. Visit friends and drive by your old home, through neighborhoods, and past landmarks. This reconnection with dear friends and fond memories will help your family bring finality to the move.

TRAVELING WITH YOUR PET

- Keep a picture of your pet on your person or in your wallet just in case you get separated from Fido or Fluffy during the move.
- Place identification tags on your pet's collar and pet carrier.
- Take your pet to the vet for an examination just before you move. Ask for advice on moving your particular pet. Specifically ask for advice on how you can help your pet through the move—what you can do before, during, and after the move to help your pet make the transition smoothly.
- Find out if you will need any health certificates for your pet to comply with local regulations in your new home, and obtain them when you visit the vet.

- If your pet is prone to motion sickness or tends to become nervous in reaction to excitement and unfamiliar surroundings, tell your veterinarian, who may prescribe medication for your pet.

- Ask for your pet's health records so you can take them to your new vet.

- If your pet is unusual—say, a ferret or a snake or other reptile—there might be laws in your new city or state regarding the transportation or housing of such an animal. Contact the department of agriculture or a local veterinarian to find out.

- Cats: It's wise to keep your cat indoors for the first two weeks until it recognizes its new surroundings as home.

- Dogs: If appropriate, walk your dog on a leash around your neighborhood to help it become familiar with its new surroundings and learn its way back home.

- If your pet will travel by plane, check with your airline regarding fees and any specific rules and regulations regarding pet transport.

- Your pet will need to travel in an approved carrier (check with your airline regarding acceptable types and sizes).

- Your airline may require a signed certificate of health dated within a certain number of days of the flight. Only your vet can produce this document.

Move Budget-Planning Guide

Housing

Home repairs $ _____

Cleaning supplies and services $ _____

Rental expenses in new city

   Application fees
   (varies—figure $15 to $35 per application) $ _____

   First and last month's rent $ _____

   Damage and security deposit $ _____

   Pet deposit $ _____

   Utility deposits $ _____

   Storage unit rental $ _____

Total.....................................**$** _____

Moving

Professional moving services or truck rental $ _____

Moving supplies $ _____

Food and beverage for volunteers $ _____

Tips for professional movers; gifts for volunteers $ _____

Moving travel:

   Airline tickets $ _____

   Fuel $ _____

   Tolls $ _____

   Meals: per meal $_____ × _____ meals $ _____

   Hotels: per night $_____ × _____ nights $ _____

Total.....................................**$** _____

(continues on next page)

Other Expenses

_____	$ _____
_____	$ _____
_____	$ _____
_____	$ _____
_____	$ _____
_____	$ _____
_____	$ _____

Total. . . . .$ _____

GRAND TOTAL. . . . .$ _____

Utilities to Cancel

Utility	Provider name and phone	Cancel date[1]
Water and sewer		
Electricity		
Gas		
Phone		
Garbage		
Cable		
Alarm service		

1. If you are selling your home, the shutoff of essential services (water, electricity, gas) will depend on the final closing and walk-through. Coordinate with your real estate agent.

Utilities to Connect

Utility	Provider name and phone	Service start date	Deposit amount required
Water and sewer			
Electricity			
Gas			
Phone			
Garbage			
Cable			
Alarm service			

Other Services to Cancel, Transfer, or Restart

Service	Provider name and phone	Service end date[1]	Service start date[1]
Subscriptions and Memberships			
Newspaper			
Memberships (health club and so on)			
Internet Service Provider			

1. If applicable

(continues on next page)

Other Services to Cancel, Transfer, or Restart			
Service	**Provider name and phone**	**Service end date**[1]	**Service start date**[1]
Government and School			
Postal mail change of address			
School records			
Voter registration			
Vehicle registration			
Financial			
Bank account[2]			
Direct deposits and withdrawals			
Safe deposit box			
Professional			
Health care (transfer doctors' and dentists' records for each family member)			
Veterinarian (transfer records)			
Cleaners (pick up your clothes)			

1. If applicable; 2. Open an account in your new town before closing your existing account.

Checklists

MOVING SUPPLIES

Packing and Unpacking

_____ Tape and tape dispenser. (The slightly more expensive gun-style dispenser is a worthwhile investment because its one-handed operation means you don't need a second person to help you hold the box closed while you do the taping.)

_____ Boxes. (It's worth it to obtain specialty boxes for your dinnerware, china set, and glasses. Specialty wardrobe boxes that allow your hanging clothes to hang during transport are another big help.)

_____ Padding such as bubble wrap.

_____ Markers.

_____ Scissors or a knife.

_____ Big plastic bags.

_____ Inventory list and clipboard.

_____ Box knife with retractable blade. (Get one for each adult.)

Loading and Moving

_____ Rope. (If nothing else, you'll need it to secure heavy items to the inside wall of the truck.)

_____ Padding blankets. (If you use your own, they may get dirty and you'll need bedding when you arrive. Padding is available for rent at most truck rental agencies.)

_____ Hand truck or appliance dolly. (Most truck rental agencies have them available for rent.)

_____ Padlock for the cargo door.

THE "NECESSARY BOX"

Eating

____ Snacks or food. (Pack enough durable items for right before you depart, your travel, and the first day in your new home—and disposable utensils, plates, cups.)

____ Instant coffee, tea bags, and so on.

____ Roll of paper towels and moistened towelettes.

____ Garbage bags.

Bathing

____ A towel for each person.

____ Soap, shampoo, toothpaste, and any other toiletries.

____ Toilet paper.

Health Items

____ First aid kit including pain relievers.

____ Prescription medicines.

Handy to Have

____ List of contact information. (Make sure you can reach relatives, the moving company, the truck driver's cell phone, and so on.)

____ Small tool kit. (You need to be able to take apart and reassemble items that can't be moved whole.)

____ Reclosable plastic bags to hold small parts, screws, bolts.

____ Spare lightbulbs. (Some bulbs in your new home might be burned out or missing.)

____ Nightlight and flashlight.

OVERNIGHT BAG

____ Enough clothes for the journey plus the first day or two in your new home.

____ Personal toiletries.

ITEMS FOR KIDS

____ Activities for the trip.

____ Favorite toys and anything else that will help children feel immediately at home in their new room.

Pet Checklist

____ Food.

____ A bottle of the water your pet is used to drinking.

____ Dishes for food and water.

____ Leash, collar, identification tags.

____ Favorite toy.

____ Medicines.

____ Bed or blanket.

____ Carrier.

____ Paper towels in case of accidents.

____ Plastic bags and a scooper.

____ Litter and litter box for your cat or rabbit.

Last Items on the Truck

CLEANING

_____ Vacuum cleaner.

_____ Cleaning supplies.

GENERAL

_____ Necessary box.

_____ Setup for kids' temporary playroom.

_____ Other items you'll need the moment you arrive.

New Home Safety Checklist

GENERAL

_____ Watch out for tripping hazards. They will be plentiful until you get everything unpacked and put away, so be careful, and keep a path clear at all times.

HEAT, FIRE, ELECTRICAL

_____ Be sure nothing gets placed too close to heaters.

_____ Test smoke, heat, and carbon monoxide detectors. Find out your fire department's recommendations regarding how many of these devices you should have and where you should place them. If you need more, go buy them (remember to buy batteries) and install them.

_____ Find the fuse or breaker box before you need to shut off or reset a circuit.

WATER

_____ Check the temperature setting on your water heater. For child safety and fuel conservation, experts recommend 120 degrees Fahrenheit.

_____ Locate the water shutoff valve in case of a plumbing problem.

Moving Task Time Line

DECISION MAKING: WEEKS 12 TO 9

_____ Consider your moving options (professional versus self-move) and get quotes.

_____ If you are being relocated by your company, find out what your company covers and what you will be responsible for doing and paying.

_____ Set a move date.

_____ Choose your moving company or truck rental agency and reserve the dates.

If You Own Your Home

_____ Decide whether you want to sell or rent it out.

_____ If you decide to sell, choose a real estate agent and put your home on the market or look into, and begin planning for, selling it yourself.

_____ If you decide to rent out your home, decide whether you want to hire a property management agency or manage the property yourself.

_____ Perform (or hire contractors to perform) home repairs.

If You Currently Rent

_____ Notify your landlord of your plans to vacate.

_____ Check into cleaning obligations and options.

Tour Your New City or Town

_____ Research your new area at the library or online at
www.monstermoving.com.

_____ Contact a real estate agent or property management agency
to help you in your search for new lodgings.

_____ Go on a school-hunting and house- or apartment-hunting
trip to your new town or city.

Additional items:

_____

_____

_____

_____

_____

_____

_____

_____

_____

_____

_____

_____

_____

_____

_____

_____

ORGANIZING, SORTING, AND NOTIFYING: WEEKS 9 TO 8

_____ Obtain the post office's change of address kit by calling 1-800-ASK-USPS or visiting your local post office or *www.usps.gov/moversnet/* (where you'll find the form and helpful lists of questions and answers).

_____ Complete and send the form.

_____ List and notify people, businesses, and organizations who need to know about your move. You may not think of everyone at once, but keep a running list and add people to your list and notify them as you remember them. As you notify them, check them off your list.

_____ Start sorting through your belongings to decide what to keep. Make plans to rid yourself of what you don't want: pick a date for a garage sale; call your favorite charity and set a date for them to come pick up donations; call your recycling company to find out what they will accept.

_____ For moving insurance purposes, make an inventory of your possessions with their estimated replacement value.

_____ If you have high-value items (such as antiques) that you expect to send with the moving company or ship separately, obtain an appraisal.

Additional items:

_____

_____

_____

_____

_____

_____

_____

FINALIZING HOUSING ARRANGEMENTS AND ESTABLISHING YOURSELF IN YOUR NEW COMMUNITY: WEEKS 8 TO 6

_____ **Home.** Select your new home and arrange financing; establish a tentative closing date or finalize rental housing arrangements.

_____ **Schools.** Find out school calendars and enrollment and immunization requirements.

_____ **Insurance.** Contact an agent regarding coverage on your new home and its contents as well as on your automobile.

_____ **Finances.** Select a bank, open accounts, and obtain a safe deposit box.

_____ **New Home Layout.** Sketch a floor plan of your new home and include room measurements. Determine how your present furniture, appliances, and decor will fit.

_____ **Mail.** If you haven't found a new home, rent a post office box for mail forwarding.

_____ **Services.** Find out the names and phone numbers of utility providers and what they require from you before they will start service (for example, a deposit, a local reference). (You can list your providers and service start dates on the checklist provided in this chapter.) Schedule service to start a few days before you arrive.

Additional items:

_____

_____

_____

_____

_____

_____

MAKING AND CONFIRMING TRANSPORTATION AND TRAVEL PLANS: WEEK 6

_____ Schedule pick-up and delivery dates with your mover.

_____ Make arrangements with your professional car mover.

_____ If you need storage, make the arrangements.

_____ Confirm your departure date with your real estate agent or landlord.

_____ Make your travel arrangements. If you will be flying, book early for cheaper fares.

_____ Map your driving trip using *www.mapblast.com* or ask your automobile club for assistance with route and accommodation information.

Additional items:

_____

_____

_____

_____

_____

_____

_____

_____

_____

_____

_____

_____

_____

_____

_____

UPROOTING: WEEKS 5 TO 4

_____ Hold your garage sale, or donate items to charity.

_____ Gather personal records from all health care providers, your
veterinarian, lawyers, accountants, and schools.

_____ Notify current utility providers of your disconnect dates and
your forwarding address. (You can list your providers and
service end dates on the checklist provided in this chapter.)

Additional items:

_____

_____

_____

_____

_____

_____

_____

_____

_____

_____

_____

_____

_____

_____

_____

_____

_____

_____

_____

_____

_____

MAKING AND CONFIRMING MOVING-DAY PLANS: WEEK 3

_____ Make arrangements for a sitter for kids and pets on moving day.

_____ Call moving-day volunteers to confirm move date and their arrival time.

_____ Obtain traveler's checks for trip expenses and cashier's or certified check for payment to mover.

_____ Have your car serviced if you are driving a long distance.

Additional items:

_____

_____

_____

_____

_____

_____

_____

_____

_____

_____

_____

_____

_____

_____

_____

_____

_____

_____

_____

_____

_____

WEEK 2

_____ If you have a pet, take it to the vet for a checkup. For more pet-moving tips, see the section earlier in this chapter on moving with pets.

_____ Arrange for transportation of your pet.

_____ If you are moving into or out of a high-rise building, contact the property manager and reserve the elevator for moving day.

_____ Reserve parking space for the professional moving van or your rental truck. You may need to obtain permission from your rental property manager or from the city.

_____ Drain oil and gas from all your power equipment and kerosene from portable heaters.

Additional items:

_____

_____

_____

_____

_____

_____

_____

_____

_____

_____

_____

_____

_____

_____

MOVING WEEK

_____ Defrost the freezer.

_____ Give away any plants you can't take with you.

_____ Pack your luggage and your necessary box for the trip (see the list provided in this chapter).

_____ Get everything but the day-to-day essentials packed and ready to go.

Additional items:

_____

_____

_____

_____

_____

_____

_____

_____

_____

_____

_____

_____

_____

_____

MOVING DAY

_____ Mark off parking space for the moving van using cones or chairs.

_____ See "Moving Day" section of chapter 5 for further to-do items.

Getting from Here to There: Moving Day and Beyond

This chapter guides you through the next stage in your move: moving day, arriving, unpacking, and settling in. Here you'll find important travel tips for both the self-move and the professional move, information related to a professional car move, and pointers for your first days and weeks in your new home.

The Professional Move

Early on moving day, reserve a large place for the moving truck to park. Mark off an area with cones or chairs. If you need to obtain parking permission from your apartment complex manager or the local government, do so in advance.

GUIDE THE MOVERS

Before work starts, walk through the house with the movers and describe the loading order. Show them the items you plan to transport yourself. (It's best if these are piled in one area and clearly marked, maybe even covered with a sheet or blanket until you're ready to pack them in your car.)

Remain on-site to answer the movers' questions and to provide special instructions.

BEFORE YOU DEPART

Before you hit the road, you will need to take care of some last-minute details:

- Walk through your home to make sure everything was loaded.
- Sign the bill of lading. But first, read it carefully and ask any questions. The bill of lading is a document the government requires movers to complete for the transportation of supplies, materials, and personal property. The mover is required to have a signed copy on hand, and you should keep your copy until the move is complete and any claims are settled.
- Follow the movers to the weigh station. Your bill will be partly based on the weight of your property moved.

UNLOADING AND MOVING IN

Be sure to take care of these details once the movers arrive at your new home:

- Have your money ready. (Professional movers expect payment in full before your goods are unloaded.)
- Check for damage as items are unpacked and report it right away.
- Unless the company's policy prohibits the acceptance of gratuities, it is customary to tip each mover. $20 is a good amount; you may want to tip more or less based on the service you receive.

The Self-Move

The following tips should help you organize and guide your help, as well as make the moving day run more smoothly:

- The day before your move, create a task list. Besides the obvious (loading the truck), this list will include tasks such as disconnecting the washer and dryer and taking apart furniture that can't be moved whole.

- Plan to provide beverages and food for your volunteers. Make it easy on yourself and provide popular options such as pizza or sub sandwiches (delivered), chilled soda pop and bottled water (in an ice chest, especially if you're defrosting and cleaning the refrigerator).

- On moving day, remember, you are only one person. So if you need to defrost the freezer or pack last-minute items, choose and appoint someone who knows your plan to oversee the volunteers and answer questions.

MOVING TIP

Draw up a detailed plan of your new home, including scale drawings of each room that show each piece of furniture you plan to take with you. Label furniture and boxes as to where they go in the new home, and have copies of the plan to put in each room there. This will give you at least a chance that most of the work of moving in will only need to be done once.

- Be sure you have almost everything packed before your help arrives. Last-minute packing creates even more chaos and it's likely that hastily packed items will be damaged during loading or transit.

- If you end up with an even number of people, it's natural for people to work in pairs because they can carry the items that require two people. If you have an odd number of people, the extra person can rotate in to provide for breaks, carry light items alone, or work on tasks you assign.

- Be sure to match a person's physical ability and health with the tasks you assign.

- Appoint the early shift to start on tasks such as disconnecting the washer and dryer and taking apart furniture (such as bed frames) that can't be moved whole.

- Before work starts, walk through the house with your volunteers and describe your loading plan.

- Know your moving truck and how it should be packed for safe handling on the road (ask the truck rental company for directions).

- Load the truck according to the directions your truck rental agency gave you. Tie furniture items (especially tall ones) to the inside wall of the truck. Pack everything together as tightly as possible, realizing that items will still shift somewhat as you travel.

Move Travel

GETTING TO THE AREA

Arriving by Plane

Los Angeles International Airport
One World Way
Los Angeles, CA 90045
(310) 646-5252

This airport, familiarly known as LAX, is the area's biggest airport. It's in west Los Angeles near the San Diego Freeway, also known as the 405.

Burbank-Glendale-Pasadena Airport
2627 North Hollywood Way
Burbank, CA 91505
(818) 840-8840

This airport is in northwest Burbank near the Golden State Freeway, also known as the 5.

John Wayne Airport
18601 Airport Way
Santa Ana, CA 92707
(949) 252-5200

The main airport for Orange County, this field lies near the Costa Mesa Freeway (the 55), the Corona Del Mar Freeway (the 73), and the San Diego Freeway (the 405).

Ontario International Airport
2500 East Airport Drive
Ontario, CA 91761
(909) 937-2700

This airport lies near the Pomona Freeway (the 60) and the San Bernardino Freeway (the 10).

Long Beach Municipal Airport
4100 Donald Douglas Drive
Long Beach, CA 90808
(562) 570-2600

MOVING TIP

Reserve a large place for the moving truck to park on the day you move out. Mark off an area with cones or chairs. If you need to obtain parking permission from your apartment complex manager or the city, do so in advance.

This airport lies near the San Diego Freeway (the 405) in Long Beach just south of the city of Lakewood.

Arriving by Car

Since Los Angeles County is north of Orange County, most routes from the north bring you into Los Angeles County, and most routes from the south bring you into Orange County.

From the northwest, along the California coast: Take the 101 Freeway south. (You can also take the 1 Freeway south; it feeds into the 101 a good distance north of Los Angeles County.) The 101 Freeway will lead you into western Los Angeles County.

From the north, through central California: Take the 5 Freeway south. (You can also take the 99 Freeway south; it feeds into the 5 just north of Los Angeles County.) The 5 Freeway will lead you into northwest Los Angeles County.

From the north, through eastern California and Nevada: Take the 395 Freeway south to the 14 Freeway in northern Kern County. (Kern County is the northern neighbor of Los Angeles County.) Then take the 14 Freeway south. It will lead you into Lancaster and other parts of northern Los Angeles County.

From the northeast, through Nevada: Take the 15 Freeway southwest until you reach the 10 Freeway in San Bernardino County. (San Bernardino County is the northeast neighbor of Los Angeles County.) Then take the 10 Freeway west. It will lead you into eastern Los Angeles County.

From the east, through central Arizona: Take the 40 Freeway west until you reach the 15 Freeway in Barstow (part of San Bernardino County). Then take the 15 Freeway south.

To reach Los Angeles County: Stay on the 15 Freeway until you reach the 10 Freeway in San Bernardino County. Then take the 10 Freeway west. It will lead you into eastern Los Angeles County.

To reach Orange County: Stay on the 15 Freeway until you reach the 91 Freeway. Then take the 91 Freeway southwest. It will lead you into northern Orange County.

From the southeast, through southern Arizona: Take the 10 Freeway west.

To reach Los Angeles County: Stay on the 10 Freeway. It will lead you into eastern Los Angeles County.

To reach Orange County: Stay on the 10 Freeway until you reach the 91 Freeway. Take the 91 Freeway southwest. It will lead you into northern Orange County.

From the south, through San Diego: Take the 5 Freeway north. It will lead you into southern Orange County.

From the west: Swim. West of Los Angeles and Orange counties is the Pacific Ocean.

Arriving by Bus

The main bus company into the area is Greyhound. Its general phone number is (800) 231-2222, and its terminals in the area are these:

1241 South Soto Street
Los Angeles, CA 90023
(323) 262-1514

1716 East Seventh Street
Los Angeles, CA 90021
(213) 629-8400

464 West Third Street
Long Beach, CA 90802
(562) 432-1842

1441 Truman Street
San Fernando, CA 91340
(818) 365-5628

1000 East Santa Ana Boulevard,
#105
Santa Ana, CA 92701
(714) 542-2215

SELF-MOVE—DRIVING A TRUCK

- A loaded moving truck handles far differently from the typical car. Allow extra space between you and the vehicle you're following. Drive more slowly and decelerate and brake sooner—there's a lot of weight sitting behind you.

- Realize that no one likes to follow a truck. Other drivers may make risky moves to get ahead of you, so watch out for people passing when it's not safe.

- Know your truck's height and look out for low overhangs and tree branches. Especially be aware of filling station overhang height.

- Most accidents in large vehicles occur when backing. Before you back, get out, walk around, and check for obstacles. Allow plenty of maneuvering room and ask someone to help you back. Ask them to stay within sight of your side view mirror—and talk over the hand signals they should use as they guide you.

- Stop and rest at least every two hours.

- At every stop, do a walk-around inspection of the truck. Check tires, lights, and the cargo door. (If you're towing a trailer, check trailer tires, door, hitch, and hitch security chain.) Ask your truck rental representative how often you should check the engine oil level.

- At overnight stops, park in a well-lighted area and lock the truck cab. Lock the cargo door with a padlock.

IF YOU'RE FLYING OR TRAVELING BY TRAIN OR BUS

- Coordinate with the moving van driver so that you arrive at about the same time.
- Plan for the unexpected such as delays, cancellations, or missed connections.
- Keep in touch with the truck driver (by cell phone, if possible), who may also experience delays for any number of reasons: mechanical problems, road construction, storms, or illness.
- Dress comfortably.
- If you are traveling with young children, dress them in bright, distinctive clothing so you can easily identify them in a crowded airport, train station, or bus terminal.

PROFESSIONAL MOVERS MAY NEED HELP, TOO

Make sure the movers have directions to your new home. Plan your travel so that you will be there to greet them and unlock. Have a backup plan in case one of you gets delayed. It is also a good idea to exchange cell phone numbers with the driver so you can stay in touch in case one of you is delayed.

TIPS FOR A PROFESSIONAL CAR MOVE

A professional car carrier company can ship your car. Alternatively, your moving company may be able to ship it in the van along with your household goods. Ask around and compare prices.

- Be sure that the gas tanks are no more than one-quarter full.
- It's not wise to pack personal belongings in your transported auto, because insurance typically won't cover those items.
- If your car is damaged in transport, report the damage to the driver or move manager and note it on the inventory sheet. If you don't, the damage won't be eligible for insurance coverage.

Unpacking and Getting Settled

You made it. Welcome home! With all the boxes and bare walls, it may not feel like home just yet, but it soon will. You're well on your way to getting settled and having life return to normal. As you unpack boxes, arrange the furniture, and hang the pictures, here are a few things to keep in mind:

- Approach unpacking realistically. It's not necessary (and probably not possible) to unpack and arrange everything on the first day.
- Find your cleaning supplies and do any necessary cleaning.
- Consider your family's basic needs (food, rest, bathing) and unpack accordingly:

    Kitchen: Start with the basics; keep less frequently used items in boxes until you decide your room and storage arrangements.

    Bedrooms: Unpack bedding and set up and make beds.

    Bathroom: Because this tends to be a small room with little space for boxes, unpack the basics early and find a place to store the still-packed boxes until you have a chance to finish.

MAINTAINING NORMALCY . . . STARTING FRESH

During the move and the days following, it's good to keep things feeling as normal as possible. But this can also be a fresh starting point: a time to establish (or reestablish) family rituals and traditions. Beyond the family, this is a time to meet and connect with new neighbors, schoolmates, and your religious or other community.

- Keep regular bedtimes and wake-up times (naps for kids if appropriate).
- If you typically eat dinner together, continue to do this, despite the chaos.
- If you typically have a regular family time—an activity or outing—don't feel bad if you must skip it one week due to move-related chores, but restart this ritual as soon as you can. In fact, your family may appreciate this special time even more in the midst of the upheaval and change.

Rome wasn't built in a day, and neither are friendships. If your move means you have to start over, take heart: persistence and work will pay off over time. Here are a few suggestions for making your first connections with people—both individuals and communities of people—in your new area.

- Encourage family members who need encouragement in making new friends.
- Provide opportunities for building friendships from day one. Take a break from unpacking and knock on doors to meet neighbors. (It's not a good idea to start a friendship by asking for help unloading, though!)
- Get involved in activities your family enjoys and make time in your schedule for people, even though moving and resettling is a hectic and busy time.
- Meet and connect with your religious or other community.

DISCOVERING YOUR COMMUNITY

Here you'll find suggestions for getting settled in your new surroundings:

- Be sure every family member gets a feel for the neighborhood and main streets; memorizes your new address; learns (or carries) new home, office, and mobile phone numbers; and knows how to contact local emergency personnel including police, fire, and ambulance.
- Go exploring on foot, bike, mass transit, or by car (turn it into a fun outing) and start learning your way around.
- Locate your local post office and police and fire stations, as well as hospitals and gas stations near your home.
- Scout your new neighborhood for shopping areas.
- Register to vote.
- If you have moved to a new state, visit the Department of Motor Vehicles to obtain your driver's license and register your vehicle (see below).
- If you haven't already done so, transfer insurance policies to an agent in your new community.

Important Local Telephone Numbers

Electricity, Gas, and Water Companies

City Agencies

Anaheim Public Utilities Department
(714) 765-3300

Burbank Public Service Department
(818) 238-3700

Fullerton Water Customer Service
(714) 738-6890

Glendale Public Service Department
(818) 548-3300

Long Beach Gas and Electric Department
(562) 570-2000

Los Angeles Department of Water & Power
(213) 481-5411
or (800) 342-5397

Pasadena Water and Power Department
(626) 744-4409

Santa Ana Water Resources
(714) 647-3320

Santa Monica Department of Environmental and Public Works Management, Utilities Division
(310) 458-8286

Regional Agencies and Companies

Metropolitan Water District of Southern California
(213) 217-6000

Orange County Water District
(714) 378-3200

Southern California Edison Company
(800) 655-4555

Southern California Gas Company
(213) 244-1200

Southern California Water Company
(909) 394-3600

Water Replenishment District of Southern California
(562) 921-5521

State Agency

California Municipal Utilities Association
(916) 441-1733

Federal Agency

U.S. Bureau of Reclamation
(916) 978-5000

Phone Companies

Los Angeles and Orange Counties have literally dozens of telecommunications carriers. The ones listed below serve the largest areas. Virtually every part of either county can get service from these companies.

AT&T
(800) 222-0300

GTE
(800) 483-1000

MCI
(800) 950-5555

Pacific Bell
(800) 310-2355

Sprint
(800) 877-7746

Cable Television Providers

In areas as big as Los Angeles and Orange counties, you'll find several cable companies, each with its own territory. Among the biggest:

Adelphia
(800) 220-7920

Cox Communications
(888) 277-6560

MediaOne
(888) 255-5789

Disposal Companies

Many if not most communities in Orange County and Los Angeles County offer trash pickup as part of their normal municipal services. But if you need other help, here are some of the area's more prominent disposal companies.

Ben Ware Waste Disposal
(714) 834-0234
or (949) 833-9901

BFI
(888) 742-5234

Bruce Metal & Salvage
(714) 543-1300
or *(714) 543-4361*

Budget Hauling
(800) 600-6604

Consolidated Disposal Services
(800) 299-4898

CR&R
(800) 826-9677

Waste Management
888 964-4968

Police and Fire Departments

With more than 100 incorporated cities in Los Angeles and Orange counties, it's impossible to list all of the police and fire department phone numbers here. But here are the numbers for some of the most prominent cities.

Police

Anaheim: (714) 765-1900

Burbank: (818) 238-3000

Costa Mesa: (714) 754-5252

Fullerton: (714) 738-6800

Garden Grove: (714) 741-5704

Glendale: (818) 548-4840

Huntington Beach: (714) 960-8825

Irvine: (949) 724-7000

Lake Forest: (949) 770-6011

Lancaster: (661) 948-8466

Long Beach: (562) 435-6711

Los Angeles (metropolitan area): (213) 626-5273

Los Angeles (San Fernando Valley): (818) 994-5273

Los Angeles (West Side): (310) 451-5273

Orange: (714) 744-7444

Palmdale: (661) 267-4300

Pasadena: (626) 744-4501

Pomona: (909) 620-2155

Santa Ana: (714) 834-4211

Santa Monica: (310) 395-9931

Torrance: (310) 328-3456

Tustin: (714) 573-3200

Fire

Anaheim: (714) 765-4000

Burbank: (818) 238-3473

Costa Mesa: (714) 549-1111

Fullerton: (714) 738-6500

Garden Grove: (714) 741-5600

MOVING TIP

Unless company policy prohibits acceptance of gratuities, it is customary to tip each professional mover. $20 is a good amount; you may want to tip more or less based on the service you receive.

If you move yourself, you might also want to give each of your volunteers a gift. Cash or a gift certificate is a nice gesture. Perhaps one of your volunteers is a plant-lover and will cheerfully accept your houseplants as a thank-you gift. It's also a good idea to supply plenty of soft drinks or water and snacks for them!

Glendale: (818) 548-4814

Huntington Beach:
(714) 536-5411

Irvine: (714) 744-0400

Lake Forest: (714) 744-0400

Lancaster: (661) 948-2631

Long Beach: (562) 570-2510

Los Angeles (metropolitan area):
(213) 485-5971

Los Angeles (San Fernando
Valley): (213) 485-5971

Los Angeles (West Side):
(213) 485-5971

Orange: (714) 288-2500

Palmdale: (661) 723-4455

Pasadena: (626) 744-4655

Pomona: (323) 881-2411

Santa Ana: (714) 647-5700

Santa Monica: (310) 458-8651

Torrance: (310) 618-2973

Tustin: (714) 744-0400

Exterminators

Southern California has a lot of pest-control companies. The following are among the most prominent.

Antimite
(800) 499-5855

Cal-Western Termite & Pest Control
(800) 858-2326

Exterminetics of Southern California
(714) 835-1887

Dewey Pest and Termite Control
(800) 697-9790

Fume-a-Pest & Termite Control
(800) 386-3273

Hydrex Pest Control
(800) 493-7392

Orkin
(800) 800-6754

Terminix
(800) 377-3787

Western Exterminator
(800) 937-8398

VEHICLE REGISTRATION

Full information is available at the California Department of Motor Vehicles's Web site, *www.dmv.ca.govnewtoca/newtoca.htm.*
Here are some excerpts that can ease the process:

Q: How long do I have to register a vehicle from another state or country?

A: Nonresident vehicle owners (recent arrivals) must register their out-of-state vehicles in California within twenty days of the date they accept employment or establish residency in California.

You may obtain a copy of the DMV's information packet which explains California's registration requirements. To request this packet, please call your local DMV.

Q: How do I transfer my registration from another state or country to California?

A: Your vehicle may be subject to California registration and license fees from the date of entry. To avoid penalties, fees must be paid within twenty days from the date the vehicle entered California.

You will need to:

• Complete an Application for Registration form Reg 343/31
• Submit your out-of-state registration certificate
• Submit your out-of-state title (if you have it)

- Provide an odometer mileage certification (if your vehicle is less than ten years old)
- Provide evidence of the California smog certification
- Bring your vehicle to a DMV office for verification of the vehicle's identification number. (For your convenience, we recommend that you schedule an appointment by calling your local DMV.)
- Pay the registration and license fees. Commercial vehicles, including pickup trucks, may also require a weight certificate.

If you brought this vehicle into California within ninety days from the date of purchase, you may also be subject to use tax.

Q: How do I register a vehicle I purchased with out-of-state plates?

A: Within twenty days of your purchase, you must apply for California registration and pay all registration and license fees.

You will need to:

- Complete an Application for Registration form Reg 343/31
- Submit the out-of-state title endorsed with the seller's signature
- Provide an odometer mileage certification signed by both the seller and the buyer
- Provide evidence of the smog certification
- Bring your vehicle to a DMV office for verification of the vehicle's identification number (For your convenience, we recommend that you schedule an appointment by calling your local DMV.)
- Pay the registration, license, and use tax fees. If the vehicle was not manufactured for sale in California, you may be required to pay a one time $300 smog impact fee, in addition to the registration, license, and use tax fees. Model year 1975 and newer gasoline-powered passenger vehicles, and 1980 and newer diesel-powered vehicles, are subject to the smog impact fee.

Q: What forms do I need to register a vehicle?

A: Application for Original Registration (REG 343/31):

This two-part application form is used for vehicles being registered for the first time and for nonresident vehicles brought into California. The completed and signed application must be submitted with the appropriate fees within twenty days of the date the vehicle is first operated in California.

This form may also be used to reregister a vehicle after it has been junked, salvaged, or removed from the department's database.

The REG 343/31 is generally submitted with other supporting documents and is not to be mailed by itself. Call (916) 657-7669 or make an appointment at your local DMV field office for more information.

Q: How can I notify the DMV when I change my address?

A: It is the law that you must notify the DMV within ten days of changing your address. There is no charge to change your address, and you may notify the DMV by any of the following ways:

1. Call any DMV office and request that a change of address form be mailed to you. It will take five days for you to receive it. Complete the information required on the form, then mail it to the address listed at the bottom of the form.

2. Download the Change of Address form DMV 14, complete the information, and mail it to the address listed at the bottom of the form.

3. Visit any DMV office, complete a change of address form, and give it to a technician. The technician will give you a Change of Address Certificate card DL 43 to complete and carry with your license.

If you do 1 or 2 above, type or write your new address in ink on a small piece of paper, sign and date it. Carry this piece of paper with your license. Do not tape or staple the change of address information to your driver license.

TAKING CARE OF THE FINANCIAL IMPLICATIONS OF YOUR MOVE

Now that you have arrived, you can take care of some of the financial and tax implications of your move. Here are some things to think about (it's also wise to consult an accountant):

- Some of your moving expenses may be tax-deductible. Prepare for tax filing by collecting receipts from your move. Also contact the Internal Revenue Service to obtain the publication and form you need. Visit *www.irs.gov* or call (800) 829-3676.
- State income tax. If your new state collects income tax, you'll need to file a state income tax form. For help with your relocation-related taxes, visit *www.monstermoving.com* and check out the "Relocation Tax Advisor."
- Other income sources may have tax implications. As you prepare to file, you'll want to consider any other sources of income and whether your new state will tax you on this income. For example, if you are paying federal income tax on an IRA that you rolled over into a Roth IRA and your new state collects income tax, you may also have to pay state income tax on your rollover IRA.

Home at Last

Once the truck is unloaded, the boxes are unpacked, and the pictures are hung, once you're sleeping in a *bed*—instead of on a loose mattress—you'll dream sweet dreams. Tomorrow, with the stress of this move slipping away behind you and the next move not even a faint glimmer on the horizon of your mind, you'll begin to discover the opportunities and savor the possibilities of your new city, new job, new school—your new home.

Getting to Know Your Town

CHAPTER 6

What's Around Town

Finding things to do in Los Angeles County and Orange County is both very easy and very hard.

It's easy because there's so much. As a center of the entertainment industry, Southern California has lots of actors, singers, dancers, and other performers showing off their talents every night. As a place that has sunshine nearly all year, the region is a paradise for hikers, bicyclists, picnickers, campers, stargazers, sunbathers, and devotees of any other kind of outdoor fun. And as a spot stuffed with suburbs and other bedroom communities, Southern California has all kinds of venues delivering fun for families.

The hard part is that the region's huge and doesn't give the confused newcomer much help. Huntington Park in Los Angeles County is nowhere near Huntington Beach in Orange County, Agoura Hills sits hours away from Laguna Hills, Emerald Bay is a long, long drive from Diamond Bar, East San Pedro lies in the western half of the region while Westminster is on the eastern side, and don't even think about Westlake and Westlake Village, or Santa Clarita, Santa Monica, and Santa Ana. Let's just say that they're not neighbors.

To make sense of the area, I've arranged the attractions in alphabetical order by type of attraction: art and culture, gyms and athletic clubs, outdoor fun, shopping, spectator sports, and so on. Then I've listed the attractions by county (Los Angeles County and Orange County), with the individual communities in alphabetical order within each county.

Finally, in its own section is a calendar of events.

And now, on to the fun.

Art Museums and Galleries

LOS ANGELES COUNTY

Crenshaw District
(City of Los Angeles)

Museum of African-American Art
Robinsons-May
40005 Crenshaw Boulevard, Third Floor
(323) 294-7071

Contemporary and historic works by Africans and African Americans

Downey

Downey Museum of Art
10419 South Rives Avenue
(562) 861-0419

www.downeyca.org/visitor/museumart.htm

Hundreds of works by artists from nearby and around the world

Downtown
(City of Los Angeles)

Museum of Contemporary Art
250 South Grand Avenue
(213) 626-2222

www.moca-la.org

Art from 1945 to the present day

Hollywood and Vicinity
(City of Los Angeles)

Barnsdall Art Park
4800 Hollywood Boulevard
(213) 485-8665

Galleries, a theater, a 1918-era Frank Lloyd Wright house, plus art workshops for all ages

Lancaster

City of Lancaster Museum/Art Gallery
44801 North Sierra Highway
(661) 723-6250

A variety of artistic and historical exhibits

Long Beach

Long Beach Museum of Art
2300 East Ocean Boulevard
(562) 439-2119

www.lbma.com

Contemporary art, video art, and a sculpture garden

Museum of Latin American Art
628 Alamitos Avenue
(562) 437-1689

www.molaa.com

Contemporary Latin American art

Pasadena

Norton Simon Museum
411 West Colorado Boulevard
(626) 449-6840

www.nortonsimon.org

European art from the 1400s to the 1900s, Asian art from the past two millennia, and other exhibits

Pacific Asia Museum
46 North Los Robles Avenue
(626) 449-2742

Artworks, costumes, and ornamental items from Asia and the Pacific Islands, plus a koi pond and Chinese garden

Pomona

Antique Row
East Second Street
(909) 623-9835

One of the West's largest antique-shop complexes, featuring furniture, prints, dolls, toys, jewelry, clothing, pottery, and other items

San Pedro (City of Los Angeles)

Angels Gate Cultural Center
Angels Gate Park
3601 South Gaffey Street,
Building A
(310) 519-0936

Art exhibits, classes, performances, and other attractions

Santa Monica

Bergamot Station
2525 Michigan Avenue
(310) 829-5854

A collection of cutting-edge galleries, primarily featuring contemporary artists

CITY FACT

L.A. County's Board of Supervisors reports that more than 65 percent of the county—2,649 square miles and more than a million people—is not part of any city. These areas have no mayor; their "city council" is the Board of Supervisors, and their cops are the county Sheriff's Department.

**Watts District
(City of Los Angeles)**

Watts Towers Art Center
1727 East 107th Street
(213) 847-4646

artscenecal.com/
WattsTowers.html

The Watts Towers, a collection of spires made from discarded bottles, ceramics, china, and industrial debris, accompanied by live performances and exhibits of visual arts

**West L.A.
(City of Los Angeles)**

Getty Center
1200 Getty Center Drive
(310) 440-7300

www.getty.edu/museum

European paintings and other works, plus lectures, concerts, and additional activities

**Wilshire District
(City of Los Angeles)**

Los Angeles County Museum of Art
5905 Wilshire Boulevard
(323) 857-6000

www.lacma.org

Eclectic collection of paintings and sculptures from the 1300s to the present day, plus a specialized Japanese pavilion

ORANGE COUNTY

Anaheim

Doll and Toy Museum/Hobby City
1238 South Beach Boulevard
(714) 527-2323

More than 3,000 dolls fill the museum, and more than twenty collectors' stores fill the surrounding Hobby City complex.

Costa Mesa

Orange County Museum of Art South Coast Plaza Gallery
3333 Bristol Street, Suite 1000
(714) 662-3366

www.ocma.net

This branch of the Orange County Museum of Art focuses on art of the twentieth century.

Fullerton

Fullerton Museum Center
301 North Pomona Avenue
(714) 738-6545

A selection of fine art and historical artifacts

Huntington Beach

Huntington Beach Art Center
538 Main Street
(714) 374-1650

Contemporary artists in various media, plus instruction, performances, and other events

Laguna Beach

Laguna Art Museum
307 Cliff Drive
(949) 494-6531

www.lagunaartmuseum.org

California Impressionists and contemporary artists

Newport Beach

Orange County Museum of Art Newport Beach
850 San Clemente Drive
(949) 759-1122

www.ocma.net
or www.ocartsnet.org/ocma

More than 6,000 works of visual art by California artists

Santa Ana

Artists Village
An area bordered by First, Fourth, Broadway, and Spurgeon streets
(714) 647-5360

Galleries, artists' studios, theaters, and more

Historical Sites, Monuments, Museums, and Recreations

LOS ANGELES COUNTY

Chino

Planes of Fame Air Museum
Chino Airport
7000 Merrill Avenue
(909) 597-3722

www.planesoffame.org

A museum of airplanes that doesn't just display them but also flies them

Crenshaw District (City of Los Angeles)

Museum in Black
Leimert Park Village
4331 Degnan Boulevard
(323) 292-9528

African art and foliage, plus African American historical artifacts

Downtown (City of Los Angeles)

Los Angeles Conservancy Historical Walking Tours
523 West Sixth Street, Suite 1216
(213) 623-2489

Guided tours of Los Angeles's old neighborhoods, shopping districts, theaters, and other points of interest

Encino (City of Los Angeles)

Los Encinos State Historic Park
16756 Moorpark Street
(818) 784-4849

Nineteenth-century structures on beautifully landscaped grounds

Hawthorne

Western Museum of Flight
Hawthorne Municipal Airport
12016 Prairie Avenue
(310) 332-6228

A collection of classic planes, plus an aviation library

Hollywood and Vicinity (City of Los Angeles)

Autry Museum of Western Heritage
Griffith Park
4700 Western Heritage Way
(323) 667-2000

www.autry-museum.org

Displays on the West from prehistory through modern days

Lancaster

Antelope Valley Indian Museum

15701 East Avenue M
(661) 946-3055

www.avim.av.org

Exhibits and displays devoted to the history and culture of Native Americans

Lomita

Lomita Railroad Museum

2137 West 250th Street
(310) 326-6255;
(310) 325-7110

www.lomita_rr.org

A replica of a New England rail station from the 1800s, including railroad cars, displays of railway equipment, and other items

Long Beach

Queen Mary

Pier J
1126 Queens Highway
(562) 435-3511;
(800) 437-2934

www.queenmary.com

Tours of the 1936 luxury liner, plus other attractions

Mission Hills (City of Los Angeles)

Mission San Fernando Rey

15151 San Fernando Mission Boulevard
(818) 361-0186

A restored, 200-year-old mission, with a tour of the mission's courtyards, gardens, church, and religious artwork

Mount Washington (City of Los Angeles)

Southwest Museum

234 Museum Drive
(323) 221-2164

www.southwestmuseum.org

Native American artwork, artifacts, and other items

Ontario

Graber Olive House

315 East Fourth Street
(909) 983-1761

www.graberolives.com

Free tours of the olive grading, curing, and canning operation, plus a museum, places to picnic, and other attractions

Pomona

Adobe de Palomares

491 East Arrow Highway
(909) 620-0264;
(909) 623-2198

www.osb.net/pomona

An 1850-era mansion, with gardens and courtyard

San Pedro
(City of Los Angeles)

Los Angeles Maritime Museum

Berth 84 at the end of 6th Street
(310) 548-7618

www.sanpedrochamber.com/
champint/lamartmu.htm

Old sailing vessels, exhibits on seagoing history, sailing equipment, and plenty of model ships

SS *Lane Victory*

Berth 94 at Catalina Terminal
Los Angeles Harbor
(310) 519-9545

www.lanevictoryship.com

A ship that served in three wars, with guided tours and displays of naval memorabilia

Santa Clarita

Heritage Junction Historic Park

24101 San Fernando Road
(661) 254-1275

Homes, schoolhouses, and other structures from the late 1800s and early 1900s, plus period artifacts

Santa Fe Springs

Heritage Park

12100 Mora Drive
(562) 946-6476

www.santafesprings.org/
historic.htm

Exhibits on local history from the indigenous people who settled the land centuries ago to antique car shows and a railroad exhibit

Santa Monica

Museum of Flying

Santa Monica Municipal Airport
2772 Donald Douglas Loop North
(310) 392-8822

www.mof.org/mof

Photos, movies, models, and actual airplanes from aviation's past and present

Torrance

Torrance Historical Society Museum
1345 Post Avenue
(310) 328-5392

Furniture, photos, clothes, and other artifacts from the past

West L.A.
(City of Los Angeles)

Museum of Tolerance
9786 West Pico Boulevard
(310) 553-8403

www.wiesenthal.com

A museum about the Nazi Holocaust and other examples of intolerance

Skirball Cultural Center
2701 North Sepulveda Boulevard
(310) 440-4500

Exhibits and programs on Jewish history and culture, including lectures and displays

Wilshire District
(City of Los Angeles)

Page Museum at the La Brea Tar Pits
5801 Wilshire Boulevard
(323) 934-7243

www.tarpits.org

A working site where paleontologists find and exhibit dinosaur remains

ORANGE COUNTY

Anaheim

Ramon Peralta Adobe
Santa Ana Canyon Road and Fairmont Boulevard
(714) 528-4260

Archaeological artifacts and historical photos of the canyon

Costa Mesa

Diego Sepulveda Adobe
Estancia Park
1900 Adams Avenue
(949) 631-5918

An authentic early-California structure, complete with period furnishings

Huntington Beach

Old World Village
7561 Center Avenue
(714) 898-3033

A Bavarian village, with cobblestone streets, ethnic dining, imported merchandise, and cultural festivals

La Habra

Children's Museum at La Habra
Portola Park
301 South Euclid Street
(562) 905-9793

www.lhcm.org

An old Union Pacific Railroad depot, this museum features vehicles and animals from the past.

CITY
FACT

The small town of Bradbury, about twenty miles northeast of downtown Los Angeles, has an unusual problem for an upscale area with exclusive, gated neighborhoods. According to journalist Joe Mozingo in the May 18, 1999, *Los Angeles Times*, black bears sometimes wander down from the nearby San Gabriel Mountains to rummage in trash cans.

Placentia

George Key Ranch Historic Site
625 West Bastanchury Road
(714) 528-4260

A nineteenth-century estate, including a house of 5,000 square feet and an orange grove

San Juan Capistrano

Mission San Juan Capistrano
Camino Capistrano at Ortega Highway
(949) 248-2048

The first settlement between San Diego and Los Angeles, this 1776-era site includes ten acres of grounds and historic buildings.

Seal Beach

Red Car Museum
Pacific Electric Park
Main Street and Electric Avenue
(562) 683-1874

Dedicated to Southern California's fondly remembered railway system

Libraries

LOS ANGELES COUNTY

Claremont

Claremont Colleges
800 Dartmouth Avenue
(909) 621-8045

One of the biggest libraries in Southern California, with special collections dealing with theater, western Americana, and other topics

Downtown
(City of Los Angeles)

Los Angeles Central Library
630 West Fifth Street
(213) 228-7000

www.lapl.org

The nexus of the L.A. City library system, with a huge collection of books and other media, two theaters, landscaped gardens, and more

University of Southern California
3551 University Avenue
(213) 740-2311

www.usc.edu

A large general collection, plus specialized collections dealing with gerontology, movies and TV, Asian studies, and other subjects

Long Beach

Long Beach Main Library
101 Pacific Avenue
(562) 570-7500

www.lbpl.org/main.html

The Long Beach library system's main library holds general collections plus special collections of sheet music and books and documents dealing with local history and genealogy.

Northridge
(City of Los Angeles)

California State University Northridge
Delmar T. Oviatt Library
18111 Nordhoff Street
(818) 677-2271

www.csun.edu

A large collection, with special sections on local history, minority studies, and women's issues

Pasadena

Pasadena Central Library
285 East Walnut Street
(626) 744-4052

A strong and varied collection, plus children's programs, film programs, literacy programs, and other activities

CITY FACT

Southern California is famous for wide, open spaces, even the ones in the sky. In the observatory atop Mount Wilson, north of Pasadena, Edwin Hubble (the namesake of the famous space telescope) discovered that the universe was expanding. A few years later, according to University of California Irvine physics professor Gregory Benford, Pasadena's Jet Propulsion Laboratory "provided the first U.S. space satellite, *Explorer I.*"

San Marino

Huntington Library, Art Collections and Botanical Gardens
1151 Oxford Road
(626) 405-2100

www.huntington.org

Galleries, a rare books library, more than 100 acres of gardens, and other attractions

Simi Valley

Ronald Reagan Presidential Library and Museum
40 Presidential Drive
(805) 410-8354;
(805) 522-8444

www.reagan.utexas.edu

The central repository for information on Ronald Reagan

West L.A.
(City of Los Angeles)

University of California Los Angeles
405 Hilgard Avenue
(310) 825-8301;
(310) 825-7143

www.ucla.edu

One of the great American university libraries, containing more than 9 million volumes, including specialized collections dealing with maps, medicine, the arts, and other topics

ORANGE COUNTY

Corona del Mar
(City of Newport Beach)

Sherman Library and Gardens
2647 East Coast Highway
Library: (949) 673-1880
Gardens: (949) 673-2261

www.cdmchamber.com

A huge complex with a considerable collection of information on the Pacific Southwest, plus botanical gardens with plants from all over the planet

Fullerton

California State University, Fullerton
Pollak Library
800 North State College Boulevard
(714) 278-2633

One of Orange County's strongest libraries, with special collections dealing with United States government history

Irvine

University of California, Irvine
University Drive
P.O. Box 19557
(949) 824-6836

www.lib.uci.edu

A library system featuring extensive Asian collections, high-tech facilities, and other advantages

CITY FACT

Brian Roberts's and Richard Schwadel's book, *L.A. Shortcuts: The Guidebook for Drivers Who Hate to Wait,* notes, "It took the *Viking II* space probe nearly one year to complete the 142,000,000-mile voyage to Mars. The inhabitants of Los Angeles drive that same amount every single day." The book also offers "The 11 Commandments of the Road," which include "Residents take precedence! Respect the locals when driving through residential areas," and "Your car is a sovereign country. Maintain a swift-handed dictatorship over passengers."

Orchestras, Opera Companies, and Other Musical Organizations

LOS ANGELES COUNTY

Downtown (City of Los Angeles)

Los Angeles Opera
Music Center
135 North Grand Avenue
(213) 972-8001;
(213) 365-3500

www.laopera.org

Great European and American operas, with an electronic sign delivering a running translation

Los Angeles Philharmonic
Music Center
135 North Grand Avenue
(213) 972-7300;
(213) 850-2000

www.laphil.org

The region's premiere orchestra, performing at both the Music Center and the Hollywood Bowl

Glendale

Glendale Symphony Orchestra
Alex Theatre
216 North Brand Boulevard
(818) 233-3123

Mozart and other kings of the classical repertoire

Long Beach

Long Beach Opera
Carpenter Performing Arts Center
California State University
Long Beach
1250 Bellflower Boulevard
(562) 439-2580

www.lbopera.org

Twentieth-century European operas and other works

Long Beach Symphony Orchestra
555 East Ocean Boulevard, #106
(562) 436-3203

www.lbso.org

An orchestra with both classics and pops programs

Pasadena

Pasadena Lyric Opera
South Pasadena Auditorium
1428 Fair Oaks Avenue
(888) 673-7248; (626) 744-9549

Popular European operas from the masters of classical music

ORANGE COUNTY

Costa Mesa

Opera Pacific
Orange County Performing Arts Center
600 Town Center Drive
(800) 346-7372;
(714) 556-2787

www.ocartsnet.org/opera_pacific

The great operas of Europe, featured from winter through spring

---

Night Life: Theaters, Concert Halls, and Clubs

If you scan this section, you'll find an odd split. Nightclubs and bars that offer entertainment are located around the L.A. city metro area. Other areas, whether in Orange County or the valleys of Los Angeles County, are primarily family bedroom communities and aren't too thick with club-hoppers. Fortunately, the entire region offers playhouses and concert venues.

LOS ANGELES COUNTY

Burbank

Starlight Bowl
1249 Lockheed View
(818) 525-3721

www.ci.burbank.ca.us

Burbank Chamber Orchestra, plus pop groups

Cerritos

Cerritos Center for the Performing Arts
12700 Center Court Drive
(562) 916-8500;
(800) 300-4345

www.cerritoscenter.com
or www.ci.cerritos.ca.us/ccpa/new_ccpa.html

Performances of opera, country, show tunes, classical, and other forms of music

Culver City

Jazz Bakery
3223 Helms Avenue
(310) 271-9039

The best in touring and local jazz performers

Downtown
(City of Los Angeles)

Al's Bar
305 South Hewitt Street
(213) 626-7213

www.alsbar.net

Old-fashioned rock 'n' roll bar, with acts that pride themselves on being hard and wild. Age twenty-one and over.

IMAX Theater
Exposition Park
700 State Drive
(213) 744-2014

A seven-story movie screen featuring documentaries and entertainment productions

Staples Center
1111 South Figueroa Street
(213) 742-7100

www.staplescenterla.com

A venue for rock, pop, and other concerts, and the home of the Kings hockey team and Lakers and Clippers basketball teams

**Music Center
of Los Angeles County**
(includes Dorothy Chandler Pavilion, Ahmanson Theatre, and Mark Taper Forum)
135 North Grand Avenue
(213) 628-2772;
(213) 972-7200

www.music-center.com

Los Angeles Master Chorale, Los Angeles Philharmonic, Los Angeles Opera, Center Theatre Group, and other companies

Glendale

Alex Theatre
216 North Brand Boulevard
(818) 243-2359

theatre.glendale.ca.us/alex

Dance and music on the cutting edge

Glendora

Haugh Performing Arts Center
Citrus Community College
1000 West Foothill Boulevard
(626) 963-9411

www.citrus.cc.ca.us/hpac/hpac.htm

A home for Broadway show tunes, performances for kids, dinner theater, movies, and performances by Citrus Community College students

Hermosa Beach

Comedy and Magic Club
1018 Hermosa Avenue
(310) 372-1193

The top comedy club of the South Bay, featuring Jay Leno and other popular comedians. Age eighteen and over.

Hollywood and Vicinity (City of Los Angeles)

The Derby

4500 Los Feliz Boulevard
(323) 663-8979

Birthplace of the swing-dance revival, featuring dance lessons, the best in modern swing bands, and a full bar. Age twenty-one and over.

Dragonfly

6510 Santa Monica Boulevard
(323) 466-6111

An old-fashioned rock club, with special nights for disco and reggae. Age twenty-one and over.

Egyptian Theater

6712 Hollywood Boulevard
(323) 466-3456

Home of the American Cinematheque, presenting classics, independent films, and other treats for the cineaste

Greek Theater

Griffith Park
2700 North Vermont Avenue
(323) 665-1927

www.nederlander.com/greek.html

An outdoor amphitheatre featuring top performing and recording acts in country, jazz, rock, and other genres

CITY FACT

On its opening day, Disneyland was a disaster. The park was jammed by thousands of people with counterfeit admission tickets; rides broke down; the water supply was inadequate; Tomorrowland was so unready that Walt Disney ordered the staff to distract park patrons from it; and in the words of *The Disney Studio Story* by Richard Holliss and Brian Sibley, "as the day got hotter, the stiletto heels worn by many of the women sank into the asphalt on Main Street."

Hollywood Bowl

2301 North Highland Avenue
(323) 850-2000

www.hollywoodbowl.org

Classics, jazz and pop—from single performances to entire festivals—in possibly the world's most famous band shell

Mann's Chinese Theater

6925 Hollywood Boulevard
(323) 464-8111; (323) 461-3331

The elaborately designed movie palace, with its famous forecourt filled with the hand prints and signatures of Hollywood stars

The Palace

1735 Vine Street
(323) 462-3000

A longtime hot spot featuring top rock bands, plus a dance floor and a cafe. Age eighteen and over.

Pantages Theatre

6233 Hollywood Boulevard
(323) 468-1770

www.nederlander.com/
pantages.html

Broadway-caliber musicals and other large-scale presentations

La Mirada

La Mirada Theatre for the Performing Arts

14900 La Mirada Boulevard
(714) 994-6310

www.cityoflamirada.org/
theahome.htm

Broadway-style musicals and other plays, plus symphonic presentations

Lancaster

Lancaster Performing Arts Center

750 West Lancaster Boulevard
(661) 723-5950

www.lpac.org

The Acting Company, Cedar Street Theatre, and touring musicians and plays

Long Beach

Terrace Theater

Long Beach Convention and Entertainment Center
300 East Ocean Boulevard
(562) 436-3661

www.longbeachcc.com

Long Beach Symphony Orchestra and other companies

North Hollywood

The Baked Potato

3783 Cahuenga Boulevard West
(818) 980-1615

A premiere (albeit tiny) jazz club, expert at booking the field's top guitarists. All ages.

Palmdale

Palmdale Playhouse

Antelope Valley Community Arts Center
38334 Tenth Street East
(661) 267-5685

www.bestintown.net/playhouse

Palmdale Youth and Community Choir, Palmdale Repertory Theatre, Palmdale Youth and Community Orchestra, Palmdale Youth and Community Dance Program, Palmdale City Players, and Desert Opera Theatre

Pasadena

Pasadena Civic Auditorium

300 East Green Street
(626) 449-7360

Home of the Pasadena Symphony, plus opera, ballet, Broadway musicals, and other events

Redondo Beach

Redondo Beach Performing Arts Center

1935 Manhattan Beach Boulevard
(310) 937-6607

www.rbpac.com

The Civic Light Opera of South Bay Cities, plus other companies and performers

San Gabriel

San Gabriel Civic Auditorium

320 South Mission Drive
(626) 308-2865

www.musictheatre.org/
sgca.html

Revivals of recent and classic Broadway musicals

Santa Monica

McCabe's

3101 Pico Boulevard
(310) 828-4403; (310) 828-4497

A guitar shop where the pros not only buy their instruments but play them: country, folk, blues, and rock. All ages.

Santa Monica Civic Auditorium

1855 Main Street
(310) 393-9961

Home of the Santa Monica Symphony and touring rock and pop acts.

The West End

1305 Fifth Street
(310) 394-4647;
(323) 656-3905

www.westendclubs.com

A dance club that calls itself "a funky good time," featuring reggae, disco, and of course funk. Age twenty-one and over.

Torrance

Center for the Arts

El Camino College
16007 Crenshaw Boulevard
(310) 329-5345

One of the South Bay's leading venues for classical music

Universal City

Universal Amphitheatre

100 Universal City Plaza
(818) 622-4440

www.uniamp.com

Big-name recording artists from all over the country

Universal City Cinemas

100 Universal City Plaza
(818) 508-0588

Arguably the region's biggest cineplex, with eighteen screens and 6,000 seats

Walnut

Mount San Antonio College Performing Arts Center

1100 North Grand Avenue
(909) 468-4050

www.mtsac.edu/
performing _arts

Choral and instrumental music performances, Broadway-style musicals and other entertainment

West Hollywood

House of Blues

8430 Sunset Strip
(323) 848-5100

www.hob.com

Blues, rock, reggae, hip-hop, country, and other street-level musical performances. Age twenty-one and over.

LunaPark

665 North Robertson Boulevard
(310) 652-0611

A hipster hangout featuring cabaret acts, alternative comedy, and other entertainment, plus three bars, a full menu, and a garden patio. Age twenty-one and over.

Viper Room

8852 Sunset Boulevard
(310) 358-1880

www.viperroom.com

Fast-rising rockers, plus a full bar and a chance to see celebrities in the audience. Age twenty-one and over.

Whisky a Go Go

8901 Sunset Boulevard
(310) 652-4202

www.whiskyagogo.com

A venerable yet still-hip club, featuring hard rock and similar kinds of music. All ages.

West L.A.
(City of Los Angeles)

Shubert Theatre

2020 Avenue of the Stars
(800) 447-7400;
(310) 201-1500

Major productions from
Broadway

UCLA Center for the Performing Arts

Royce Hall
University of California, Los
Angeles
405 Hilgard Avenue
(310) 825-4401

www.performingarts.ucla.edu

A vast variety of performances
in music, dance, spoken word,
and other media

Wilshire District
(City of Los Angeles)

Silent Movie

611 North Fairfax Avenue
(323) 655-2520

One of America's few silent-
movie houses, with silent and
talkie classics

Wiltern Theatre

3790 Wilshire Boulevard
(213) 380-5005

Rock, pop, country, and other
musical acts

Woodland Hills

Valley Cultural Center

21550 Oxnard Street, #470
(818) 704-1358

www.valleycultural.org

Home of the San Fernando
Valley Symphony Orchestra, featuring classical concerts, jazz
shows, and other performances
in an outdoor setting

CITY FACT

L.A. is the world capital of self-storage facilities, wrote journalist Gregory Rodriguez in a 1998 issue of *Los Angeles* magazine. "The country's youth are proba-bly more mobile than ever. One third of twenty-somethings moved in the last year. Young Latinos and westerners are more likely than other Americans to change their residence."

ORANGE COUNTY

Costa Mesa

Orange County Performing Arts Center
600 Town Center Drive
(714) 556-2787

www.ocpac.org

Jazz, ballet, classical, show tunes, rock, musical theater, and other entertainment

Fullerton

Plummer Auditorium
California State University, Fullerton
201 East Chapman Avenue
(714) 870-3739

www.fullerton.edu/root/paweb/ts193.html

Jazz, show tunes, Broadway-style musicals, and more

Huntington Beach

Huntington Beach Playhouse
7111 Talbert Avenue
(714) 375-0696

www.user-friendly.com/playhouse/hb.html

Plays by Shakespeare and modern playwrights

Irvine

Bren Events Center
University of California, Irvine
100 Bren Events Center

Student shows of music and dance from around the world, plus other events

www.bren.uci.edu

Irvine Meadows Amphitheatre
8808 Irvine Center Drive
(949) 855-2863

www.avalonconcerts.com

A variety of well-known musical acts

Newport Beach

Newport Theatre Arts Center
2501 Cliff Drive
(949) 631-0288

www.employees.org/~jillkat/newport.htm

Revivals of Broadway comedies, dramas, and musicals

Other Cultural Attractions

LOS ANGELES COUNTY

Claremont

Brackett Observatory and Millikan Planetarium
Pomona College
610 North College Avenue
(909) 621-8724

www.astronomy.pomona.edu

Shows and other programs dealing with the stars and planets

Downtown and Vicinity (City of Los Angeles)

California African American Museum
Exposition Park
600 State Drive
(213) 744-7432

www.caam.ca.gov

Artworks and historical objects from African American culture past and present

California Science Center
Exposition Park
700 State Drive
(213) 744-7400

www.casciencectr.org

Interactive, hands-on exhibits on a variety of sciences and technologies

El Pueblo de Los Angeles Historic Monument and Olvera Street
845 North Alameda Street
(213) 628-1274; (213) 485-6855

A Mexican-style marketplace plus houses from Los Angeles's past, on the site of the city's first settlements

Natural History Museum of Los Angeles County
Exposition Park
900 Exposition Boulevard
(213) 763-3466

www.nhm.org

Millions of specimens alive and dead, including dinosaur skeletons and an insect zoo

Hollywood and Vicinity (City of Los Angeles)

Griffith Observatory
Griffith Park
2800 East Observatory Road
(323) 664-1191

www.griffithobservatory.org

Planetarium shows, a view of the cosmos through the observatory's giant telescope, and other attractions

Pasadena

Kidspace Museum
390 South El Molino Avenue
(626) 449-9144

Interactive museum for kids under ten, including hands-on exhibits on technology and the environment

Santa Clarita

Warmuth Honey House
17262 Sierra Highway
(661) 252-2350

A beekeeping and honey museum

Torrance

Torrance Cultural Arts Center
3330 Civic Center Drive
(310) 781-7150

www.ci.torrance.ca.us

Gallery, theater, garden, and shopping areas

ORANGE COUNTY

Fullerton

Muckenthaler Cultural Center
1201 West Malvern Avenue
(714) 738-6595

Educational activities, theatrical performances, and an art gallery, specializing in multicultural works

Newport Beach

Newport Harbor Nautical Museum
151 East Pacific Coast Highway
(949) 673-7863

www.newportnautical.org

Artifacts and displays dealing with the harbor and life on the sea

Santa Ana

Discovery Museum of Orange County
3101 West Harvard Street
(714) 540-0404

Hands-on exhibits, historical artifacts, an educational garden, and more

Discovery Science Center
2500 North Main Street
(714) 542-2823; (714) 540-2001

www.discoverycube.org or www.go2dsc.com

Science-based shows and exhibits, a laser theater, and other attractions

Gyms and Athletic Clubs

You'd expect a land famous for beaches and movie stars to produce great bodies, and you'd be right. While their cousins in cold climates can hide their bodies inside layers of flannel, heavy wool, and puffy, down-filled coats, Southern Californians wear clothes appropriate for more temperate temperatures. If they gain weight, the rest of the world can see it right away.

Consequently, many people here work hard to get in shape and stay there. Southern California has lots of gyms, athletic clubs, weight rooms, and other body shops.

The best way to find a club that suits you is to ask your friends where they go (assuming that they do go; not everyone does). The next best way is simply to go from club to club and tour the facilities.

Here are some of the area's most popular athletic clubs. They have branches throughout most or all of Southern California.

Bally Total Fitness
(800) 695-8111

www.ballyfitness.com

A chain with gyms all over the area, featuring aerobic programs, swimming pools, circuit training, free weights, running tracks, racquetball, and other amenities

Gold's Gym
(310) 392-6004

www.goldsgym.com

A place known for muscle building, with cardiovascular training, personal training, nutrition analysis, and other features

LA Fitness
(800) 523-4863

www.lafitness.com

Cross training, aerobics, racquetball, basketball, weight training, saunas, and other attractions

Powerhouse Fitness & Aerobics Center
(248) 476-2888

www.powerhousegym.com

Aerobics, sports medicine, massage therapy, kick boxing, weights, tanning center, and other facilities

Spectrum Club
(310) 479-5200

Weight training, aerobics, swimming, basketball, racquetball, and other facilities

24 Hour Fitness
(800) 204-2400

www.24HourFitness.com

Swimming, basketball, weight lifting, bicycling, treadmills, stair climbers, and other attractions

World Gym
(310) 450-0080; (800) 544-7441

www.worldgym.com

Weights, cardiovascular training, stretching, and other facilities

Amusement Parks

LOS ANGELES COUNTY

Industry

Malibu Speed Zone
17817 Castelton Street
(888) 662-5428

A chance to race fearfully fast cars, plus food and arcade games

Pomona

Fairplex
1101 West McKinley Avenue
(909) 623-3111

www.fairplex.com

Swap meets, home and garden events, car races and shows, arts and crafts shows, and the Los Angeles County Fair

San Dimas

Raging Waters
111 Raging Waters Drive
(909) 802-2200

www.ragingwaters.com

Water rides, beaches, lagoons, and other attractions

Santa Monica

Pacific Park
380 Santa Monica Pier
(310) 260-8744

www.pacpark.com

A park on a pier, with rides, food vendors, games, and other attractions

Unincorporated Area near Santa Clarita

Six Flags Magic Mountain
26101 Magic Mountain Parkway
(818) 367-5965;
(661) 255-4100

www.sixflags.com/
magicmountain

Roller coasters, a water park, Bugs Bunny World for young kids, and other entertainments

Universal City

Universal Studios Hollywood
100 Universal City Plaza
(818) 622-3801; (818) 508-9600; (818) 622-3036

www.universalstudios.com

A studio tour, plus rides based on famous movies and TV series

ORANGE COUNTY

Anaheim

Disneyland
1313 Harbor Boulevard
(714) 781-4565

www.disney.go.com/disneyland/

"The happiest place on earth," the prototype for almost every other theme park, with rides, specialty foods, shopping, and (very important) convenient places to sit when you're tired.

Buena Park

Knott's Berry Farm
8039 Beach Boulevard
(714) 220-5200

www.knotts.com

Shops, restaurants, rides (especially roller coasters), and historical-themed areas such as the Old West Ghost Town and the Indian Trails

Huntington Beach

Adventure Playground
Huntington Central Park
Golden West Street
(714) 536-5486

A tree house, tire swings, a rope bridge, a sandbox, a rafting pond, a mud slide, and equipment for kids to build anything they like

Irvine

Wild Rivers Waterpark
8770 Irvine Center Drive
(949) 768-9453

Water slides and other wet rides, wave pools, hot springs, and other water-based attractions

Newport Beach

Balboa Fun Zone
600 East Bay Avenue
(949) 673-0408

Arcades, a Ferris wheel, a carousel, laser tag, bumper cars, and more

Beaches

Call the phone numbers for any beach before you visit it; parking can get very tight, the weather at the beach can get much cooler than it gets inland, and the waters may be too polluted (or full of riptides) for safe swimming.

Since some beaches don't have an address with a specific street number as a house or business would, some of the addresses listed below are those of the main lifeguard stations.

LOS ANGELES COUNTY

Hermosa Beach

Hermosa County Beach
15100 Pacific Coast Highway
(310) 372-2166

Swimming, volleyball, food vendors, and fishing, among other things

Long Beach

Long Beach City Beach
2100 East Ocean Boulevard
(562) 570-1360

Swimming, volleyball, hiking, sailing, wind surfing, fishing, a launch ramp for jet skis, a sailing center, and other attractions

Malibu

Nicholas Canyon Beach
33904 Pacific Coast Highway
(310) 457-9891

Fishing, picnicking (with barbecues), swimming, surfing, and more

Zuma Beach
30050 Pacific Coast Highway
(310) 457-9891

Volleyball, fishing, surfing, swimming, and playgrounds, among other things

Manhattan Beach

Manhattan County Beach
2200 Strand
(310) 372-2166

Swimming, surfing, snorkeling, fishing, volleyball, and other attractions

Marina del Rey and Playa del Rey

Dockweiler State Beach
12001 Vista del Mar
(310) 372-2166; (310) 322-7036

Surfing, swimming, picnicking, a campground for recreational vehicles, a playground, and food vendors

Pacific Palisades

Will Rogers State Beach

15100 Pacific Coast Highway
(310) 451-2906;
(818) 880-0350

Volleyball, swimming, bodysurfing, conventional surfing, gymnastics, a bicycle path, and a playground

Redondo Beach

Redondo County Beach

100 Esplanade
(310) 372-2166

Surfing, swimming, diving, fishing, volleyball, a bicycle trail, a walking path, food vendors, souvenir stands, and other attractions

San Pedro

Cabrillo Beach

3720 Stephen M. White Drive
(310) 372-2166

Volleyball, swimming, fishing, surfing, scuba diving, picnicking, a playground, food vendors, and a marine museum

Santa Monica

Santa Monica State Beach

1622 Ocean Front Walk
(310) 305-9545;
(310) 394-3266;
(310) 451-2906

Volleyball, gymnastics, bodysurfing, conventional surfing, a bicycle and skate trail, a playground, and other attractions

MOVING TIP

Take family heirlooms, fragile items, and sensitive electronic devices in a car, not the truck.

Venice (City of Los Angeles)

Venice Beach

Ocean Front Walk
(310) 451-2906;
(310) 394-3266;
(310) 392-4687 ext. 6

A playground, a basketball court, a weight-lifting area (this is the home of Muscle Beach), bicycle and skate trail, plus an eclectic boardwalk with food vendors, souvenir stands, and street performers

ORANGE COUNTY

Corona del Mar
(City of Newport Beach)

Corona del Mar Beach

Ocean Boulevard
(949) 722-1611

Skin diving, tide pools, barbecue pits, picnic areas, volleyball courts, and more

Dana Point

Doheny State Beach

23500 Dana Point Harbor Drive
(949) 496-6171

Swimming, surfing, fishing, camping, volleyball courts, picnic sites with barbecues, and other attractions

Huntington Beach

Bolsa Chica State Beach

Pacific Coast Highway
(714) 846-4660;
(714) 846-3460

Volleyball, bird watching, bicycle and skate path, barbecue fire pits, and recreational-vehicle campground

Laguna Beach

Laguna Beach

175 North Pacific Coast Highway
(949) 494-6571

Picnic area, playground, basketball courts, volleyball courts, and a boardwalk

Newport Beach

Newport Beach

Ocean Front south of Newport Boulevard
(949) 722-1611

Picnicking, volleyball, swimming, fishing, and other activities

Seal Beach

Seal Beach

906 Ocean Avenue
(562) 431-1531

Fishing, dining, surfing, wind surfing, and other activities

Sunset Beach

Sunset Beach

Pacific Avenue between Anderson Avenue and Warner Avenue
(949) 509-6683

Bike and skate path, playground, and other attractions

Parks

LOS ANGELES COUNTY

Agoura

Paramount Ranch
Cornell Road
(818) 597-9192;
(805) 370-2301

www.nps.gov/samo

Home of the *Dr. Quinn, Medicine Woman* television show, with places to picnic, hike, and ride horses

Arcadia

Angeles National Forest
701 North Santa Anita Avenue
(626) 574-1613

An immense area, containing mountains, trails for hiking and bicycling, ski areas, and a vast variety of wildlife

Harbor City (City of Los Angeles)

Ken Malloy Harbor Regional Park
25820 Vermont Avenue
(310) 548-7515

A lake, a playground, picnic areas, barbecues, and a hiking trail, plus other attractions

Hollywood and Vicinity (City of Los Angeles)

Griffith Park
4730 Crystal Springs
(323) 913-4688

America's biggest urban park, with museums, an observatory, the Los Angeles Zoo, the Greek Theatre, picnic areas, tennis courts, and trails for walkers and horseback riders

Irwindale

Santa Fe Dam Recreation Area
15501 East Arrow Highway
(626) 334-1065

Campsites, picnic areas, trails for walking and bicycling, and a lake for fishing, boating, and swimming

Lancaster

Saddleback Butte State Park
17102 East Avenue J
(661) 942-0662

www.calparksmojave.com/saddleback

Campgrounds, picnic areas, trails for hikers and equestrians, and other attractions

Long Beach

El Dorado Park East

7550 East Spring Street
(562) 570-1771

Paths for bicycling and hiking, playgrounds, picnic areas, campgrounds, lakes, and other attractions

El Dorado Park West

2800 Studebaker Road
(562) 570-3225

Baseball fields, tennis courts, playgrounds, a basketball court, a roller hockey rink, and picnic areas

San Dimas

San Dimas Canyon Nature Center

1628 North Sycamore Canyon Road
(909) 599-7512

Hiking trails, a museum with live animals, wildlife fairs, and other items

San Pedro
(City of Los Angeles)

Angels Gate Park

3601 South Gaffey Street
(310) 548-7705

www.laharbor-watts.org

Soccer field, basketball court, swimming pool, and other

attractions, including a military museum

Santa Clarita

William S. Hart Museum and Regional Park

24151 North San Fernando Road
(661) 259-0855

Campground, picnic area, trains for hikes and horseback rides, and a museum devoted to Western and Native American culture

South El Monte

Whittier Narrows Recreation Area

750 South Santa Anita Avenue
(626) 575-5600

www.lathingstodo.com/
whitnaro.htm

Fields for baseball and soccer; ranges for skeet shooting and archery; picnic areas; lakes for fishing; trails for horseback riding, hiking, and bicycling; and other attractions

Unincorporated Area near Malibu

Leo Carrillo State Park

35000 Pacific Coast Highway
(818) 880-0350

Two thousand acres of beach, tide pools, nature trails, campgrounds, and other attractions

Unincorporated Area near Santa Clarita

Placerita Canyon Nature Center
19152 Placerita Canyon Road
(661) 259-7721
www.parks.co.ca.la.us.
Nature walks, hiking trails, animal shows, and historic sites

Valyermo

Devil's Punchbowl County Natural Area
28000 Devil's Punchbowl Road
(661) 944-2743
Hiking trails, striking geological formations, picnic areas, and a nature center

Vasquez Rocks

Vasquez Rocks Natural Area
107000 West Escondido Canyon Road
(661) 268-0840
Picnic areas, rock-climbing areas, and trails for hiking and horseback riding

Ventura County near Malibu

Point Mugu State Park
9000 West Pacific Coast Highway
(818) 880-0350
Campsites; beaches; mountains; trails for equestrians, hikers, and bicyclists; and other attractions

ORANGE COUNTY

Fountain Valley

Mile Square Regional Park
(714) 962-5549
Picnic areas, bicycle trails, playgrounds, lakes, and a recreation center featuring racquetball, tennis, and basketball

Huntington Beach

Huntington Central Park
(714) 960-8847
A lake, a trail for horseback riding, horseshoe pits, a fitness course, picnic areas, and restaurants

Laguna Niguel

Laguna Niguel Regional Park
(940) 831-2791
Picnic areas; tennis courts; amphitheater; volleyball courts; horseshoe pits; trails for hiking, horseback riding, and cycling; and a lake stocked for fishing

Lake Forest

Whiting Ranch Wilderness Park

(949) 589-4729

Nature walks, hiking, cycling, and horseback riding, among other activities

MOVING TIP

Moving to a new school can be tough on kids, but there are ways to make it easier. "The best way to deal with the anxiety of that first day [at a new school] is to get your kids—no matter what age— inside their new school before it opens," says *Time* magazine columnist Amy Dickinson, reporting the views of clinical psychologist Peter Sheras. "At the very least, a careful look around school may prevent the mortification of getting lost on the first day."

Rancho Santa Margarita Vicinity

O'Neill Regional Park

(949) 858-9365

Campground, equestrian areas, playground, arboretum, hiking trails, and other attractions

Unincorporated Area near Brea, Yorba Linda, and Chino Hills

Chino Hills State Park

4721 Sapphire Street
(909) 780-6222

cal-parks.ca.gov/

Picnic areas, campgrounds and trails for hikers, bicyclists, and equestrians

Unincorporated Area near Laguna Beach and Newport Beach

Crystal Cove State Park

(949) 494-3539;
(800) 444-7275

Hiking, bicycling, horseback riding, camping, scuba diving, and other activities

Wildlife Preserves, Botanical Gardens, and Zoos

LOS ANGELES COUNTY

Arcadia

The Arboretum of Los Angeles County
301 North Baldwin Avenue
(626) 821-3222

More than 120 acres of plants from around the world (especially the tropics), plus historic buildings

Claremont

Rancho Santa Ana Botanic Garden
1500 North College Avenue
(909) 625-8767

www.rsabg.org

Thousands of species of California plants, plus classes in gardening and other attractions

Hollywood and Vicinity (City of Los Angeles)

Los Angeles Zoo
Griffith Park
5333 Zoo Drive
(323) 644-6400; (323) 644-4273

www.lazoo.org

More than a thousand creatures, plus animal shows and a park for picnicking and other recreation

La Canada Flintridge

Descanso Gardens
1418 Descanso Drive
(818) 952-4400; (818) 952-4401

www.Descanso.com

Roses, camellias, oaks, and other flora, plus koi ponds, picnic grounds, a walking trail, and other items

Lancaster

California Poppy Reserve
15101 West Lancaster Road
(661) 724-1180

www.calparksmojave.com/poppy

Thousands of poppies (California's state flower) and other attractions

Long Beach

Long Beach Aquarium of the Pacific
100 Aquarium Way
(562) 590-3100;
(562) 951-1683

www.aquariumofpacific.org

More than 500 species of ocean life in about fifty exhibit tanks, with a total of more than 12,000 specimens

Montebello

Montebello Barnyard Zoo

Grant Rea Park
600 Rea Drive
(323) 887-4595

www.barny.qpg.com

Hayrides, pony cart rides, and train rides, plus a collection of farm animals for kids to meet

Rolling Hills Estates

South Coast Botanic Garden

26300 Crenshaw Boulevard
(310) 544-6815

Over 2,000 kinds of plants from across the globe, plus a lake and stream

San Pedro (City of Los Angeles)

Cabrillo Marine Aquarium

3720 Stephen White Drive
(310) 548-7562

www.cabrilloaq.org

Replicas of Southern California's ocean habitats, more than thirty aquariums, and other attractions

Santa Catalina Island

Santa Catalina Island Visitors Bureau

(310) 510-1520

Catalina (hardly anyone refers to it by its full name) lies less than thirty miles off the mainland. It offers camping, golf, fishing, shopping, dining, and tours of its striking wildlife.

ORANGE COUNTY

Dana Point

Orange County Marine Institute

24200 Dana Point Harbor Drive
(949) 496-2274

Displays, exhibits, cruises, tide pools, and more, all dealing with ocean life

Laguna Niguel

Niguel Botanical Preserve

Crown Valley Community Park
29751 Crown Valley Parkway

A twenty-acre preserve with plants from the Mediterranean, Australia, Chile, and other areas

Orange

Tucker Wildlife Sanctuary
29322 Modjeska Canyon Road
(714) 649-2760

More than 150 species of birds, plus rodents, reptiles, and other creatures

Santa Ana

Santa Ana Zoo
Prentice Park
1894 East Chestnut Avenue
(714) 835-7484; (714) 647-6575

More than 200 creatures, plus a Children's Zoo, an aviary, and a rain-forest exhibit

Other Attractions—and Things Found Only in Southern California

LOS ANGELES COUNTY

Burbank

NBC Television Studios
3000 West Alameda Avenue
(818) 840-3537

Tours of the home of *The Tonight Show,* including the wardrobe and set-construction departments

Warner Brothers Studios
4000 Warner Boulevard
(818) 972-8687; (818) 954-1744

www.warner.com
or www.studio-tour.com

A behind-the-scenes tour, including famous sets and the studio's own museum

Commerce

Commerce Casino
6131 Telegraph Road
(213) 721-2100; (714) 879-2100

More than 200 gaming tables, featuring poker, blackjack, baccarat, and other games

Culver City

Museum of Jurassic Technology
9341 Venice Boulevard
(310) 836-6131

A bizarre collection of unusual art, little-known historical artifacts, curiosities of science, and other items

Downtown
(City of Los Angeles)

Angels Flight Railway
351 Hill Street
(213) 626-1901

The world's shortest (and possibly steepest) railway

Chinatown
Bordered by North Alameda Street, Bernard Street, Cesar E. Chavez Avenue, and Figueroa Street
(213) 617-0396

Shopping, dining, nightclubbing, and other activities with a Chinese flair

Little Tokyo
244 South San Pedro Street and surrounding streets
(213) 628-2725;
(213) 620-0570

Shops, restaurants, galleries, cultural institutions, and more, all in Japanese style

Museum of Neon Art
501 West Olympic Boulevard
(213) 489-9918

www.neonmona.org

New and classic neon sculpture, electrical displays, and kinetic artworks

Edwards Air Force Base

Edwards Air Force Base
(661) 277-3517

www.edwards.af.mil

Tours of the base, plus the Air Force Flight Test Museum and the NASA Flight Research Center

Hollywood and Vicinity
(City of Los Angeles)

Hollywood Walk of Fame
Hollywood Boulevard between Gower Street and La Brea Avenue, and Vine Street between Sunset Boulevard and Yucca Street
(323) 469-8311

Thousands of star-shaped emblems embedded in the sidewalk, most of them bearing names of show-business personalities

Paramount Pictures

5555 Melrose Avenue
(323) 956-1777

Tours of sound stages and the departments devoted to costumes, props, and other items

Long Beach

Shoreline Village

401–435 Shoreline Drive
(562) 435-2668

Shops, restaurants, a boardwalk, street musicians, and other attractions

Marina del Rey
(City of Los Angeles)

Fisherman's Village

13755 Fiji Way
(310) 823-5411

Waterfront restaurants and stores, plus harbor cruises and boat rentals

Venice

Venice Beach

Ocean Front Walk
(310) 451-2906; (310) 394-3266;
(310) 392-4687 ext 6

A playground, a basketball court, a weight-lifting area (this is the home of Muscle Beach), bicycle and skate trail, plus an eclectic

boardwalk with food vendors, souvenir stands, and street performers

Wilshire District
(City of Los Angeles)

Carole and Barry Kaye Museum of Miniatures

5900 Wilshire Boulevard
(323) 937-6464

www.museumofminiatures.com

Tiny, tiny items including replicas of famous buildings

Koreatown

Olympic Boulevard between Crenshaw Boulevard and Vermont Avenue
(323) 936-7141

A neighborhood featuring Korean restaurants and stores, the Korean-American Museum, and the Korean Cultural Center

ORANGE COUNTY

Fullerton

Air Combat U.S.A.
P.O. Box 2726
(800) 522-7590

www.aircombat.com

A NATO fighter/trainer where guests engage in airborne battles

Garden Grove

Crystal Cathedral
12141 Lewis Street or 13280 Chapman Avenue
(714) 971-4000;
(714) 971-4069

www.crystalcathedral.org
or www.newhopeon-line.com

A huge, all-glass church, nationally famous because of its TV worship services

Huntington Beach

Huntington Beach International Surfing Museum
411 Olive Avenue
(714) 960-3483

Surfboards, surf-music album covers, and other surfing memorabilia

Newport Beach

Balboa Pavilion
400 Main Street
(949) 673-5245

Located on the scenic Balboa Peninsula, this area offers restaurants, shopping, sightseeing cruises, and sport-fishing trips

Orange

Fairhaven Memorial Park
1702 East Fairhaven Avenue
(714) 633-1442

A resting place known for its 1916 mausoleum and vast arboretum

GameWorks
The Block at Orange
20 City Drive
(714) 939-9690

www.gameworks.com

Interactive games of all kinds

Restaurants

As you would expect, this region is full of restaurants. This section provides both the major chains (which have locations throughout the area) and some of the best individual restaurants. The price range is broken down as follows:

★ = Inexpensive

★★ = Moderate

★★★ = Expensive

★★★★ = Very Expensive

LOS ANGELES COUNTY

Chains and Multiple Locations in the County

Baja Fresh Mexican Grill ★

Mexican

Locations include Beverly Hills, Burbank, Long Beach, Manhattan Beach, Marina del Rey, Pasadena, Studio City, West Side, Westlake Village, Westwood, and Woodland Hills

California Pizza Kitchen ★

Italian

Locations include Beverly Hills, Brentwood, Burbank, Downtown Los Angeles, Encino, Glendale, Manhattan Beach, Marina del Rey, Pasadena, Studio City, and West Hollywood

Houston's ★★

American

Locations include Century City, Manhattan Beach, Pasadena, and Woodland Hills

In-N-Out Burger ★

American

Locations all over Southern California

Islands ★

California Asian

Locations include Beverly Hills, Burbank, Encino, Glendale, Manhattan Beach, Marina del Rey, Pasadena, Torrance, West L.A., and Woodland Hills

Johnny Rockets ★

American

Locations include Beverly Hills, Burbank, Century City, Encino, Hollywood, Long Beach, Manhattan Beach, Pasadena, Santa Monica, and West Hollywood

Koo Koo Roo ★

American

Locations include Beverly Hills, Brentwood, Burbank, Downtown Los Angeles, Encino, Hancock Park, Manhattan Beach, Marina del Rey, Pasadena, Santa Monica, Venice, West Hollywood, and West Side

La Salsa ★

Mexican

Locations include Beverly Hills, Brentwood, Burbank, Pasadena, Redondo Beach, Santa Monica, Sherman Oaks, Studio City, West Hollywood, and Westwood

Louise's Trattoria ★

Italian

Locations include Beverly Hills, Brentwood, Glendale, Hancock Park, Los Feliz, Hollywood, Pasadena, Rancho Park, Redondo Beach, Santa Monica, Studio City, and Valencia

McCormick and Schmick's ★★

Seafood

Locations include Beverly Hills, Downtown Los Angeles, El Segundo, and Pasadena

Noah's New York Bagels ★

Deli/Bakery

Locations include Beverly Hills, Brentwood, Hollywood, Marina del Rey, Pasadena, Santa Monica, Sherman Oaks, Studio City, West Hollywood, and Westwood

Tony Roma's ★

American

Locations include Arcadia, Beverly Hills, Burbank, Encino, Glendale, Northridge, Pasadena, Redondo Beach, Universal City, and West Side

Beverly Hills and Vicinity

Arnie Morton's of Chicago ★★★

435 South La Cienega Boulevard
Los Angeles
(310) 246-1501

American

Chaya Brasserie ★★★

8741 Alden Drive
Los Angeles
(310) 859-8833

Continental

El Torito Grill ★
9595 Wilshire Boulevard
Beverly Hills
(310) 5543-1896
Southwestern

Lawry's the Prime Rib ★★
100 North La Cienega Boulevard
Beverly Hills
(310) 652-2827
American

Matsuhisa ★★★★
129 North La Cienega Boulevard
Beverly Hills
(310) 659-9369
Japanese

Regent Beverly Wilshire
★★★
Regent Beverly Wilshire Hotel
9500 Wilshire Boulevard
Beverly Hills
(310) 275-5200
French

Spago Beverly Hills ★★★★
176 North Canon Drive
Beverly Hills
(310) 385-0880
Californian

Calabasas

Saddle Peak Lodge ★★★
419 Cold Canyon Road
(818) 222-3888
American

Downtown (City of Los Angeles)

Taix ★
1911 Sunset Boulevard
(213) 484-1265
French

Water Grill ★★
554 South Grand Avenue
(213) 891-0900
Seafood

Encino (City of Los Angeles)

Delmonico's Seafood Grille
★★
16538 Ventura Boulevard
(818) 986-0777
Seafood

Hollywood and Vicinity (City of Los Angeles)

Citrus ★★★
6703 Melrose Avenue
(323) 857-0034
California French

Le Chardonnay ★★★
8284 Melrose Avenue
(323) 655-8880
French

Patina ★★★★
5955 Melrose Avenue
(323) 467-1108

California Continental

Malibu and Vicinity

Gladstone's 4 Fish ★★★★
17300 Pacific Coast Highway
Los Angeles
(310) 573-0212

Seafood

Granita ★★★
Malibu Colony Plaza
23725 West Malibu Road
Malibu
(310) 456-0488

Mediterranean

Marina del Rey (City of Los Angeles)

Cafe del Rey ★★★
4451 Admiralty Way
(310) 823-6395

California Asian

Pasadena

Parkway Grill ★★
510 South Arroyo Parkway
(626) 795-1001

Californian

Pinot Restaurant ★★★
897 Granite Drive
(626) 792-1179

French

Yujean Kang's ★★★
67 North Raymond Avenue
(626) 585-0855

Chinese

Redondo Beach

Chez Melange ★★
Palos Verdes Inn
1716 Pacific Coast Highway
(310) 540-1222

Eclectic

Santa Monica

Border Grill ★★
1445 Fourth Street
(310) 451-1655

Mexican

Broadway Deli ★
1457 Third Street Promenade
(310) 451-0616

Deli

Chinois on Main ★★★
2709 Main Street
(310) 392-9025

Franco-Asian

Drago ★★★
2628 Wilshire Boulevard
(310) 828-1585
Italian

Rockenwagner ★★★
2435 Main Street
(310) 399-6504
Eclectic

Valentino ★★★★
3115 Pico Boulevard
(310) 829-4313
Italian

**Sherman Oaks
(City of Los Angeles)**

Cafe Bizou ★★
14016 Ventura Boulevard
(818) 788-3536
French

Joe Joe's ★★
13355 Ventura Boulevard
(818) 990-8280
Californian

South Pasadena

Shiro ★★★
1505 Mission Street
(626) 799-4774
California Asian

**Studio City
(City of Los Angeles)**

Art's Deli ★
12224 Ventura Boulevard
(818) 762-1221
Deli

Pinot Bistro ★★★
12969 Ventura Boulevard
(818) 990-0500
French

**Venice
(City of Los Angeles)**

Chaya Venice ★★
110 Navy Street
(310) 396-1179
Asian

Joe's ★★★
1023 Abbot Kinney Boulevard
(310) 399-5811
Californian

West Hollywood

The Ivy ★★★
113 North Robertson Boulevard
(310) 274-8303

American

Locanda Veneta ★★★
8638 West Third Street
(310) 274-1893

Italian

L'Orangerie ★★★★
903 North La Cienega Boulevard
(310) 652-9770

French

The Palm ★★★
9001 Santa Monica Boulevard
(310) 550-8811

American

West L.A.
(City of Los Angeles)

Apple Pan ★
10801 West Pico Boulevard
(310) 475-3585

American

Bel-Air Hotel ★★★★
701 Stone Canyon Road
(310) 472-1211

California French

Four Oaks ★★★
2181 North Beverly Glen
Boulevard
(310) 470-2265

French

Il Moro ★★
11400 West Olympic Boulevard
(310) 575-3530

Italian

Junior's ★
2379 Westwood Boulevard
(310) 475-5771

Deli

Wilshire District
(City of Los Angeles)

Cafe Pinot ★★
7400 West Fifth Street
(213) 239-6500

California French

Campanile ★★★
624 South La Brea Avenue
(323) 938-1447

Mediterranean

Pink's Famous Chili Dogs ★
709 La Brea Avenue
(323) 931-4223

American

ORANGE COUNTY

Chains and Multiple Locations in the County

Baja Fresh Mexican Grill ★

Mexican

Locations include Anaheim Hills, Brea, Costa Mesa, Irvine, Laguna Hills, Laguna Niguel, and Santa Ana

In-N-Out Burger ★

Hamburgers

Locations all over Southern California

Koo Koo Roo ★

American

Locations include Aliso Viejo, Costa Mesa, Irvine, Laguna Hills, Tustin, and Yorba Linda

La Salsa ★

Mexican

Locations include Anaheim Hills, Brea, Costa Mesa, Irvine, Newport Beach, Orange, and Santa Ana

Peppino's ★

Italian

Locations include Aliso Viejo, Laguna Niguel, Lake Forest, Mission Viejo, Orange, and Tustin

Ruby's ★

American

Locations include Balboa, Corona del Mar, Costa Mesa, Fullerton, Huntington Beach, Irvine, Laguna Beach, Laguna Hills, Mission Viejo, San Juan Capistrano, Santa Ana, Seal Beach, Tustin, and Yorba Linda

Souplantation ★

American

Locations include Brea, Costa Mesa, Fountain Valley, Garden Grove, Laguna Niguel, and Tustin

Brea

Crocodile Café ★

Brea Marketplace
975 East Birch Street
(714) 529-2233

American

La Vie en Rose ★★★

240 South State College Boulevard
(714) 529-8333

French

Buena Park

Mrs. Knott's Chicken Dinner ★

Knott's Berry Farm
8039 Beach Boulevard
(714) 220-5080

American

Costa Mesa

Rainforest Café ★

South Coast Plaza
3333 Bristol Street
(714) 424-9200

American

Troquet ★★★

South Coast Plaza
3333 Bristol Street
(714) 708-6865

French

Dana Point

Harbor House Café ★

34157 Pacific Coast Highway
(949) 496-9270

American

Ritz-Carlton Laguna Niguel ★★★★

1 Ritz-Carlton Drive
(949) 240-5008

Continental

Fullerton

Angelo and Vinci's Ristorante ★

550 North Harbor Boulevard
(714) 879-4022

Italian

Summit House ★★★

2000 East Bastanchury Road
(714) 671-4111

American

Huntington Beach

Louise's Trattoria ★

300 Pacific Coast Highway
(714) 960-0996

Italian

Irvine

Chanteclair ★★★

18912 MacArthur Boulevard
(949) 752-8001

French

Gaucho Grill ★

3041 Michelson Drive
(949) 251-9111

Argentinean

Il Fornaio ★★

18051 Von Karman Avenue
(949) 261-1444

Italian

7

Laguna Beach

Las Brisas ★★
361 Cliff Drive
(949) 497-5434

Mexican

Splashes ★★★
Surf & Sand Hotel
1555 South Coast Highway
(949) 497-4477

Mediterranean

Zinc Cafe & Market ★★
350 Ocean Avenue
(949) 494-6302

Californian

La Habra

Cafe El Cholo ★
840 East Whittier Boulevard
(714) 525-1320

Mexican

Newport Beach

Cheesecake Factory ★
Newport Fashion Island
1141 Newport Center Drive
Newport Beach
(949) 720-8333

American

Five Crowns ★★★
3801 East Pacific Coast Highway
Newport Beach
(949) 760-0331

Continental

The Ritz ★★★
Newport Fashion Island
880 Newport Center Drive
Newport Beach
(949) 720-1800

Continental

Santa Ana

Gustaf Anders ★★★
South Coast Plaza Village
1651 Sunflower Avenue
(714) 668-1737

Swedish

Sunset Beach

Harbor House Café ★
16341 Pacific Coast Highway
(562) 592-5404

American

Tustin

Zov's Bistro & Bakery Café ★★
Enderle Center
17440 East 17th Street
(714) 838-8855

Mediterranean

Shopping Areas

Crossroads of the World in Hollywood claims to be the very first shopping mall. It's almost certainly America's first roofless, open-air mall—or rather, it was; it's now a collection of offices.

However you slice it, Southern California has had a long and ambitious history of places that will take your money. Following are some of the more noteworthy ones.

LOS ANGELES COUNTY

Beverly Hills

Rodeo Drive
Rodeo Drive between Wilshire and Santa Monica boulevards

World-famous designers' shops: Dior, Tiffany, Gucci, Armani, and more

Commerce

Citadel Factory Stores
5675 East Telegraph Road
(323) 888-1724

wwwcitadelfactorystorescom

Outlets and factory shops for Eddie Bauer, Ann Taylor, Old Navy, and other clothiers

Culver City

Fox Hills Mall
200 Fox Hills Mall
(310) 390-7833

hahncompany.com

More than 100 shops and restaurants

Downtown
(City of Los Angeles)

Fashion District
110 Ninth Street, Suite C625
(213) 488-1153

www.dpoa.com

More than 1,000 shops and other purveyors of things to wear

Hollywood and Vicinity

Melrose Avenue shops
Melrose Avenue between Fairfax and La Brea avenues

A street filled with ultra-trendy fashion, plus hip record stores, restaurants, and other attractions

Glendale

Glendale Galleria
135 Glendale Galleria
(818) 240-9481

www.glendalegalleria.com

Nordstrom, Macy's, Robinsons May, JC Penney, and more than 200 specialty stores, restaurants, and service companies

Ontario

Ontario Mills Mall
1 Mill Circle
(909) 484-8300

www.ontariomillsmall.com

Possibly the largest mall in Southern California, with more than 100 stores, plus food services, thirty movie screens, a GameWorks entertainment complex, a skate park, and even a police station

Pasadena

Old Town Pasadena
Bordered by Arroyo Parkway, Pasadena Avenue, Walnut Street, and Del Mar Boulevard
(626) 795-5952

Block after block of chic stores, popular restaurants, and other establishments

Santa Monica

Third Street Promenade
Third Street south of Wilshire Boulevard
(310) 393-8355

Open-air pedestrian mall, with upscale restaurants and shops, plus street performers and other attractions

Torrance

Del Amo Fashion Center
Hawthorne Boulevard (Del Amo Fashion Square)
(310) 542-8525

Macy's, Robinson's May, JC Penney, and Sears, plus more than 300 restaurants, specialty stores, service providers, and other businesses

Universal City (City of Los Angeles)

Universal Studios CityWalk
100 Universal Center Drive
(818) 822-4455

www.universalstudios.com/citywalk

Specialty shops, restaurants, nightclubs, a multiplex movie theater, and other attractions

West Hollywood

Beverly Center
8500 Beverly Boulevard
(310) 854-0700

Macy's, Bloomingdale's, and dozens of other stores, plus restaurants and movie theaters

West L.A. (City of Los Angeles)

Century City Shopping Center & Marketplace

10520 Santa Monica Boulevard
(310) 277-3898

Bloomingdale's, Macy's, and more than 150 restaurants, specialty stores, and movie theaters

ORANGE COUNTY

Costa Mesa

South Coast Plaza

3333 Bristol Street
(714) 435-2000, (800) 782-8888

www.southcoastplaza.com

Macy's, Nordstrom, Robinsons-May, Saks Fifth Avenue, Sears, and more than 200 stores, restaurants, theaters, and service companies

Santa Ana

MainPlace Santa Ana

2800 North Main Street
(714) 547-7000

www.mainplacesantaana.com

Macy's, Nordstrom, Robinsons-May, and nearly 200 specialty stores and restaurants

Newport Beach

Fashion Island

1045 Newport Center Drive
(714) 721-2000

Macy's, Neiman-Marcus, Robinsons-May, and more than 200 specialty stores and fine restaurants

Spectator Sports

At this writing, Los Angeles has no NFL football team—but it's got just about everything else.

LOS ANGELES COUNTY

Carson

California State University Dominguez Hills Toros
1000 East Victoria Street
(310) 516-3300
www.csudh.edu/athletics

Men's baseball, golf, and softball; women's volleyball, tennis, and cross country; and men's and women's soccer and basketball

Downtown and Vicinity (City of Los Angeles)

Los Angeles Avengers
Staples Center
1111 South Figueroa Street
(310) 473-7999
www.laavengers.com

The city's own arena football team

Los Angeles Clippers
Staples Center
1111 South Figueroa Street
(213) 745-0500
www.clippers.com

The less prominent (but still enjoyable) of the area's two NBA teams

Los Angeles Dodgers
Dodger Stadium
1000 Elysian Park
(323) 224-1500
www.dodgers.com

Los Angeles's professional baseball team

Los Angeles Kings
Staples Center
1111 South Figueroa Street
(888) 546-4752
www.lakings.com

The area's top hockey team

Los Angeles Lakers
Staples Center
1111 South Figueroa Street
(213) 742-7400
www.nba.com/lakers

The area's top professional basketball team

University of Southern California Trojans

3551 University Avenue
(213) 740-4672

www.usctrojans.com

Men's baseball and football; women's soccer; and men's and women's basketball, tennis, volleyball, and water polo

Inglewood

Los Angeles Sparks

Great Western Forum
3900 West Manchester Boulevard
(877) 447-7275

www.wnba.com/sparks

The area's professional women's basketball team

Lancaster

Lancaster Jethawks

45116 Valley Central Way
(661) 726-5400

www.jethawks.com

Lancaster's minor league baseball team

Long Beach

California State University Long Beach 49ers

1250 Bellflower Boulevard
(562) 985-4949

www.longbeachstate.com

Women's soccer, softball, and tennis; men's baseball; and men's and women's basketball, cross country, golf, volleyball, track and field, and water polo

Long Beach Ice Dogs

300 East Ocean Boulevard
(562) 436-4259

www.icedogshockey.com

Long Beach's professional hockey team

Northridge

California State University Northridge Matadors

81111 Nordhoff Street
(818) 885-4200

www.gomatadors.com

Men's baseball, softball, and football; women's tennis; and men and women's basketball, cross country, golf, soccer, track and field, swimming, and volleyball

Pasadena

Los Angeles Galaxy

Rose Bowl
1010 Rose Bowl Drive
(626) 432-1540

www.lagalaxy.com

The area's top professional soccer team

Pomona

California State Polytechnic University Pomona Broncos
3801 West Temple Avenue
(909) 869-7659

www.csupomona.edu/~athletic/

Men's and women's basketball, cross country, tennis, soccer, and track and field; women's volleyball; and men's baseball

West L.A. (City of Los Angeles)

University of California Los Angeles Bruins
405 Hilgard Avenue
(310) 825-4321

www.uclabruins.com

Men's and women's basketball, cross country, volleyball, soccer, water polo, tennis, golf, and track and field; women's gymnastics, swimming, and diving; and men's football, baseball, and softball

ORANGE COUNTY

Anaheim

Anaheim Angels
Edison Field
2000 East Gene Autry Way
(714) 634-2000

www.angelsbaseball.com

Orange County's professional baseball club

The Mighty Ducks
Arrowhead Pond of Anaheim
2695 East Katella Avenue
(714) 704-2400

www.mightyducks.com

Orange County's professional hockey team

Fullerton

California State University Fullerton Titans
800 North State College Boulevard
(714) 278-2783

sports.fullerton.edu

Men's baseball and wrestling; women's gymnastics, softball, volleyball, and tennis; and men's and women's basketball, fencing, soccer, track, and cross country

Irvine

University of California Irvine Anteaters

University Drive
(949) 833-5011

www.athletics.uci.edu/home/sportsinfo/sports.html

Men's and women's basketball, soccer, tennis, volleyball, water polo, crew, and rowing; and men's baseball, golf, sailing, swimming and diving, cross country, and track and field

Santa Ana

Orange County Zodiac

Santa Ana Municipal Stadium
6th and Flower Streets
(949) 348-4880; (714) 571-4232

www.oczodiac.com

Orange County's professional soccer team

Video Rentals

Southern California is video heaven. If it's on film or tape, you can probably get it here.

One reason is Hollywood. People in the entertainment business were naturally among the first to buy VCRs, DVDs, and other equipment, and they wanted things to watch on them. Entire stores have sprung up to specialize in cinematic rarities, cult favorites, and neglected classics alongside mainstream movies.

What's more, the area's diversity brings in items from other places. Imagine the items that you can get from Video Discoteca Guadalajara, New Hawaii Video, Nhut Tran Video, Ala-Eldeen Arabic Video, and other stores.

There are far too many individual video stores to list here. While the selection is immense, it can get intimidating. What if you're new in town and just want a popcorn movie for Saturday night?

Most people in that position look to the chain stores. The region's main chain is Blockbuster (and its daughter chain, Wherehouse). Your local phone book should list at least half a dozen Blockbuster stores within easy distance.

Hollywood Video runs second to Blockbuster. They're not quite as ubiquitous, though. While San Dimas has two Hollywood Video stores at last count, there are none in Lancaster or Palmdale—each of which has about three times San Dimas's population.

Tower is probably third in line. Although it's best known as a chain of record stores, many Tower outlets carry videos as well. They cater to a younger, hipper audience than Blockbuster or Hollywood Video, and they may carry movies that you can't find at the other stores. Tower stores abound in the central sections of the region, but outlying towns—such as those of the luckless Antelope Valley—are less likely to have them.

Then there are the local chains, which cover selected areas of Southern California. The Antelope Valley, for instance, has Modern Video, with locations in Acton, Lancaster, Palmdale, and elsewhere. 20/20 Video is a popular chain. It has branches in parts of the San Fernando Valley (Burbank, Glendale, Studio City, Van Nuys, Reseda), metropolitan Los Angeles (Hollywood, Huntington Park, South Gate, West Hollywood, the West L.A., and the Wilshire District), and the beach communities (Pacific Palisades and Santa Monica), among other places.

The San Fernando Valley has Video Stage, with locations in Canoga Park, Sun Valley, Tarzana, and Van Nuys. The Valley also includes Video Market, with stores in Arleta, North Hollywood, and North Hills.

In metropolitan Los Angeles and nearby vicinities, you can find Best Video, located in South Gate, East Los Angeles, and Highland Park. There's also Super Video, in Bell, South Gate and Hollywood, plus Video Empire in Bell Gardens, central L.A., Huntington Park, and Cudahy. Another set of metro L.A. stores is Video Express, with locations in Culver City, Boyle Heights, and East Los Angeles, among other places.

Finally, there's Star Video, in East Los Angeles, Hollywood, Maywood, the Wilshire District, and the downtown area. There are also Star Video shops in such inland Orange County communities as Anaheim, Fullerton, and Fountain Valley.

Calendar of Events

Southern California loves a party. Every group in the region has its celebrations, and usually they invite everyone else to join in. Following are some of the more noteworthy annual events.

Bear in mind, though, that some events don't take place every year; they can be postponed or just plain canceled due to lack of funds, poor planning, inappropriate weather, or any number of other reasons. Always call ahead before going to any event.

JANUARY

New Year's Day

Tournament of Roses Parade
Orange Grove Boulevard
Pasadena
(626) 449-4100

A parade of floats covered in flowers

Rose Bowl
Rose Bowl Stadium
Pasadena
(626) 577-3100

The region's premier college football game, wherein the top Pac 10 team takes on the top Big 10 team

Martin Luther King, Jr., Day Celebrations

King Day Parade
Crenshaw District (City of Los Angeles)
(323) 298-8777

A parade honoring King

Martin Luther King Junior Day Festival
Long Beach
(562) 570-6816

Martin Luther King Junior Celebration
Palmdale Playhouse
Palmdale
(661) 449-4100

JANUARY OR FEBRUARY (THE DATES VARY)

Chinese New Year
Chinatown: (213) 617-0396
Los Angeles Zoo: (323) 666-4650

Chinese-Americans celebrate the New Year with parades, street fairs, and other excitement.

Tet
Golden West College
Huntington Beach
(714) 895-8367
Cultural Court of Little Saigon
Westminster
(714) 891-7883

Tet is the Vietnamese New Year, celebrated with ethnic food and entertainment.

FEBRUARY

Mardi Gras
El Pueblo de Los Angeles Historic Monument
Downtown Los Angeles
(213) 628-1274

New Orleans isn't the only town with a Mardi Gras. L.A.'s version, naturally, offers a touch of Latin American flavor.

Queen Mary Scottish Festival
Queen Mary
Long Beach
(562) 435-3511

Scottish music, dance, and food

Festival of the Whales

Dana Point
(800) 290-3262

A street fair, displays and exhibits dealing with whales, and other celebrations

African American History Month Celebrations

Los Angeles: (323) 295-0521
Pasadena: (626) 795-9311
Santa Ana: (949) 440-8943

Local governments and other organizations put on shows and educational events to commemorate African American history.

MARCH

Los Angeles Marathon

Los Angeles
(310) 444-5544

www.LAMarathon.com

A running, walking, and wheelchair-rolling race from downtown through a variety of neighborhoods

Patriot's Day Parade

Laguna Beach
(949) 494-1018

An old-fashioned celebration of local pride

Return of the Swallows/Fiesta de las Golindrinas

Mission San Juan Capistrano
(949) 248-2048; (949) 493-1976

Once a year, flocks of swallows land at the mission, and flocks of humans land there to celebrate their return.

APRIL

Toyota Grand Prix of Long Beach
Long Beach
(562) 436-9953; (562) 981-2600; (888) 827-7333

One of America's biggest race-car competitions, and possibly the biggest to run on city streets

Newport-Ensenada Race
Newport Beach Harbor
Newport Beach
(714) 771-0691; (714) 650-1351; (949) 435-9553

One of the area's most popular boat races, featuring hundreds of yachts and other watercraft

Hollywood Bowl Easter Sunrise Service
Hollywood
(323) 850-2000

Congregates fill the Bowl for a non-denominational service.

There are other sunrise services in Santa Ana and Whittier.

In addition, there are Easter egg hunts in Calabasas, Claremont, Costa Mesa, Knott's Berry Farm (Buena Park), Newport Beach, Santa Ana, Tustin, Whittier, and other communities.

MAY

Strawberry Festival
Village Green Park
Garden Grove
(714) 638-0981
A parade, musical performances, and other events. Oh, and lots of strawberries.

Cinco de Mayo

El Pueblo de Los Angeles Historic Monument
Downtown Los Angeles
(213) 625-5045

Celebrating the victory of the Mexicans over French invaders in 1862, this celebration—the region's biggest Cinco de Mayo event—offers food, music, dance, and other kinds of fun. Other Cinco de Mayo celebrations take place in Anaheim, Irvine, Santa Ana, San Clemente, and other communities.

Children's Day

Japanese American Cultural and Community Center
Little Tokyo
(213) 628-2725

Based on a holiday popular in Asia (particularly Japan), Children's Day in Los Angeles features arts and crafts, martial arts demonstrations, performing arts, food, and other attractions.

Similar or related events also take place in Anaheim, Downey, La Habra, Pacific Palisades, and other communities.

JUNE

A Taste of Orange County

El Toro Marine Corps Air Station
Irvine
(949) 753-1551
Local restaurants and other food providers offer samples of their best. Events include wine tastings, activities for children, and live music.

Gay Pride Weekend

West Hollywood
(323) 969-8302; (323) 860-0701
Dancing, entertainment, exhibitors offering everything from clothes to political pamphlets, and a parade

JULY

Orange County Fair
Orange County Fair Grounds
Costa Mesa
(714) 708-3247; (714) 751-3247
Rides, live entertainment, and other attractions

Festival of the Arts and Pageant of the Masters
Irvine Bowl Amphitheater
Laguna Beach
(949) 494-1145; (800) 487-3378
A large art show, plus live tableaus recreating great works of art

Sawdust Festival
Laguna Beach
(949) 494-3030
More than 150 local artists' work on display, plus food and entertainment

Independence Day Celebrations

Southern California goes all out for the Fourth of July; hardly any other day of the year gets as many celebrations.

Queen Mary
Long Beach
(562) 435-3511

One of the biggest shows of the season, with a fireworks display and live entertainment

Huntington Beach
(714) 374-1535; (714) 969-3492; (714) 536-5486; (714) 960-8899

Huntington Beach does the Fourth up big, with fireworks displays, a parade, and more. Not all of these affairs are in one place or run by the same organization, so planning your Independence Day may take a few calls.

<u>Other Independence Day celebrations take place in:</u>

Los Angeles County

Antelope Valley and Vicinity: Lancaster, Palmdale

Los Angeles Valleys and Vicinity: Agoura Hills, Burbank, Calabasas, Northridge, Pasadena, San Fernando, Sun Valley, Thousand Oaks

Beach Communities and Vicinity: Lawndale, Marina del Rey, Pacific Palisades, Rancho Palos Verdes, Santa Monica, Torrance

Metropolitan Los Angeles and Vicinity: Culver City, Dodger Stadium, Hollywood

East Los Angeles County: Claremont, Ontario, Pomona, Walnut, West Covina

Southeast Los Angeles County and Vicinity: Chino Hills , Montebello, Santa Fe Springs, Whittier

Catalina Island

Orange County

North Orange County Inland Communities: Anaheim, Buena Park (Knottís Berry Farm)

Central Orange County Beach Communities: Newport Beach

Central Orange County Inland Communities: Santa Ana, Tustin

South Orange County Beach Communities: Dana Point, San Clemente

South Orange County Beach Communities: San Juan Capistrano

AUGUST

Nisei Week Japanese Festival

Japanese American Cultural and Community Center
Little Tokyo
(213) 687-7193

Nisei means "Japanese American," and Nisei Week celebrates Japanese American life and culture with arts and crafts, a street fair, live entertainment, and other attractions.

Catalina Ski Race
Long Beach
(909) 352-8658; (714) 894-3498

A huge water-ski race, involving more than 100 boats, from Long Beach to Catalina Island and back

SEPTEMBER

International Street Fair
Orange
(714) 532-6260

Folk dancing, ethnic music, international foods, and more

Los Angeles County Fair
Los Angeles County Fairplex
Pomona
(909) 623-3111

Billed as the world's largest county fair, with livestock shows, carnival rides, live entertainment, food, and more

Mexican Independence Day Celebration
Olvera Street
Los Angeles
(213) 625-5045

Historic exhibits, Mexican food, arts and crafts, and other attractions

Other Mexican Independence Day celebrations take place in Commerce, Santa Ana, San Fernando, and South Gate.

SEPTEMBER AND OCTOBER

Oktoberfest
Old World Village
Huntington Beach
(714) 895-8020; (714) 898-3033; (714) 897-1470

One of the region's largest celebrations of oom-pa-pah bands and all other things German

Other Oktoberfests take place in Anaheim, Cypress, and Torrance.

OCTOBER

Knott's Scary Farm
Knott's Berry Farm
Buena Park
(714) 220-5200

The wholesome park goes terrifying, with ghostly decor and Halloween-themed shows.

Shipwreck
Queen Mary
(562) 435-3511

The grand old cruise ship is turned into a haunted vessel.

Other Halloween events take place in these areas:
Los Angeles County

Los Angeles Valleys and Vicinity: Calabasas, Northridge, Universal Studios

Beach Communities and Vicinity: Long Beach, Torrance

Metropolitan Los Angeles and Vicinity: Los Angeles Zoo, West Hollywood

East Los Angeles County: Claremont, Covina, Walnut

Southeast Los Angeles County and Vicinity: Cudahy, Norwalk, Santa Fe Springs, Whittier

Orange County

North Orange County Inland Communities: Anaheim, Cypress

Central Orange County Beach Communities: Newport Beach

Central Orange County Inland Communities: Santa Ana, Tustin

South Orange County Beach Communities: Dana Point

South Orange County Inland Communities: San Juan Capistrano

NOVEMBER

Doo Dah Parade
Pasadena
(626) 449-3689

A satire on the Rose Parade, with outlandish floats, bizarre marchers, and general wackiness.

NOVEMBER AND DECEMBER

Southern California doesn't get a lot of snowy white Christmases, but the locals make up the difference in enthusiasm. From the day after Thanksgiving to the day of Christmas, Christmas (and Hanukkah and Kwanzaa) overtakes the region.

Parades
Hollywood Christmas Parade
(323) 469-8311

One of the season's first and biggest Christmas parades, complete with celebrities and Santa Claus.

Other Christmas parades take place in Chatsworth, Covina, Disneyland, Downey, Glendora, Granada Hills, Pomona, and Whittier. Long Beach, Huntington Beach, Marina del Rey, and Newport Beach put a special twist on the event by holding boat parades.

Tree Lightings
Fashion Island Christmas Tree Lighting Ceremony
Newport Beach
(949) 722-1611; (949) 720-3300

One of the area's biggest trees goes up in lights.

Other tree lightings take place in Costa Mesa, Covina, Lancaster, Lawndale, Norwalk, San Dimas, San Fernando, San Gabriel, San Juan Capistrano, Tustin, and Valencia.

Additional Events

El Pueblo de Los Angeles Historic Monument

Las Posadas

(213) 485-9777; (213) 625-5045

A Latino-tinged event, with a candlelight walk commemorating the journey of Joseph and Mary to Bethlehem

Other holiday events take place in:

Los Angeles County

Los Angeles Valleys and Vicinity: La Canada, San Gabriel, Thousand Oaks, Universal Studios

Los Angeles County Beach Communities and Vicinity: Pacific Palisades

Metropolitan Los Angeles and Vicinity: Culver City, Los Angeles Music Center, Los Angeles Zoo

East Los Angeles County: Azusa, Claremont, Glendora

Southeast Los Angeles County and Vicinity: Santa Fe Springs, Whittier

Orange County

North Orange County Beach Communities: Huntington Beach

North Orange County Inland Communities: Anaheim, Buena Park, Fullerton, Garden Grove, La Habra, Orange

Central Orange County Beach Communities: Newport Beach

Central Orange County Inland Communities: Irvine, Lake Forest, Santa Ana, Westminster

South Orange County Beach Communities: Dana Point

South Orange County Inland Communities: San Juan Capistrano

Free Events

Many if not most of the events listed in the Calendar are free. So are most of the parks and beaches (though they may charge for parking).

A number of other events are free, too. You can find a list at Southern California Freebies (*www.geocities.com/heartland/6295/freebie.html*). Here are some of the most noteworthy.

LOS ANGELES COUNTY

Downtown and Vicinity (City of Los Angeles)

Los Angeles County Arts Commission
Musicians Trust Fund Performances
374 Hall of Administration
(213) 974-1343

www.lacountyarts.org/free.html

At public sites all over the county, musicians play for free.

Museum of Contemporary Art
250 South Grand Avenue
(213) 633-5334

www.moca-la.org

Once a week during the summer, the museum puts on jazz shows by some of the field's best performers. And on Thursdays, admission to the museum is free from 5 P.M. to 8 P.M.

Duarte

Justice Brothers Racing Museum
2734 East Huntington Drive
(626) 359-9174

www.justicebrothers.com/jb6.htm

A museum dedicated to racing cars, motorcycles, and other high-speed automotive memorabilia

Hollywood (City of Los Angeles)

Hollyhock House
Barnsdall Art Park
4800 Hollywood Boulevard
(213) 485-8665

A chance to tour a classic Frank Lloyd Wright home

San Pedro

Shakespeare by the Sea
(310) 217-7596

www.ghog.com/seashakespeare

Free performances of classic theater

Universal City

Audiences Unlimited
100 Universal City Plaza
(818) 753-3470

www.tvtickets.com

Free tickets to television-show tapings

Vasquez Rocks

Vasquez Rocks Natural Area
10700 West Escondido Canyon Road
(661) 268-0840

A free place for picnics and hikes

West L.A.
(City of Los Angeles)

Armand Hammer Museum of Art and Cultural Center
10899 Wilshire Boulevard
(310) 443-7000

Admission to this museum is free on Thursday evenings from 6 P.M. to 9 P.M.

Getty Center

1200 Getty Center Drive
(310) 440-7300

www.getty.edu/museum

European paintings and other works, plus lectures, concerts, and additional activities

Wilshire District
(City of Los Angeles)

Los Angeles County Museum of Art
5905 Wilshire Boulevard
(323) 857-6000

www.lacma.org

Much like the Museum of Contemporary Art, LACMA puts on its own Friday-night summer jazz series. Admission to the museum is free on the second Tuesday of each month.

Public Transportation

Once you know where you want to go, how do you get there?

If you don't drive, you'll need help—lots of it. Here are some of the organizations that provide it.

If you're from a town that depends on public transportation, brace yourself. L.A. isn't a mass-transit town. Oh, the authorities try mightily, installing subways and upgrading buses, but mass transit in L.A. is generally for people who cannot drive a car or afford to buy one.

If you're in one of those categories, or you simply don't want to drive, here are some organizations that can get you around the region.

The main transit organization for most of Los Angeles County and some of Orange County is the Metropolitan Transportation Authority (MTA). The MTA's main number is (800) 266-6883.

In addition, there's Metrolink, a system of commuter trains that connects the cities of Lancaster, Los Angeles, Oceanside, Oxnard, Riverside, San Bernardino, and San Juan Capistrano. Its number is (800) 371-5465.

Finally, Amtrak runs trains among the cities of Orange, Los Angeles, Santa Ana, Anaheim, Fullerton, and other communities. Its number is (800) 872-7245.

Other useful numbers:

LOS ANGELES COUNTY

Antelope Valley and Vicinity

Antelope Valley Transit Authority
(661) 945-9445

Santa Clarita Transit
(800) 266-6883

Conejo Valley, San Fernando Valley, and San Gabriel Valley

Foothill Transit
(for San Gabriel Valley and parts of East Los Angeles County)
(800) 743-3463

Los Angeles Department of Transportation
Commuter Express/DASH buses
(818) 808-2273

Beach Communities

Long Beach Transit
(562) 591-2301

Torrance Transit System
(310) 618-6266

CITY FACT

The county of Los Angeles says that its city with the largest population is, naturally, Los Angeles, with nearly 3,800,000 people. The city with the smallest population is Vernon, just south of downtown L.A., with fewer than 100 citizens.

Metropolitan Los Angeles and Vicinity

Culver City Bus
(310) 253-6500

Los Angeles Department of Transportation
Commuter Express/DASH buses
(213) 808-2273; (310) 808-2273

Santa Monica Municipal Bus Lines
(310) 451-5444

West Hollywood CityLine
(800) 447-2189

Southeast Los Angeles County

Carson Circuit
(310) 952-1779

East Los Angeles County

Foothill Transit
(for San Gabriel Valley and parts of East Los Angeles County)
(800) 743-3463

ORANGE COUNTY

Serving much of Orange County is the Orange County Transportation Authority. Its buses cover not only Orange County but also poke into Riverside County. Its numbers are (714) 636-7433 (for north and central Orange County) and (800) 636-7433 (for south Orange County).

Shuttle Services

Unless you have lots of generous-spirited loved ones or you can afford limousines, you'll sooner or later take a shuttle to or from the airport. Here are some of the more prominent services.

LOS ANGELES COUNTY

Antelope Valley and Vicinity

Prime Time Shuttle
(800) 733-8267

World Shuttle Services
(661) 257-0472

Conejo Valley, San Fernando Valley, and San Gabriel Valley

Roadrunner Shuttle
(805) 389-8196;
(800) 247-7919

SuperShuttle
(626) 443-6600

Valley Shuttle and Limousine Service
(818) 999-2088;
(877) 999-2088

World Shuttle Service
(818) 830-8250;
(888) 992-8600

Beach Communities

Express Shuttle
(888) 800-6543

SuperShuttle
(310) 782-6600; (323) 775-6600;
(909) 467-9600

Metropolitan Los Angeles and Vicinity

Metropolitan Express
(800) 338-3898

SuperShuttle
(310) 782-6600; (323) 775-6600

Southeast Los Angeles County

Express Shuttle
(800) 342-9949

East Los Angeles County

L.A. Crown
(310) 827-4463;
(800) 559-4463

SuperShuttle
(626) 443-6600

ORANGE COUNTY

North Orange County Beach Communities

Advantage
(714) 557-2465

Karmel Shuttle
(888) 995-7433

North Orange County Inland Communities

New Shuttle Express
(877) 977-3748

Southern California Coach
(714) 978-6415; (800) 232-6224

Central Orange County Inland Communities

Advantage
(714) 557-2465; (800) 752-5211

Airport Bus
(800) 772-5299

Karmel Shuttle
(888) 995-7433

New Shuttle Express
(877) 977-3748

Superior Shuttle
(714) 973-1100

South Orange County Beach Communities

Superior Shuttle
(949) 240-0505

CITY FACT

In Orange County, even when things are bad, they're not so bad. The county usually experiences strong economic growth. The worst fall-off in nearly twenty years took place from 1992 to 1993, when annual median family income fell almost 4 percent—to $54,380. The biggest growth, by the way, came from 1988 to 1989, when income jumped more than 9 percent, from $45,176 to $49,916.

Taxicabs

Most people in Southern California don't take cabs. They don't need to: They drive their own cars.

Besides, cabs are very expensive. The law sets cab rates so that cabbies can't legally cut their prices. Since cabs charge by the mile (or fraction thereof), and travel in SoCal means covering a lot of miles, cabbing in L.A. is primarily for people who are drunk, rich, from out of town, or some combination of the three.

But if your car's in the shop or you for another reason need a cab (and we all do sooner or later), here are some of the better established cab companies and co-ops.

LOS ANGELES COUNTY

Antelope Valley

Yellow Cab/Checker Cab of Antelope Valley
(661) 267-9850; (888) 804-8294

On the Go Cab Co.
(661) 951-0154; (661) 951-7176; (888) 317-8294

Conejo Valley, San Fernando Valley, and San Gabriel Valley

On the Go Cab Co.
(888) 317-8294

United Taxi
(818) 780-1234

Yellow Cab Co.
(626) 331-3825; (800) 305-8254; (800) 340-8294; (818) 361-6959; (909) 622-1313

Beach Communities

United Independent Taxi
(310) 414-0411; (310) 821-1000; (800) 822-8294

Metropolitan Los Angeles and Vicinity

Yellow Cab Co.
(310) 208-2912; (800) 200-1053

Independent Taxi Company
(310) 659-8294; (323) 666-0050; (800) 521-8294

United Independent Taxi
(213) 483-7600; (310) 821-1000; (323) 653-5050; (800) 411-0303; (800) 822-8294

Southeast Los Angeles County

All Destinations Taxi
(562) 809-4447

Fiesta Taxi
(888) 834-3782

East Los Angeles County

AAA Yellow Cab
(626) 333-8294;
(800) 345-8294

Yellow Cab Co.
(800) 305-8294

ORANGE COUNTY

North Orange County Beach Communities

AM-PM Taxi/Fiesta Taxi
(800) 400-7313; (888) 834-3782

North Orange County Inland Communities

AM-PM Taxi/Fiesta Taxi
(800) 400-7313; (888) 834-3782

A Taxi Cab
(800) 200-0000; (800) 469-8294

California Yellow Cab
(714) 671-6000; (714) 704-4900;
(800) 935-5692; (877) 935-5692

South Coast Cab
(714) 750-8294; (800) 482-9422

Yellow Cab Company
(714) 535-2211; (800) 535-2211

Central Orange County Beach Communities

South Coast Cab
(800) 582-9422; (949) 675-1213

Central Orange County Inland Communities

California Yellow Cab
(714) 285-0205; (800) 935-5692;
(877) 935-5692; (949) 261-9096

Coast Yellow Cab
(800) 400-8294

Yellow Cab
(800) 829-4743; (800) 331-3772;
(949) 263-8888; (949) 951-8294

South Orange County Beach Communities

Yellow Cab
(949) 376-0092

CHAPTER 7

What's Out of Town

L os Angeles County and Orange County are so big and varied that you can easily spend a year without leaving them. But sometimes, even the happiest resident wants to get out of town—albeit without necessarily going too far. And the most chauvinistic native must admit that the surrounding areas have attractions that simply don't exist in the two counties.

That's what this chapter is about. Moving roughly from north to south, with a few detours along the way, it catalogs the most popular destinations in the rest of Southern California.

Not every destination is in easy driving distance, though. San Diego, for example, lies less than seventy road miles from San Clemente, in the southernmost tip of Orange County; but it's more than 300 miles from Gorman, in northwest Los Angeles County. The Channel Islands lie much closer to L.A. County's Westlake Village than they do to Orange County's Trabuco Canyon. And Palm Springs is a lot closer to Pomona than to Huntington Beach. So always check a map before hopping into the car and setting off for parts unknown.

That said, let's take a look at those parts.

Northwest

CARPINTERIA

Carpinteria State Beach

Highway 224 off the 101 Freeway
(805) 684-2811

cal-parks.ca.gov/DISTRICTS/
channel/csp514.htm

Carpinteria's about three hours up the 101 Freeway from metropolitan Los Angeles, and many consider its state beach to be worth the trip. Visitors can camp overnight, play in the beach's tidepools, swim, picnic, or enjoy other beach activities. Parents should note that this beach is renowned for calm, riptide-free waters.

Channel Islands

Channel Islands National Park
1901 Spinnaker Drive
Ventura
(805) 658-5700; (805) 658-5730

The Channel Islands lie about twenty miles off the Santa Barbara Coast. Of the eight Channel Islands, five are available to visit. Anacapa Island is full of wildflowers and sea mammals, and has a museum and nature trail. Santa Barbara Island is a great place for bird watching and nature hikes. San Miguel Island is perhaps the most exotic, with picturesque fossil formations and the world's widest variety of seals and sea lions. Santa Rosa has hundreds of archaeological sites and a considerable variety of wildlife. And Santa Cruz, the largest of the islands at more than 60,000 acres, is varied and beautiful; it's owned partly by the National Park Service and partly by the environmentally minded Nature Conservancy. All five islands feature campgrounds.

OXNARD

Oxnard, named after its founder, has an ugly sounding name, but it's a fun town to visit. Sitting less than two hours from metropolitan Los Angeles (via the 101 or 1 Freeway), Oxnard offers a fine mix of business, culture, outdoor sports, and park land.

Gull Wings Children's Museum

418 West Fourth Street
(805) 483-3005

Hands-on activities and exhibits, computers, a farmers' market, a medical room, a campground, a puppet theater, a geological dig, and other attractions.

Oxnard State Beach Park

Near Harbor Boulevard and Channel Islands Boulevard
(805) 385-7950

Trails for bikes and feet, sandy shores, picnic areas, and other attractions dot this park's sixty-plus acres.

SANTA BARBARA

About three hours up the 101 Freeway from Los Angeles, Santa Barbara is clean, beautiful, and affluent. It's no coincidence that Ronald Reagan came there to escape his White House duties. With its gorgeous countryside, charming Spanish-colonial architecture, and friendly atmosphere, Santa Barbara is a great place to unwind. The city offers all kinds of athletic activities, and its shopping, lodging, and dining are first-rate, if pricey. If you want fun on the cheap, a stroll through the handsome town, beaches, or parklands is almost always available.

Andree Clark Bird Refuge

Highway 101 at East Corbel Boulevard
(805) 564-5437; (805) 964-1468

ceres.ca.gov/wetlands/geo_info /so_cal/andree_clark.html

Home for huge numbers of beautiful birds, plus a park, a picnic area, a lagoon, a bicycle path, and other attractions, all at no charge.

El Capitan State Beach

About twenty miles northwest of Santa Barbara
(805) 968-1033; (805) 968-3294

cal-parks.ca.gov/DISTRICTS/ channel/ecsb527.htm

El Capitan has tide pools, sycamore and oak groves, a creek, a bike trail, and places for swimming, fishing, surfing, picnicking, and camping.

Mission Santa Barbara

2291 Laguna Street
(805) 682-4713

www.sbmission.org

A National Historic Landmark still in use as a Catholic parish, Mission Santa Barbara is so lovely that it's been called "Queen of the Missions." It contains gardens, a museum, a chapel, and an old cemetery.

MOVING TIP

Stacy Phillips, move-in coordinator at a retirement community south of Orange County, offers advice on moving, as quoted by writer Marsha Kay Seff in the *San Diego Union-Tribune*. Among her recommendations:

- Don't wait until a crisis forces you to move. Start early and take your time.
- Leave throw rugs behind; they're safety hazards.
- Bring your favorite chair.
- Instead of moving all of your possessions or throwing them out, store some for a while to see if you really need or miss them.

Moreton Bay Fig Tree
Chapala Street and Montecito Street
(805) 962-5339

Possibly the largest tree of its kind in America, this monster—well over a century old—is more than seventy-five feet high, with a trunk almost thirteen feet in diameter and branches that spread out more than 150 feet.

Refugio State Beach
About twenty-five miles northwest of Santa Barbara
(805) 968-1033;
(805) 968-3294

cal-parks.ca.gov/DISTRICTS/
channel/rsb527.htm

Refugio has fishing, trails, picnic areas, campgrounds, and other attractions. It's one of the area's most popular beaches.

Santa Barbara Botanic Garden
1212 Mission Canyon Road
(805) 682-4726

www.sbbg.org

More than 1,000 species of California plants are here, as are scenic trails and gorgeous ocean views. The Botanic Garden offers classes, workshops, field trips, tours, a library, a nursery, a herbarium, and other plant-related facilities.

Santa Barbara County Courthouse

1100 Anacapa Street
(805) 962-6464

One of the town's most beautiful buildings, the courthouse has an eighty-foot clock tower (from which you can get a majestic view of the area) plus gardens with places to picnic and unusual plants.

Santa Barbara Museum of Natural History

2559 Puesta del Sol Road
(805) 682-4711

www.sbnature.org/intro2.htm

"The Museum offers a close look at the story of the region's birth, geology and minerals, native wildlife, rich marine life and the culture of the Chumash Indians," says its Web site. There's also a planetarium, an art gallery, a library, and other attractions.

Santa Barbara Zoological Gardens

500 Ninos Drive
(805) 962-6310; (805) 963-5695

www.santabarbarazoo.org

This zoo is home to more than 600 animals, plus a carousel, a gift store, and other attractions.

Sea Center

211 Stearns Wharf
(805) 962-0885

www.sbnature.org/seacentr.htm

"Experience the blow of a blue whale, see the beauty of the kelp forest and touch the spines of a sea urchin," say the official words of the Sea Center. In this facility devoted to marine life, visitors can learn about ocean creatures in an enjoyable atmosphere.

Stearns Wharf

State Street at the waterfront
(805) 564-5518

A place for fishing, shopping, dining, boat charters, and even a small museum, all on an old-fashioned wooden wharf.

SIMI VALLEY

Ronald Reagan Presidential Library and Museum
40 Presidential Drive
(805) 410-8354;
(805) 522-8444

www.reagan.utexas.edu

Less than an hour down the 118 Freeway from metropolitan Los Angeles (depending on traffic), this spot is the central repository for information on Ronald Reagan. It offers exhibits, programs, a full-scale replica of the Oval Office, interactive displays, and a superb view of the surrounding mountains and valleys.

VENTURA

In promoting itself to visitors, Ventura has called itself "the relaxation destination." Given the considerable number of places to take it easy in Southern California, any place that calls itself the spot for relaxation faces some tall competition. Still, Ventura doesn't do so badly: It's got beautiful beaches and quite a few cultural and historic places to visit. It's about two hours from metropolitan Los Angeles via the 101 Freeway.

Albinger Archaeological Museum
113 East Main Street
(805) 648-5823

Near the Mission San Buenaventura is a dig site, and that site has produced the contents of this museum: 3,500 years' worth of artifacts from the Chumash Indians and their predecessors in the region, all the way up to the early 1900s. What's more, admission to the museum is free.

McGrath State Beach
About five miles south of Ventura
(805) 654-4744

With a wide variety of feathered and flying species, McGrath is a great site for bird watching. It also has campgrounds, a nature trail, and places to fish and surf (although surfers should watch out for riptides).

Mission San Buenaventura
210 East Main Street
(805) 653-0323

www.ca-missions.org

A trip into the past, the San Buenaventura Mission offers authentic architecture and artifacts from the eighteenth and nineteenth centuries. It includes a church that's still in use, a museum, and other attractions.

Ventura County Museum of History and Art
100 East Main Street
(805) 653-0323

www.vcmha.org

From a collection of horse-drawn farm equipment to a historical research library, the Ventura County Museum of History and Art offers almost anything that you'd want to know or see about Ventura County's past.

North

ROSAMOND

Exotic Feline Breeding Compound and Feline Conservation Center
Rosamond Boulevard
(661) 256-3332;
(661) 256-3793

www.cathouse-fcc.org

This facility, well over an hour up Highway 14 from metropolitan Los Angeles, offers dozens of leopards, tigers, and other exotic cats in a preserve for anyone to see. It protects rare specimens and offers educational opportunities for children and adults.

East

BIG BEAR

The Big Bear Lake area is one of the more popular getaways for people tired of the flatlands in L.A. County and Orange County. At elevations above 8,000 feet, the area offers outdoor recreation, stunning mountain vistas, and some of the cleanest air in Southern California. Even getting there is beautiful: You'll take Highway 18, known as the

Rim of the World Scenic Byway for its mountainside vistas. (If you're coming from metropolitan Los Angeles, give yourself three or more hours for the journey: Highway 18 is a twisty one.) Big Bear isn't long on museums or other aspects of high culture, but you can't have everything.

CITY FACT

When she moved from Iowa to California, novelist Jane Smiley (*Moo*; the Pulitzer Prize-winning *A Thousand Acres*) found that even the people who remodeled her house had a California difference. "You have to listen to and appreciate the workmen's discussions of their life journeys and goals," she told *Metropolitan Home* magazine. "In Iowa, they never say a word about anything, much less about life journeys."

Big Bear Lake

Highway 18 at Highway 38 in San Bernardino County
(909) 866-5831

www.bigbear.net

Fishing, boating, skiing, snowboarding, hiking, mountain biking—these are only a few of the things that you can do at, on, or near Big Bear Lake. For extra enjoyment, you can rent a cabin for a weekend or longer from one of the many real estate agents who specialize in that trade.

Snow Summit Mountain Resort

880 Summit Boulevard
(909) 866-5766

www.snowsummit.com

This resort is one of the region's most popular places to ski and snowboard. With several chairlifts and considerable amounts of man-made snow, everyone who wants to ski gets a chance—although it can take a while; the resort can become very crowded.

JOSHUA TREE

Joshua Tree National Park

74485 National Park Drive
(760) 367-5500

www.nps.gov/jotr/home.html#

Three to four hours (depending on traffic) down the 10 and 62 freeways from metropolitan Los Angeles, Joshua Tree is a great place to camp, hike, picnic, mountain bike, bird watch, try your hand (and feet) at rock climbing, go horseback riding, or just stare at the park's gorgeous fields of wildflowers. Park rangers lead tours and provide other sources of information about the park.

LAKE ARROWHEAD

Lake Arrowhead

Arrowhead Lake Association
Highway 189 at Highway 173
(909) 337-2595

www.lakeassociation.com

www.lakearrowhead.org

www.lakearrowhead.com

www.lakearrowhead.net

Lake Arrowhead, about two hours down Highway 18 from metropolitan Los Angeles, isn't a city. It's an unincorporated part of San Bernardino County, and much of it is controlled by the Arrowhead Lake Association, a group of local property owners. The lake and the surrounding areas offer camping, hiking, ice skating, skiing on snow and water, and other recreation. Cabins are available for short-term rental, making Lake Arrowhead an excellent spot for a few days out of town.

PALM SPRINGS AND VICINITY

About an hour and a half to two hours down the 10 Freeway from metropolitan Los Angeles, Palm Springs is a resort town in the middle of a desert. Its popularity among the rich and retired has made it an expensive place to visit, but if you like golf, tennis, mineral hot springs and spas, and other tony diversions, Palm Springs is the place for you.

Even if you're on a budget, you can find workably priced fun in Palm Springs. The warm weather and the desert scenery are free, and there are other attractions that won't strain your wallet too far.

MOVING TIP

The Better Business Bureau says that moving companies generate more complaints than most other businesses. Journalist John Godfrey has looked into the matter. To avoid problems, he recommends:

- When you ask moving companies for estimates, get *binding* estimates. Otherwise, the true cost may be much higher than the estimate.

- If the movers pack for you, watch them. Because they charge for each box, they may use more boxes than necessary.

- Ask the moving company to provide insurance that guarantees full replacement value for whatever the company damages or loses.

Indian Canyons
Agua Caliente at Indian Reservation
(760) 325-5673;
(760) 325-3400

The Indian Canyons offer some of Palm Springs' most remarkable sights: waterfalls, streams, palm forests, picturesque rock formations, miles of old trails, and other attractions.

Mount San Jacinto State Park
Near Highway 243
(909) 659-2607

cal-parks.ca.gov/DISTRICTS/
colorado/msjs616.htm

Mount San Jacinto State Park is more than 13,000 acres of places to picnic, ski, and camp. Its mountains run up to 10,000 feet high, and there are more than fifty miles of hiking trails. Because it sits primarily in high elevations, the park can get cold even in summer, providing a contrast to Palm Springs' desert temperatures.

Oasis Waterpark
1500 South Gene Autry Trail
(760) 327-0499

www.oasiswaterresort.com/
waterpark/index.htm

A water park in the desert? Of course. Covering more than twenty acres, Oasis Waterpark offers water slides, an innertube ride, a wave-action pool, and other soggy fun for the family.

Palm Springs Aerial Tramway
Tramway Road
(888) 515-8726;
(760) 325-1391

www.pstramway.com

Get the view from 8,500 feet by riding this airborne cable car that travels from the desert floor into the mountains. The tram takes its passengers up near Mount San Jacinto Wilderness State Park, which offers hiking trails, campgrounds, and a ski center.

Palm Springs Desert Museum
101 Museum Drive
(760) 325-0189

www.psmuseum.org

The visual arts, the performing arts, and the sciences get celebrated at this museum. In addition, the museum offers a sculpture garden, lectures, films, and other attractions.

South

CARLSBAD

Carlsbad, a couple of hours' drive down the 5 Freeway from metropolitan Los Angeles, is a great escape. For beaches and lagoons and coves, for golf and tennis, and for shopping (particularly antiquing) and dining, Carlsbad is one of the region's best towns.

Carlsbad State Beach
100 Tamarack Avenue
(800) 444-7275

This beach, though not as well known as its neighbor to the south (see following), is a good place to fish, swim, surf, and skin dive. If you'd rather stay dry, you can simply stroll the nearby boardwalk or enjoy a beach picnic.

Legoland
Interstate 5 and Cannon Road
(760) 918-5346

www.legolandca.com

Everything is made of LEGOs at Legoland, or at least that's how it seems. Whimsical sculptures and reproductions of great monuments are among the attractions here, along with rides, workshops, and other features for kids.

South Carlsbad State Beach

4000 Carlsbad Boulevard
(760) 438-3143; (800) 444-7275

cal-parks.ca.gov/DISTRICTS/
sandiego.scsb652.htm

Surfers, swimmers, and skin divers love this beach, as do campers and picnickers. It's surrounded by high bluffs which make for some gorgeous ocean views.

ESCONDIDO

San Diego Wild Animal Park

15500 San Pasqual Valley Road
(760) 747-8702

www.sandiegozoo.org/wap/
homepage.php3?siteloc=3

A huge wildlife preserve lying about two to three hours' drive down the 15 Freeway from metropolitan Los Angeles, the Wild Animal Park has more than 3,500 animals native to Asia and Africa and other far-off lands. The park offers tours; shops; restaurants; shows featuring birds, elephants, and other beasts; plus other attractions.

OCEANSIDE

Oceanside Visitor and Tourism Information Center

926 North Coast Highway
(760) 721-1101

www.oceansidechamber.com

Oceanside, about two hours down the 5 Freeway from metropolitan Los Angeles, is something of an enigma. It's a fairly popular place, but it's popular for nothing in particular.

Unlike other Southern California cities, Oceanside has no hugely famous attractions to pull people to the city. Virtually everyone in Southern California seems to have visited San Diego's Sea World or its remarkable zoo. Even the smaller cities—quite a few of them, anyway—have famous tourist sites. But many people who go out of their way to visit Escondido's Wild Animal Park, Big Bear's Snow Summit, or Carlsbad's Legoland have never heard of Oceanside's Mission San Luis Rey de Francia, its California Surf Museum, or its enormous Municipal Pier. They have heard of nearby Camp Pendleton Marine Corps Base, which covers more than 100,000 acres, but they usually don't think of the base as a tourist attraction. (As it happens, the base does offer tours.)

What draws people to Oceanside is not any of these attractions. What draws them to Oceanside is . . . Oceanside.

The town has the pleasant diversions mentioned, plus some of the best surfing beaches in Southern California. While it lacks the "must-see" attractions of other towns, Oceanside is a splendidly pleasant place to spend a weekend.

SAN DIEGO

About three hours (depending on traffic) down the 5 Freeway from metropolitan Los Angeles, San Diego has long billed itself as "America's Finest City." One of the country's most populous towns, it has usually kept political and ethnic conflict under more control than comparable metropoli. People from livelier cities may find San Diego bland, repressed, or narrow, but even they'll readily agree that the town is a great place to vacation. For scenic beauty, outdoor activities (especially water sports), and family attractions—from an outstanding zoo to the country's biggest annual comic book convention—San Diego is hard to outdo.

CITY FACT

Orange County schools average better than Los Angeles County schools, if you trust their Scholastic Aptitude Test scores. In 1998, according to the reference volume *California Cities, Towns and Counties*, Orange County's average score on the verbal section of the SAT was 526; the math was 553. Los Angeles County scored 467 on verbal, 498 on math.

La Jolla and Vicinity

Sitting in the northern part of San Diego, La Jolla (Spanish for "the jewel") is quite the sophisticated area, full of fancy shops and home to the University of California San Diego. In keeping with this combination of wealth and youth, the area offers some of the state's finest surfing and other beach attractions.

Black's Beach

(Also known as Torrey Pines City Beach)
Torrey Pines Scenic Drive
(858) 755-2063

www.sannet.gov/lifeguards/
beaches.cove.shtml

If you want to go nude, go Black's. It's the area's most famous and very unofficial nude beach. Atop the nearby tall cliffs is the Torrey Pines Glider Port, where hang gliders and other flying creatures take off. The cliffs make getting to Black's difficult, but once you're there, you're likely to have a good time, provided that you watch out for the water's riptides and strong currents.

MOVING TIP

California's public schools have dropped in quality in recent years. Consequently, you may want your kids to attend private school. If your company is transferring you, see if it will contribute to the kids' tuition. "Paying school tuition for children of executives stationed abroad is fairly standard," writes reporter Timothy Schellhardt in the *Wall Street Journal*. "But Eric Steiner, executive vice president of Fairchild Corp., got a $25,225 tuition reimbursement when he moved with his two children from Virginia to California."

La Jolla Cove

1100 Coast Boulevard
(619) 221-8901

www.sannet.gov/lifeguards/beac
hes.cove.shtml

Although small, La Jolla Cove is very popular for its sheer scenic beauty, with sandstone cliffs and sparkling water. It's not far from La Jolla's shopping and restaurants, and it offers great spots for picnicking, scuba diving, and snorkeling.

Museum of Contemporary Art

700 Prospect Street
(858) 454-3542

www.mcasd.org

Paintings, drawings, sculptures, video, and other visual arts are the focus of this institution. Its permanent collection houses more than 3,000 works created in the past fifty years.

Stephen Birch Aquarium Museum

Scripps Institution of Oceanography
University of California San Diego
2300 Expedition Way
(858) 534-3474

aquarium.ucsd.edu

This establishment offers more than thirty marine tanks with Pacific Ocean creatures of almost all kinds, a tide pool, displays of underwater life, and more. If you like fish, this is Mecca.

Torrey Pines State Beach

North Torrey Pines Road
(858) 755-2063

cal-parks.ca.gov/DISTRICTS/
sandiego/tpsb631.htm

A fine place to picnic, surf, fish, and swim, the Torrey Pines State Beach also offers great sightseeing due to its nearby red bluffs and its proximity to Torrey Pines State Reserve (see following entry).

Torrey Pines State Reserve

Carmel Valley Road
(858) 755-2063

parks.ca.gov/districts/sandiego/t
psr630.htm

This park's 2,000 acres include a considerable range of native plant life, a lagoon for migrating seabirds, high cliffs, deep ravines, ocean views, a visitor center, miles of hiking trails, and guided nature walks.

Metropolitan San Diego

San Diego is justly famous for its outdoor attractions—its parks and beaches—and it has cleverly melded them with its cultural attractions. The city puts museums in its public parks, and it offers outdoor theme parks that combine education and entertainment.

Balboa Park

1549 El Prado
(619) 239-0512

www.balboapark.org

More than just a park, the 1,200-acre Balboa Park contains museums of art, science, history, and other subjects; a theater; the San Diego Zoo; a sports complex; a rose garden; and more.

Cabrillo National Monument

1800 Cabrillo Memorial Drive
(619) 557-5450

www.nps.gov/index.html

This park, named after the first European to discover San Diego, has a museum, a lighthouse, the remains of an old fort, and other historical items. Situated on the Pacific Ocean, it is an excellent place for whale watching and offers tide pools, a hiking trail, educational programs, and other facilities.

Mission Bay Park

Mission Boulevard
(619) 221-8901

www.sannet.gov/park-and-recreation/missbay.shtml

At more than 4,000 acres, Mission Bay is said to be the west coast's biggest water park. The park has beaches, boat docks, boat rentals, paths for walking and bicycling, basketball courts, playgrounds, and places for windsurfing, water skiing, swimming, volleyball, softball, and other activities. It also contains the famous Sea World theme park.

Old Town San Diego State Historic Park

San Diego Avenue and Twiggs Street
(619) 220-5422

cal-parks.ca.gov/DISTRICTS/sandiego/otsdshp667.htm

This park recreates nineteenth-century San Diego life. It includes a schoolhouse, a black-smith's shop, a newspaper office, a stable, and a mansion. It also has shops, restaurants, and a museum.

Pacific Beach

(619) 272-4300 (Pacific Beach Chamber of Commerce)

One of San Diego's most popular beaches (if not the most popular of all), Pacific Beach is a magnet for young, active people. It has a boardwalk, restaurants, shops, a path for bicycles and pedestrians, and Crystal Pier, a 1920s-era fishing pier.

Reuben H. Fleet Science Center

Balboa Park
1875 El Prado
(619) 238-1233

www.rhfleet.org

A full-scale science complex, including a giant IMAX theater, hands-on exhibit galleries, a full-motion simulator to demonstrate high-powered rides, and quite a few other attractions

San Diego Maritime Museum

1306 North Harbor Drive
(610) 234-9153

www.sdmaritime.com

A celebration of seafaring, including the sailing ship *Star of India,* the steam yacht *Medea,* and the ferryboat *Berkeley,* the Maritime Museum is a tribute to San Diego's long history as a seaport.

MOVING TIP

Label your boxes with the room to which their contents are going, not with the room from which they came. This is particularly helpful if you are moving into a larger home. It will cut down on excessive shuffling around once you begin unpacking.

San Diego Museum of Man

Balboa Park
1350 El Prado
(619) 239-2001

www.museumofman.org

This anthropological museum contains folk art, ancient artifacts, and other finds. Permanent exhibits include "Life and Death on the Nile: Sun Gods and Mummies in Ancient Egypt," "Kumeyaay: Indians of San Diego," "Early Man," "Life Cycles and Ceremonies," "Primates Past and Present," and "Peoples of the Southwest."

MOVING TIP

If your new home is on a narrow or twisty road, make sure that your moving van can reach your front door. *Money* magazine reports that when one young family moved into Orange County's Silverado Canyon, "the United Van Lines trucks ... couldn't maneuver down the road to their new home. Everything had to be transferred onto a smaller U-Haul truck."

San Diego Zoo
2920 Zoo Drive
Balboa Park
(619) 234-3153

www.sandiegozoo.org/zoo/
homepage.php3?siteloc=2

A hundred acres of animals, the San Diego Zoo houses nearly 4,000 beasts and more than 6,000 species of plant life, plus shops and restaurants.

Sea World Adventure Park
500 Sea World Drive
(619) 222-6363

www.4adventure.com/
seaworld/sw_california/
swcframe.html

Prepare to get wet at this theme park that features ocean-themed shows and rides. The park also provides educational opportunities amid all the fun.

CHAPTER 8

Volunteer and Community Involvement

For all their reputation as sun-baked hedonists, lots of Southern Californians get deeply involved in improving their communities.

Forming or joining organizations to help others has quite a history in the area. It may stretch a point to say that the missionaries who settled in the area were a community-service organization—the natives who already lived there may have had a different opinion about the newcomers' activities—but these days, there are lots of clubs, societies, organizations, federations, and other groups out to do good.

Here is detailed information about some of the area's most prominent volunteer groups. Most of the organizations have too many branches, chapters, or affiliates throughout Southern California to list here, so this chapter includes only the addresses and phone numbers of national, state, or regional headquarters, whose staffers will be happy to direct you to the nearest division.

AIDS Project Los Angeles

1313 North Vine Street
Los Angeles, CA 90028
(323) 993-1600

www.apla.org

"Treatment and prevention education as well as advocates on behalf of people living with AIDS and AIDS-related legislation"—that, in APLA's own words, is the organization's mission. APLA helps people who have AIDS, works to prevent people from getting it, and gets involved with governmental attempts to fight the disease.

The American Legion of California

401 Van Ness Avenue, Room 117
San Francisco, CA 94102-4587
(415) 431-2400

www.legion.org
or www.calegion.org

This patriotic group helps such youth groups as the Child Welfare Foundation, Children's Miracle Network, McGruff Safe Kids Program, Boy Scouts of America, and the National High School Oratorical Contest.

American Lung Association of California

424 Pendleton Way
Oakland, CA 94621
(800) 586-4872;
(510) 638-5864

www.californialung.org

Volunteers participate in anti-smoking education and advocacy efforts, spread instruction and news about air pollution and lung problems, aid children who suffer from asthma to learn more about the disease, and help others who suffer from lung ailments.

CITY FACT

According to CalTech and the United States Geological Survey, Southern California usually experiences one to five earthquakes per day. Most of them are so small that you wouldn't feel them unless you were standing atop the epicenter. Since 1979, all the biggest quakes (magnitude 5.6 or more) have occurred between 2 A.M. and 9 A.M.

Americorps

Western Campus
2650 Truxton Road
San Diego, CA 92106-6001
(800) 942-2677
  (national headquarters)
(619) 524-0749
  (Western Campus)
www.nationalservice.org/statepr
ofiles/ca_intro.htm

The domestic Peace Corps, Americorps offers more than 200 service projects, from building homes to tutoring children to organizing neighborhood watch groups. Some of the groups listed in this chapter have worked with or received funding from Americorps.

Amnesty International

Western Region
Southern California Cluster
9000 West Washington Boulevard,
2nd Floor
Culver City, CA 90232
(800) 266-3789
  (national headquarters);
(310) 815-0450
  (Southern California Cluster)
www.amnesty_volunteer.org/
usa/scal

Amnesty International calls itself "a worldwide grassroots activist organization working impartially for the release of all prisoners of conscience, fair and prompt trials for political pris-

oners, and an end to torture and executions."

The Arthritis Foundation

Southern California Chapter
4311 Wilshire Boulevard,
Suite 530
Los Angeles, CA 90010-3775
(213) 954-5750; (800) 954-2873
www.arthritis.org/offices/sca

Orange County/Long Beach Branch
17155 Newhope Street, Suite A
Fountain Valley, CA 92708
(714) 436-1625; (800) 452-2832

The Arthritis Foundation sponsors research and other efforts to combat arthritis. Volunteers participate in support groups, exercise classes, and self-help classes, among other activities.

Big Brothers/Big Sisters of America

Big Brothers of Greater Los Angeles
1486 Colorado Boulevard
Los Angeles, CA 90041
(323) 258-3333
www.bigbrothersla.org

Big Sisters of Los Angeles
6022 Wilshire Boulevard,
Suite 202
Los Angeles, CA 90036
(323) 933-5749
www.bigsistersla.org

Big Brothers/Big Sisters of Orange County
14131 Yorba Street,
Suite 200
Tustin, CA 92780
(714) 544-7773

www.bigbrooc.org

"Making a big difference, one child at a time" (to quote the organization's motto), this group matches adult mentors to children who need a grown-up's companionship and guidance. There are also Big Brother and Big Sister organizations especially for Catholics and Jews.

California Federation of Women's Clubs
4946 East Yale,
Suite 102
Fresno, CA 93727
(559) 456-3557

www.cfwc.org

The CFWC is part of an international community-service organization that provides programs such as child abuse prevention, youth leadership training, opportunities for people with disabilities, literacy and reading programs, highway and vehicle safety, and more.

Easter Seals Southern California
1801 East Edinger Avenue,
Suite 190
Santa Ana, CA 92705
(714) 834-1111

www.essc.org

Easter Seals organizations help the disabled with activities such as the After-School Program (recreational activities for children), Behavior Management (to help disabled people improve their independence and self-control), the Brain Injury Program (support services for brain-injury survivors), and several other offerings.

Fair Housing Congress of Southern California
Fair Housing Councils of Los Angeles County
3600 Wilshire Boulevard, Suite 426
Los Angeles, CA 90010
(213) 365-7184

www.fairhousing.com/fhcsc

Fair Housing Council of Orange County
201 South Broadway
Santa Ana, CA 92701-5633
(714) 569-0825

"Our goal is the eradication of illegal housing discrimination," says the FHC. Volunteers help people who have suffered from discrimination get help and satisfaction. The group is involved with community education, political advocacy, and other activities.

Habitat for Humanity International

National Headquarters
121 Habitat Street
Americus, GA 31709-3498
(800) 422-4828

www.habitat.org

Working with churches, companies, foundations, and other groups, Habitat for Humanity builds houses for the needy. Volunteers go out with wood, hammer, and nails, and construct livable shelters for the poor.

Kiwanis International

California Headquarters
P.O. Box 6369
Oakland, CA 94603
(510) 562-7055

www.kiwanis.org

Kiwanis specializes in serving the children of the world, according to its motto. (One of its top recent campaigns, for example, has been to eliminate iodine deficiency disorder.) The organization has Circle K orga-

nizations for young adults on college campuses and Key Clubs for high school students.

League of United Latin American Citizens

California LULAC
11591 Candy Lane
Garden Grove, CA 92840
(714) 636-7576

www.california lulac.org

California's oldest Latino civil rights organization, LULAC fights for social and economic opportunity for Hispanic Americans. The organization places special emphasis on programs that promote education as a means for cultural growth and development, as well as civil liberties and voting rights.

Lions Clubs International

National Headquarters
300 22nd Street
Oak Brook, IL 60532-8842
(630) 571-5466

www.lions.org

Lions Clubs operate and/or support a variety of programs, including diabetes awareness programs, aid for the deaf, and international youth camps. There is an especially strong emphasis on help for the blind, including the Southern

California Eye Institute and the Lions Project for Canine Companions for Independence.

Meals on Wheels Association of America

National Headquarters
1414 Prince Street, Suite 202
Alexandria, VA 22314
(800) 677-1116;
(703) 548-5558

www.projectmeal.org

Meals on Wheels Santa Monica/Malibu/Pacific Palisades
609 Arizona Avenue
Santa Monica, CA 90401
(310) 394-5133;
(310) 394-7558

Meals on Wheels delivers hot food to anyone who is house-bound, particularly the elderly and infirm. Its Web site doesn't list all of the many local MOW chapters, but the Santa Monica chapter, listed here, can direct you to the one nearest you.

Mothers Against Drunk Driving

MADD California State
P.O. Box 601008
Sacramento, CA 95860
(916) 481-6233;
(800) 426-6233

www.madd.org

MADD Los Angeles County
P.O. Box 451217
Westchester, CA 90045
(310) 215-2905; (818) 509-2022

www.gran-net.com/madd/ca/lacounty

MADD Orange County
17772 Irvine Boulevard, Suite 103
Tustin, CA 92780
(714) 838-6199

www.itstime.com/madd

Recruiting not just mothers but all groups of people, MADD works to get drunk drivers off the road, to punish those who are on the road, and to raise public awareness of drunken driving. The organization is deeply involved in national and local politics, assistance to victims of drunk drivers, and other programs.

National Multiple Sclerosis Society

Southern California Chapter
2440 South Sepulveda Boulevard,
Suite 115
Los Angeles, CA 90064
(800) 344-4867
  (national headquarters)
(310) 479-4456
  (Southern California Chapter)

www.nmss.org

This group helps people with the crippling disease multiple sclerosis. NMSS funds research into treatment, sets up educational and informational programs, organizes physical and emotional health programs, and provides self-help and support groups, among other things.

Retired and Senior Volunteer Program (RSVP)

Southern California Region
11150 West Olympic Boulevard,
Suite 670
Los Angeles, CA 90064
(310) 235-7421

sites.tier.net/rsvp

A national agency that places volunteers in their fifties and older to help with day care for children, infants, or adults; visiting and counseling; office work; education; and other programs, from crocheting to computers.

Rotary International

National Headquarters
One Rotary Center
1660 Sherman Avenue
Evanston, IL 60201
(847) 866-3000

www.rotary.org

A group with programs that range from Preserve Planet Earth to Urban Peace to Drug and Alcohol Abuse Prevention, Rotary is one of the largest, most widespread, and oldest community-service groups.

MOVING TIP

Family, neighbors, friends, and co-workers make excellent movers. Plan on two persons for every 1,000 square feet of current living space. Double this figure if you are moving to and from two-story structures.

Salvation Army Southern California

900 West James Wood Avenue
Los Angeles, CA 90015
(213) 896-9160;
(213) 553-3277;
(323) 221-5620

www.salvationarmy-socal.org

Possibly the most famous volunteer organization, the venerable Salvation Army has forty sites in Southern California. It collects toys for needy children, runs homeless shelters, offers training and education, and organizes other programs.

Shelter for the Homeless

15161 Jackson Street
Midway City, CA 92655-1432
(714) 897-3221

www.shelterforthehomeless.org

For more than a decade, Shelter for the Homeless has helped people without homes get job training, education, counseling, child care, and, of course, places to live. It is one of the few organizations on this list founded and based in Southern California.

Sierra Club

Angeles Chapter (Los Angeles)
3435 Wilshire Boulevard,
Suite 320
Los Angeles, CA 90010-1904
(213) 387-4287

Orange County Office
230 East 17th Street, Suite 206
Costa Mesa, CA 92627
(949) 631-3140

www.sierraclub.org

The original environmental group, the Sierra Club has nearly 50,000 members in Los Angeles County and Orange County. Volunteers get involved in activities aimed at raising environmental consciousness among citizens and government leaders.

Trauma Intervention Programs, Inc.

Headquarters
P.O. Box 892050
Temecula, CA 92589
(909) 600-8652

www.geocities.com/Heartland/
Forest/4961

TIP volunteers go to emergency sites to help family members, witnesses, and others whom governments and other organizations may ignore: the ones who aren't the immediate victims of the emergencies but who suffer nonetheless.

Volunteer Center of Los Angeles

8134 Van Nuys Boulevard,
Suite 200
Van Nuys, CA 91402
(818) 908-5066

www.volunteers.org/connection

This organization, which operates primarily in the northern parts of Southern California, is a multiservice agency offering programs such as parenting classes, teen counseling, English as a Second Language education, citizenship exam instruction, Urban Foresters in Training, and Youth in Service to Youth.

Finding the Essentials

CHAPTER 9

Important Places to Know

There is more than enough of everything in Southern California. Whether you want your shirts scrubbed or your soul cleansed, the region offers a sometimes overwhelming range of choices.

The best way to find a good pharmacy, grocery, dry cleaner, or other essential establishment is to ask the people around you—neighbors, coworkers, and so on. Almost everyone has a favorite place to recommend.

In the meantime, the following lists will get you on your way. The lists are not complete. This book has room to list only a representative smattering of places in the most prominent or fastest-growing communities.

Nevertheless, the lists will give you a good start. Jump on in.

Cleaners and Laundries

LOS ANGELES COUNTY

Burbank

Gilbert Cleaners
409 North Glenoaks Boulevard
(818) 846-1750

Downtown Los Angeles and Vicinity

Bowers & Sons Cleaners
2509 South Central Avenue
(213) 749-3237

CITY FACT

The power of Disneyland, aerospace, and other factors shows up in Orange County's housing statistics. In 1950, according to the national census, the county had fewer than 6,000 housing units. Ten years later, it had more than 200,000.

Glendale

Swiss Cleaners
1219 North Central Avenue
(818) 244-7744

Lakewood

Dutch Dry Cleaners
5933 South Street
(562) 866-6212

La Mirada

Imperial Cleaners
15065 Imperial Highway
(562) 947-1337

Lancaster

Antelope Valley Express Dry Cleaners
131 East Avenue J
(661) 942-5199

Century Express Cleaners
1874 East Avenue J
(661) 723-7331

2849 West Avenue L
(661) 722-4995

George's Cleaners
44759 North Beech Avenue
(661) 942-4124

Lancaster Square Cleaners
44209 North 10th Street West
(661) 942-6416

41939 North 50th Street West
(661) 943-2218

Long Beach

Foasberg Cleaners
640 East Wardlow Road
(562) 426-7345

3337 East Broadway
(562) 439-2222

Gaylord Cleaners
1232 Obispo Avenue
(562) 494-0086

Ontario

24 K Cleaners
2410 South Grove Avenue
(909) 947-7790

Palmdale

A Pro Cleaners
533-K East Palmdale Boulevard
(661) 267-2664

3005 East Palmdale Boulevard
(661) 272-1515

George's Cleaners
38729 North Tierra Subida
(661) 273-3011

Pasadena

Magic Cleaners
89 North Lake Avenue
(626) 796-1975

'Round the Clock Cleaners
827 East Colorado Boulevard
(626) 793-3919

Pomona

Quality Cleaners
2001 South Garey Avenue
(909) 465-5852

Quality Cleaners
2260 South Garey Avenue
(909) 591-2857

Santa Fe Springs

G&M Cleaners
14515 Valley View
(562) 404-9747

Santa Monica

Metropolitan Drive Thru Cleaners & Laundry
2003 Lincoln Boulevard
(310) 452-3443

Plaza Dry Cleaners
1011 Wilshire Boulevard
(310) 395-2417

Torrance

Classic Cleaners
2833 Pacific Coast Highway
(310) 530-5331

MOVING TIP

Drive your rental truck around the block a few times and practice parking. You'll gain confidence and feel more comfortable when navigating highways. When the truck is full, however, it may handle differently, so make a trial run or two around the block after you've finished loading.

South Bay Suede Cleaners
4215 Spencer
(310) 370-6288

la.digitalcity.com/
sbsspecialtycleaners

ORANGE COUNTY

Anaheim

West Anaheim Cleaners
1272 South Magnolia Avenue
(714) 826-4580

White Horse Cleaners
5655 East La Palma Avenue
(714) 970-8494

Van Nuys
(City of Los Angeles)

Princess Cleaners
16055 Vanowen Street
(818) 785-2788

Westlake
(City of Los Angeles)

Chapman Cleaners
3450 West 6th Street
(213) 386-6816

Westwood
(City of Los Angeles)

Sterling Cleaners
1600 Westwood Boulevard
(310) 474-8525

Westland Cleaners & Laundry
1363 Westwood Boulevard
(310) 479-5725; (310) 478-7642

Whittier

Walt's Cleaners
8002 Greenleaf Avenue
(562) 693-0161; (562) 698-7119

Dana Point

Dana Point Cleaners
33611 Del Obispo
(949) 661-6252

Fullerton

Crown Cleaners
1956 North Placentia Avenue
(714) 524-3452

Fullerton Elite Cleaners
138 West Wilshire Avenue
(714) 525-5971

Garden Grove

Julie's Drycleaner
12904 Harbor Boulevard
(714) 530-8301

Huntington Beach

The Boardwalk Cleaners
16851 Algonquin Street
(714) 846-0015

Seacliff Cleaners
2119 Main Street
(714) 960-4406

Laguna Niguel

Celebrity Cleaners
28221-C Crown Valley Parkway
(949) 831-2979

Lake Forest

Cleaner in Motion
22500 Muirlands Boulevard,
Suite A
(949) 830-2333

CITY FACT

While many people come to Southern California to get famous, other celebrities were born here, including actors Shirley Temple (Santa Monica), Marilyn Monroe (Los Angeles), and Robert Redford (Santa Monica); chef Julia Child (Pasadena); tennis star Pancho Gonzalez (Los Angeles); politicians Richard Nixon (Yorba Linda) and Adlai Stevenson (Los Angeles); General George Patton (San Gabriel); and astronaut Sally Ride (Los Angeles).

Muirlands 1-Day Cleaner & Laundry
24322 Muirlands Boulevard
(949) 837-7952

Orange

Santiago Hills Cleaners
8500 East Chapman Avenue
(714) 288-1100

Santa Ana

Accent Cleaners
3767 South Plaza Drive
(714) 754-4008

Tustin

Tustin Cleaning Center
18331 Irvine Boulevard, #D
(714) 730-3844

Tustin Ranch Cleaners
13313 Jamboree Road
(714) 838-3930

Hospitals

Hospitals marked with an asterisk have emergency facilities.

LOS ANGELES COUNTY

Beverly Hills and Vicinity

Cedars-Sinai Medical Center*
8700 Beverly Boulevard
(310) 423-3277; (310) 855-4898;
(310) 855-4000

Burbank

**Providence Saint Joseph
Medical Center***
501 South Buena Vista Street
(818) 843-5111

Chino

Chino Valley Medical Center*
5451 Walnut Avenue
(909) 464-8600

Downtown/Central City (City of Los Angeles)

**California Hospital Medical
Center Los Angeles***
1401 South Grand Avenue
(213) 748-2411

www.chmcla.com

Duarte

**City of Hope National Medical
Center**
1500 East Duarte Road
(626) 359-8111

www.cityofhope.org

Encino

**Encino-Tarzana Regional
Medical Center***
16237 Ventura Boulevard
(818) 708-5140

Glendale

Glendale Memorial Hospital & Health Center*
1420 South Central Avenue
(818) 502-1900; (818) 502-2201

Granada Hills
(City of Los Angeles)

Granada Hills Community Hospital*
10445 Balboa Boulevard
(818) 360-1021

Hollywood
(City of Los Angeles)

Edgemont Hospital
4841 Hollywood Boulevard
(323) 913-9000; (323) 913-2900

Lancaster

Lancaster Community Hospital*
43830 North 10th Street West
(805) 948-4781

Long Beach

Long Beach Community Medical Center*
1720 Termino Avenue
(562) 498-4536; (562) 498-4511

lbcommunity.com

Long Beach Memorial Medical Center*
2801 Atlantic Avenue
(562) 933-2000

Ontario

Vencor Hospital Ontario*
550 North Monterey Avenue
(909) 391-0333

Pasadena

Huntington Memorial Hospital*
100 West California Boulevard
(626) 397-5000

MOVING TIP

Make sure you have arranged to obtain your children's birth certificates and immunization records prior to moving. In most districts, children cannot be registered in school without them.

Saint Luke Medical Center*
2632 East Washington Boulevard
(626) 797-1141

Pomona

Pomona Valley Hospital Medical Center*
1798 North Garey Avenue
(909) 865-9500

CITY FACT

The cost of living is high in Southern California: about 15 percent above the national average, according to the Economic Research Institute. Still, it ranks below places like San Francisco (approximately 25 percent above average) and Manhattan (about 40 percent above average).

www.tenethealth.com/encino-tarzana

Torrance

Little Company of Mary Hospital*
4101 Torrance Boulevard
(310) 540-7676

Van Nuys (City of Los Angeles)

Van Nuys Hospital
15220 Vanowen Street
(818) 787-0123

Westlake

Good Samaritan Hospital*
1225 Wilshire Boulevard
(or 616 Witmer Street)
(213) 977-2121

www.goodsam.com

Santa Monica

Saint John's Health Center*
1328 22nd Street
(310) 829-5511

Tarzana (City of Los Angeles)

Encino-Tarzana Regional Medical Center*
18321 Clark Street
(818) 881-0800;
(818) 708-5140

Westwood

UCLA Medical Center*
10833 Le Conte Avenue
(310) 825-9111

Wilshire District (City of Los Angeles)

Midway Hospital Medical Center*
5925 San Vicente Boulevard
(323) 938-3161

ORANGE COUNTY

Anaheim

Martin Luther Hospital*
1830 West Romneya Drive
(714) 491-5200

Corona

Corona Regional Medical Center-Main*
800 South Main Street
(909) 737-4343; (909) 736-6240

Costa Mesa

College Hospital Costa Mesa
301 Victoria Street
(949) 642-2734

Fullerton

Saint Jude Medical Center*
101 East Valencia Mesa Drive
(714) 992-3000; (714) 992-3909

Garden Grove

Garden Grove Hospital*
12601 Garden Grove Boulevard
(714) 537-5160

Huntington Beach

Columbia Huntington Beach Hospital and Medical Center*
17772 Beach Boulevard
(714) 842-1473

Irvine

Irvine Medical Center*
16200 Sand Canyon Avenue
(949) 753-2000
www.tenethealth.com

Laguna Beach

South Coast Medical Center*
31872 Coast Highway
(949) 499-1311; (949) 499-7223

Los Alamitos

Los Alamitos Medical Center*
3751 Katella Avenue
(562) 598-1311

Mission Viejo

Mission Hospital Regional Medical Center*
27700 Medical Center Road
(949) 364-1400
www.mhmrc.com

Newport Beach

Hoag Memorial Hospital Presbyterian*
One Hoag Drive
(949) 645-8600
www.hoag.org

Orange

Chapman Medical Center*
2601 East Chapman Avenue
(714) 633-0011

Children's Hospital of Orange County*
455 South Main Street
(714) 997-3000; (714) 532-8405

Santa Ana

Coastal Communities Hospital*
2701 South Bristol Street
(714) 754-5454

Santa Ana Hospital Medical Center
1901 North Fairview Street
(714) 554-1653

Tustin

Tustin Hospital & Medical Center*
14662 Newport Avenue
(714) 838-9600

Groceries

As a region of immigrants, health nuts, and trend enthusiasts, Southern California offers a considerable spectrum of grocery stores and supermarkets. Don't come here looking for a Kroger, Tesco, Piggly Wiggly, or Publix store, though. Those stores haven't saturated Southern Cal as they have other areas.

Instead, you'll find food and other staples at these chains:

Albertson's
www1.albertsons.com/corporate/

This popular chain, more than sixty years old and located in more than thirty-five states, has stores all over Southern California.

Bristol Farms
www.bristolfarms.com

Bristol Farms stores sell gourmet and specialty foods in Brentwood, Century City, Hollywood, Long Beach, Manhattan Beach, Mission Viejo, Newport Beach, Rolling Hills, South Pasadena, Westlake Village, Westwood, and elsewhere.

Gelsons

www.gelsons.com

Gelsons is known for high quality and high prices. The stores tend to land in affluent areas, primarily in Los Angeles County, and they offer both everyday and fancy foods.

Pavilions

www.pavilions.com

An upscale supermarket—some stores have their own greenhouses or wine stewards—this chain has about thirty stores in the region.

Ralphs

www.ralphs.com

One of the area's most ubiquitous chains, Ralphs is a strong, mainstream supermarket with more than seventy locations all over Southern California.

7-Eleven

www.7-eleven.com

The prototypical convenience store is everywhere in Southern California.

Smart & Final Iris

www.smartandfinal.com

Shop where the restaurants do, buying in bulk and getting discounts. Smart & Final has more

CITY FACT

Los Angeles County is the most populous county in the United States. (Take that, New York!) According to the county's Web site, L.A. County has more people than all but eight states.

than seventy locations all over Southern California.

Stater Brothers

Known best for their meat, Stater Brothers is a full-service supermarket with locations in most of Southern California.

Trader Joe's

www.traderjoes.com

A quirky place, Trader Joe's offers discounted foods and wines from both famous brands and companies that you've never heard of. It has more than thirty stores in the area.

Vons

www.valueplus.com

This is a well-stocked supermarket, with locations all over Southern California.

Whole Foods Market

www.wholefoods.com

Whole Foods calls itself "the world's largest retailer of natural and organic foods." It has stores in Beverly Hills, Brentwood, Costa Mesa, Glendale, Pasadena, Redondo Beach, Sherman Oaks, Torrance, Tustin, West Hollywood, West Los Angeles, and Woodland Hills.

Pharmacies

For a place filled with people who take pride in being healthy via natural means such as exercising and eating right, Southern California dispenses a lot of drugs. The following list is by no means comprehensive, but it's a start.

LOS ANGELES COUNTY

Burbank

Burbank Tower Pharmacy
500 East Olive Avenue
(818) 843-2241

Rite Aid
1505 West Olive Avenue
(818) 846-7843

Chino

Gemmel Pharmacy of Chino
12163 Central Avenue
(909) 627-1581

Rite Aid
12059 Central Avenue
(909) 627-4012

Downtown/Central City (City of Los Angeles)

Horton & Converse Pharmacy
735 South Figueroa Street
(213) 623-2838

Rite Aid
501 South Broadway
(213) 628-8997

Sav-On Drugs
201 North Los Angeles Street
(213) 620-1494

Glendale

Ideal Pharmacy
1155 North Central Avenue
(818) 246-1739

Rite Aid
531 Glendale Avenue
(818) 241-9770

Western Drug
501 Western Avenue
(818) 242-5887

Hollywood (City of Los Angeles)

Ideal Pharmacy
7095 Hollywood Boulevard
(323) 851-6800

Rite Aid
6130 West Sunset Boulevard
(323) 467-4201

Lancaster

Burns Pharmacy
866 West Lancaster Boulevard
(661) 942-1461

Mel's Prescription Pharmacy
1324 West Avenue J
(661) 948-7577

Williams Pharmacy
1035 West Avenue I
(661) 948-4575

Long Beach

Abrams & Clark
3841 Atlantic Avenue
(562) 427-7901

Rite Aid
4402 Atlantic Avenue
(562) 423-0036

CITY FACT

In the 1990s, the hardest economic changes in California occurred in Los Angeles County. The state Legislative Analyst's Office revealed that the county lost more than 300,000 jobs—more than 100,000 in aerospace alone—but made gains in transportation, apparel, and services. Since 1997, construction of offices, industrial buildings, and retail stores has jumped by over a third.

Walgreens Pharmacy
3590 Atlantic Avenue
(562) 424-3963

Ward's Pharmacy
653 Long Beach Boulevard
(562) 437-0678

Ontario

Gemmel Pharmacy of Ontario
143 North Euclid Avenue
(909) 986-1129

Rite Aid
1050 North Mountain Avenue
(909) 984-3309

Palmdale

Ana Verde Pharmacy
1037 East Palmdale Boulevard
(661) 273-5553

Pasadena

California Pharmacy
555 South Lake Avenue
(626) 792-3156

Phoenix Pharmacy
2523 East Washington Boulevard
(626) 791-760

Pomona

Rite Aid
611 East Holt Avenue
(909) 623-2948

Walgreens Pharmacy
795 East Foothill Boulevard
(909) 624-3017

Santa Monica

Airport Pharmacy
3250 Pico Boulevard
(310) 450-7555

Drugtown Pharmacy
802 Seventh Street
(310) 393-9821

Horton & Converse Pharmacy
2001 Santa Monica Boulevard
(310) 829-3401

Torrance

Fox Drug
1327 El Prado
(310) 328-7244; (800) 770-3784

Medical Arts Pharmacy
20911 Earl Street
(310) 214-8282

Medical Centre Pharmacy
4201 Torrance Boulevard
(310) 540-3312

Rite Aid
240 West Sepulveda Boulevard
(310) 325-0868

855 West Sepulveda Boulevard
(310) 830-1943

1237 West Carson Street
(310) 320-4534

Van Nuys
(City of Los Angeles)

Milton's Pharmacy
14444 Burbank Boulevard
(818) 787-3600

Rite Aid
17266 Saticoy Street
(818) 345-1543

7110 Sepulveda Boulevard
(818) 782-7430

7239 Woodman Avenue
(818) 781-7127

Venice
(City of Los Angeles)

Rite Aid
888 Lincoln Boulevard
(310) 396-2838

Sav-On Drugs
219 Lincoln Boulevard
(310) 392-3983

Westlake
(City of Los Angeles)

Horton & Converse Pharmacy
201 South Alvarado Street
(213) 413-2424

Rite Aid
650 South Alvarado Street
(213) 413-2458

Westwood
(City of Los Angeles)

Rite Aid
1101 Westwood Boulevard
(310) 209-0708

Super Drug Westwood
1465 Westwood Boulevard
(310) 477-1746

CITY FACT

From 1990 to 1998, the city of Corona increased its population from almost 76,000 to about 113,000—a rise of nearly 50 percent. The U.S. Census Bureau has called Corona the fastest-growing city in Southern California and the seventh fastest-growing city in the entire United States.

ORANGE COUNTY

Anaheim

Alpha Drugs
515 South Beach Boulevard
(714) 821-8959

1240 South Magnolia Avenue
(714) 220-0373

Park Professional Pharmacy
9541 Ball Road
(714) 772-7451

Pharmacy Plus
1012 North Euclid Street
(714) 533-1337

Rite Aid
921 South Brookhurst Street
(714) 772-0240

Vista Drug
931 South Euclid Street
(714) 533-1337

White Front Pharmacy
523 West Chapman Avenue
(714) 750-5851; (714) 750-5853

Corona

Rite Aid
1208 Magnolia Avenue
(909) 278-4200

Sav-On Drugs
1183 Magnolia Avenue
(909) 272-4427

Costa Mesa

Ramsay Rexall Drugs
2246 Newport Boulevard
(949) 646-7744

Rite Aid
233 East 17th Street
(949) 646-4960

Dana Point

Longs Drugs
32575 Street of the Golden
Lantern
(949) 248-4801

Fullerton

Longs Drugs
2251 North Harbor Boulevard
(714) 871-7021

Rite Aid
1725 West Orangethorpe Avenue
(714) 525-8432

Garden Grove

Dial Drug
12015 Euchel
(714) 636-6901

Rite Aid
13822 Brookhurst Street
(714) 530-3136

9661 Chapman Avenue
(714) 530-4730

Walgreens Pharmacy
12002 Harbor Boulevard
(714) 663-2850

Huntington Beach

Rite Aid
21132 Beach Boulevard
(714) 536-8359

5881 Warner Avenue
(714) 846-5291

Walgreens Pharmacy
17502 Beach Boulevard
(714) 842-7365

9500 Garfield Avenue
(714) 593-1352

Irvine

Park Pharmacy
250 East Yale Loop, Suite C
(949) 551-7195

Lake Forest

Walgreens Pharmacy
24382 Muirlands Boulevard
(949) 598-9088

Mission Viejo

Cal-Med Pharmacy
24031A Marguerite Parkway
(949) 586-1700

Longs Drugs
27750 Santa Margarita Parkway
(949) 770-9933

Tower Pharmacy
26732 Crown Valley Parkway
(949) 364-1200

Newport Beach

Exclusive Pharmacy
4501 Birch Street
(949) 660-7244

Rite Aid
6767 Westminster Boulevard
(714) 897-8521

Orange

Longs Drugs
8520 East Chapman Avenue
(714) 633-5545

Walgreens Pharmacy
111 South Main Street
(714) 289-3650

Watson Drug
116 East Chapman Avenue
(714) 532-6315

Santa Ana

Walgreens Rxpress
3000 South Bristol Street
(714) 427-3986

Wagner Pharmacy
12254 East McFadden Avenue
(714) 547-3590

Tustin

Tustin Community Pharmacy
14642 Newport Avenue
(714) 669-4000

Walgreens Rxpress
13348 Newport Boulevard
(714) 505-6021

Houses of Worship

Southern Californians aren't all New Age crystal devotees or Hollywood sharpies who worship only Mammon. The region is filled with traditional Baptists, Lutherans, Catholics, and Christians of all types, plus Jews, Moslems, Buddhists, and Sikhs.

LOS ANGELES COUNTY

Burbank

Baptist

Calvary Baptist Church
724 South Glenoaks Boulevard
(818) 846-6723

Valley Baptist Church of Burbank
2201 West Alameda Avenue
(818) 845-7871

Catholic

Saint Finbar Catholic Church
2010 West Olive Avenue
(818) 846-6251

Christian Science

Christian Science Church
116 South San Fernando Boulevard
(818) 846-3316

Jewish

Burbank Temple Emanu El
1302 North Glenoaks Boulevard
(818) 845-1734

Temple Beth Emet Reform
600 North Buena Vista Street
(818) 843-4787

Latter-day Saints

Reorganized Church of Jesus
801 South 6th Street
(818) 843-9787

Lutheran

Christ Lutheran Church
2400 West Burbank Boulevard
(818) 846-4415

First Lutheran Church
1001 South Glenoaks Boulevard
(818) 848-7432

Methodist

Burbank First Methodist Church
700 North Glenoaks Boulevard
(818) 845-1531

Magnolia Park United Methodist Church
2828 West Magnolia Boulevard
(818) 846-2866

Presbyterian

First Presbyterian Church
521 East Olive Avenue
(818) 842-5103

Westminster Presbyterian Church
542 North Buena Vista Street
(818) 842-5264

Other Denominations

First Christian Church
221 South 6th Street
(818) 845-7459

Chino

Baptist

Pipeline Avenue Baptist Church
11548 Pipeline Avenue
(909) 628-1706

MOVING TIP

Don't forget to make proper arrangements for the transfer of your medical records. Your physician, dentist, optometrist, and veterinarian will have files containing prescriptions, dental x-rays, and immunization history. Contact the American Medical Records Association to determine your state's procedure.

Victory Baptist Church
14132 San Antonio Avenue
(909) 597-3314

Catholic

Saint Margaret Mary Catholic Church
12686 Central Avenue
(909) 627-8466

Latter-day Saints

Church of Jesus Christ of Latter-day Saints
6726 Chino Avenue
(909) 590-9309

Lutheran

Immanuel Lutheran Church in Chino
5648 Jefferson Avenue
(909) 628-2823

Methodist

Chino United Methodist Church
12909 6th Street
(909) 628-1107

Other Denominations

Centrepointe Christian Fellowship
12986 Central Avenue
(909) 393-5882

First Christian Reformed Church
6159 Riverside Drive
(909) 591-9111

New Hope Christian Fellowship
13333 Ramona Avenue
(909) 628-8612

Downtown/Central City (City of Los Angeles)

Baptist

Fundamentalist Baptist Tabernacle
1329 South Hope Street
(213) 744-9999

Catholic

Cathedral of Saint Vibiana
114 East 2nd Street
(213) 624-3941

Jewish

Sharie Tefilah
556 South Broadway
(213) 488-5148

Methodist

Centenary United Methodist Church
300 South Central Avenue
(213) 617-9097

La Plaza United Methodist Church
115 Paseo De La Plaza
(213) 628-5773

Glendale

Baptist

First Southern Baptist Church
725 North Central Avenue
(818) 246-2408

Catholic

Incarnation Catholic Church
1001 North Brand Boulevard
(818) 242-2579

Christian Science

First Church of Christ, Scientist
1320 North Brand Boulevard
(818) 242-1493

Jewish

Temple Sinai of Glendale
1212 North Pacific Avenue
(818) 246-8101

Latter-day Saints

Church of Jesus Christ of Latter-day Saints
1524 Canada Boulevard
(818) 242-2179

Lutheran

Saint Matthew's Lutheran Church
1920 West Glenoaks Boulevard
(818) 842-3138

Methodist

Emmanuel United Methodist Church/North Glendale United Methodist Church
1015 North Central Avenue
(818) 244-1979; (818) 242-6813

Presbyterian

Hana Presbyterian Church
1707 Victory Boulevard
(818) 265-1281

Other Denominations

Call to Prayer Church Ministry
229 North Central Avenue
(818) 500-8343

Central Christian Church
1479 East Broadway
(818) 242-4169

Glendale Christian Fellowship
632 West Stocker Street
(818) 247-3663

www.gncf.org

Hollywood

Baptist

Community Missionary Baptist Church
1313 North Edgemont Street
(323) 913-2085

First Baptist Church
6682 Selma Avenue
(323) 464-7343

First Southern Baptist Church
1528 North Wilton Place
(323) 466-9631

Catholic

Saint Ambrose Church
1281 North Fairfax Avenue
(323) 656-4433

Christian Science

5th Christian Science Church
7107 Hollywood Boulevard
(323) 876-7770

Jewish

Ahavas Yisroel Synagogue
731 North La Brea Avenue
(323) 937-1247

Temple Israel of Hollywood
7300 Hollywood Boulevard
(323) 876-8330

CITY FACT

The Comparative Guide to U.S. Suburbs
says that Beverly Hills has the region's
highest per capita income, followed by
Palos Verdes Estates, San Marino, Malibu,
and Newport Beach. The lowest-income
communities are Coachella, Cudahy, Bell
Gardens, Lennox, and East Los Angeles.

Latter-day Saints

Church of Jesus Christ of Latter-day Saints
1552 North Normandie Avenue
(323) 665-1352

Lutheran

Hope Lutheran Church of Hollywood
6720 Melrose Avenue
(323) 938-9135

Methodist

Crescent Heights United Methodist Church
1296 North Fairfax Avenue
(323) 656-5336

Presbyterian

West Hollywood Presbyterian Church
7350 West Sunset Boulevard
(323) 874-6646

Sikh

Sikh Temple
1966 North Vermont Avenue
(323) 665-7707

Other Denominations

Bible Christian Church
240 North Virgil Avenue, #16A
(213) 389-4864

Lancaster

Baptist

Harvest Community Church
42309 10th Street West
(661) 942-2803

www.harvestonline.com

Valley Baptist Church
44818 20th Street West
(661) 942-7322

Catholic

Sacred Heart Catholic Church
45007 Cedar Avenue
(661) 942-4830

Christian Science

Christian Science Church
44802 Fern Avenue
(661) 942-9926

Latter-day Saints

Church of Jesus Christ of Latter-day Saints
3140 West Avenue K
(661) 943-0023

Church of Jesus Christ of Latter-day Saints
1701 West Lancaster Boulevard
(661) 940-0082

Jewish

Beth Knesset Bamidbar
1611 East Avenue J
(661) 942-4415

Lutheran

Our Savior's Lutheran Church
1821 West Lancaster Boulevard
(661) 948-4115

Our Shepherd Lutheran Church
42521 20th Street West
(661) 943-1025

Methodist

Lancaster United Methodist Church
918 West Avenue J
(661) 942-0419

Presbyterian

Lancaster Presbyterian Church
1661 West Lancaster Boulevard
(661) 948-1661

Other Denominations

All People Christian Center
825 West Avenue J
(661) 949-7060

Antelope Valley Christian Center
304 West Lancaster Boulevard
(661) 949-7200

Long Beach

Baptist

Bibleway Baptist Church
2501 Pacific Avenue
(562) 432-7227

First Providence Baptist Church
801 East Hill Street
(562) 426-5840

Catholic

Saint Cornelius Church
5500 East Wardlow Road
(562) 421-8966

Christian Science

Fourth Church of Christ Scientist
3629 Atlantic Avenue
(562) 424-5562

Jewish

Temple Beth Shalom
3635 Elm Avenue
(562) 426-6413

Latter-day Saints

Church of Jesus Christ of Latter-day Saints
6979 Orange Avenue
(562) 633-0931

Lutheran

First Lutheran Kindergarten
905 Atlantic Avenue
(562) 437-8532

Methodist

First United Methodist Church
507 Pacific Avenue
(562) 437-1289

Presbyterian

Community Presbyterian Church
6380 Orange Avenue
(562) 423-0451

Other Denominations

Rock Christian Fellowship
901 Olive Avenue
(562) 432-6715

Ontario

Baptist

Calvary Baptist Church
730 North Mountain Avenue
(909) 986-0412

South Euclid Baptist Church
1960 South Euclid Avenue
(909) 986-5059

Buddhist

Buddhist Temple of America
5615 Howard Street
(909) 391-9012

Catholic

Saint George Catholic Church
325 West E Street
(909) 983-2637

Christian Science

First Church of Christ Science
1429 North Euclid Avenue
(909) 460-4907

Jewish

Temple Sholom of Ontario
963 West 6th Street
(909) 983-9661

Latter-day Saints

Church of Jesus Christ of Latter-day Saints
3450 East Creekside Drive
(909) 923-9215

Church of Jesus Christ of Latter-day Saints
522 West Francis Street
(909) 983-9419

Lutheran

First Lutheran Church of Ontario
203 East G Street
(909) 986-5178

MOVING TIP

Encourage your children to pack their own clothing and toys. However, when the truck is being loaded and unloaded, have a relative, close friend, or trusted baby-sitter keep the children away from the action.

Methodist

First United Methodist Church
918 North Euclid Avenue
(909) 986-6641

Presbyterian

Westminster Presbyterian Church
East G Street and North Sultana Avenue
(909) 986-5121

Other Denominations

Church of God of Prophecy
1130 South Campus Avenue
(909) 467-5010

Palmdale

Baptist

Baptist Church
38433 30th Street East
(661) 273-4473

Catholic

Saint Mary's Catholic Church
1600 East Avenue R4
(661) 947-3306

Christian Science

Christian Science Society
3030 East Avenue R8
(661) 947-6661

Latter-day Saints

Church of Jesus Christ of Latter-day Saints
2120 East Avenue R
(661) 273-9076

Lutheran

Saint Stephen's Lutheran Church
1737 East Avenue R
(661) 947-6451

Methodist

Palmdale United Methodist Church
39055 10th Street West
(661) 947-3103

Moslem

Masjid of Antelope Valley
1125 East Palmdale Boulevard
(661) 224-1111

Presbyterian

First Presbyterian Church
1850 East Avenue R
(661) 273-4424

Other Denominations

Christ's Church of the Valley
2714 East Avenue R
(661) 947-9570

Palmdale Christian Fellowship
950 East Palmdale Boulevard
(661) 947-8839

Pasadena

Baptist

First Baptist Church
75 North Marengo Avenue
(626) 793-7164

Mount Moriah Baptist Church
372 East Orange Grove Boulevard
(626) 792-4305; (626) 585-9486

Catholic

Saint Andrew's
311 North Raymond Avenue
(626) 792-4183

Mater Dolorosa
651 North Sierra Madre
Boulevard
(626) 564-1158

Christian Science

Christian Science Church
550 East Green Street
(626) 793-5151

Jewish

Pasadena Jewish Temple & Center
1434 North Altadena Drive
(626) 798-1161

Latter-day Saints

Church of Jesus Christ of Latter-day Saints
770 Sierra Madre Villa Avenue
(626) 351-0309

Lutheran

Hill Avenue Grace Lutheran Church
73 North Hill Avenue
(626) 792-4169

Messiah Lutheran Church
570 East Orange Grove Boulevard
(626) 795-7748

MOVING TIP

Keep items designated for commercial storage together, either in the front or rear of the truck, depending on whether the first stop is your new home or the storage facility.

Methodist

First United Methodist Church
500 East Colorado Boulevard
(626) 796-0157

Scott United Methodist Church
444 North Orange Grove Boulevard
(626) 795-7511

Other Denominations

New Harvest Christian Fellowship
2007 East Foothill Boulevard
(626) 793-3098

Vision Christian Fellowship
464 East Walnut Street
(626) 304-2688

Pomona

Baptist

First Baptist Church of Pomona
601 North Garey Avenue
(909) 629-5277

White Avenue Baptist Church
675 South White Avenue
(909) 622-2234

Catholic

Saint Joseph's Catholic Church
1150 West Holt Avenue
(909) 629-410

Jewish

Temple Beth Israel
3033 North Towne Avenue
(909) 626-1277

www.tbipomona.org

Latter-day Saints

Church of Jesus Christ of Latter-day Saints
175 West Willow Street
(909) 623-9182

Lutheran

Saint Paul's Lutheran Church
610 North San Antonio Avenue
(909) 623-6368

Methodist

Covenant United Methodist Church
1750 North Towne Avenue
(909) 622-3969

Primm AME Church
1956 South Towne Avenue
(909) 627-0818

Presbyterian

First Presbyterian Church
401 North Gibbs Street
(909) 622-1542

South Hills Presbyterian Church
1170 Fremont Street
(909) 629-0492

Santa Monica

Baptist

Mount Hermon Baptist Church
1827 Pico Boulevard
(310) 450-1777

Catholic

Saint Anne's Catholic Church
2013 Colorado Avenue
(310) 829-4411

Jewish

Kehillat Ma'arav
1715 21st Street
(310) 829-0566

Santa Monica Synagogue
1448 18th Street
(310) 453-4276

Latter-day Saints

Church of Jesus Christ of Latter-day Saints
1257 Centinela Avenue
(310) 828-1718

Lutheran

Saint Paul's Lutheran Church
958 Lincoln Boulevard
(310) 451-1346

Mount Olive Lutheran Church
1343 Ocean Park Boulevard
(310) 452-1116

Methodist

First United Methodist Church
1008 11th Street
(310) 395-7292

Presbyterian

First Presbyterian Church
1220 2nd Street
(310) 451-1303

Other Denominations

Santa Monica Four Square Church
2221 Lincoln Boulevard
(310) 396-9800

Vineyard Christian Fellowship
2716 Ocean Park Boulevard, #3082
(310) 581-9924

Torrance

Baptist

Bethel Baptist Church
1501 West Carson Street
(310) 320-8505

Crenshaw Baptist Church
18749 Crenshaw Boulevard
(310) 323-2115

Catholic

Saint Catherine Laboure Church
3846 Redondo Beach Boulevard
(323) 323-8900

Christian Science

Christian Science Church
1409 Marcelina Avenue
(310) 328-2324

Latter-day Saints

Church of Jesus Christ of Latter-day Saints
2000 Artesia Boulevard
(310) 323-5510

Lutheran

First Evangelical Lutheran Church
2900 West Carson Street
(310) 320-9920

CITY FACT

For a small town, West Hollywood is crowded. Nando Travel, a British travel advisory firm, notes that the city's 1.9 square miles contain more than 100 restaurants.

Methodist

Hope United Methodist Church
3405 Artesia Boulevard
(310) 323-1012

Presbyterian

Torrance First Presbyterian Church
1880 Crenshaw Boulevard
(310) 618-2222

Other Denominations

South Bay Seventh-Day Church
4400 Del Amo Boulevard
(310) 670-4222

South Bay Vineyard Christian Fellowship
22301 South Western Avenue, #103
(310) 328-2251

Van Nuys (City of Los Angeles)

Baptist

Korean Valley First Baptist Church
15520 Sherman Way
(818) 779-0247

Catholic

Saint Bridget of Sweden Church
16711 Gault Street
(818) 782-7180

Christian Science

Christian Science Church
14654 Hamlin Street
(818) 785-1866

Jewish

Chabad of North Hollywood
13079 Chandler Boulevard
(818) 989-9539

Latter-day Saints

Church of Jesus Christ of Latter-day Saints
14001 Burbank Boulevard
(818) 989-1462

Lutheran

First Lutheran Church
6952 Van Nuys Boulevard
(818) 989-5844

Methodist

Van Nuys United Methodist Church
6260 Tyrone Avenue
(818) 785-3256

Presbyterian

Presbyterian Church
14701 Friar Street
(818) 786-6230

Other Denominations

Church of the Valley
6565 Vesper Avenue
(818) 786-4070

Venice

Baptist

Second Community Baptist Church
1041 Abbot Kinney Boulevard
(310) 392-5632

Catholic

Saint Mark's Catholic Church
940 Coeur D'Alene Avenue
(310) 821-5058

Christian Science

Christian Science Church
132 Brooks Avenue
(310) 396-1390

Jewish

Mishkon Tephilo Synagogue
206 Main Street
(310) 399-9652

Lutheran

First Lutheran Church-Venice
815 Venice Boulevard
(310) 821-2740

Methodist

Venice United Methodist Church
1020 Victoria Avenue
(310) 391-2314

Other Denominations

Hope Christian Fellowship
1400 Riviera Avenue
(310) 392-5144

Westlake
(City of Los Angeles)

Baptist

Berendo Street Baptist Church
975 South Berendo Street
(213) 383-4982

Salem Baptist Church
729 South Park View Street
(213) 738-1077

Buddhist

Buddhist Peace Temple
1131 South Hoover Street
(213) 736-0077

Catholic

Our Lady of Loretto
250 North Union Avenue
(213) 483-3013

Precious Blood Church
435 South Occidental Boulevard
(213) 389-8439

Christian Science

3rd Christian Science Church
730 South Hope Street
(213) 623-2185

Lutheran

Angelica Lutheran Church
1345 South Burlington Avenue
(213) 382-6378

New City Parish
1340 South Bonnie Brae Street
(213) 387-9037

Methodist

Echo Park United Methodist Church
1226 North Alvarado Street
(213) 484-8214

Presbyterian

Los Angeles Presbyterian Church
2533 West 3rd Street
(213) 386-4790

Other Denominations

Congregational Christian Church
2400 West Temple Street
(213) 383-4321

Joy Christian Fellowship
1645 Beverly Boulevard
(213) 977-1067

Reigning with Jesus Christian Church
1925 West Temple Street
(213) 413-1243

Westwood (City of Los Angeles)

Catholic

Saint Martin of Tours
11967 West Sunset Boulevard
(310) 476-7403

Christian Scientist

28th Church of Christ Scientist
1018 Hilgard Avenue
(310) 208-8189

Jewish

Sinai Temple
10400 Wilshire Boulevard
(310) 474-1518

Latter-day Saints

Church of Jesus Christ of Latter-day Saints
10777 Santa Monica Boulevard
(310) 475-7018

Lutheran

University Lutheran Chapel
10915 Strathmore Drive
(310) 208-4579

Methodist

Westwood United Methodist Church
10497 Wilshire Boulevard
(310) 475-4818

Presbyterian

University Presbyterian Church
900 Hilgard Avenue
(310) 208-3991

Westwood Presbyterian Church
10822 Wilshire Boulevard
(310) 474-4535

CITY FACT

Orange County is the newest of the Southern California counties, having been incorporated in 1889. Until then, it had been part of Los Angeles County, which was incorporated in 1850.

Other Denominations

Westwood Hills Christian Church
10808 Le Conte Avenue
(310) 208-8576

ORANGE COUNTY

Anaheim

Baptist

First Baptist Church of Anaheim
701 West Broadway
(714) 774-4444

Catholic

Annunciation Byzantine Catholic Church
319 North Harbor Boulevard
(714) 533-6292

Jewish

Temple Beth Emet
1770 West Cerritos Avenue
(714) 772-4720
www.tbe-anaheim.org

Latter-day Saints

Church of Jesus Christ of Latter-day Saints
2446 West Orange Avenue
(714) 826-3390

Lutheran

Mighty Fortress Lutheran Church
1557 West Katella Avenue
(714) 995-6301

Prince of Peace Missouri Synod
1421 West Ball Road
(714) 774-0993

Methodist

Anaheim United Methodist Church
1000 South State College Boulevard
(714) 776-5710

West Anaheim United Methodist Church
2045 West Ball Road
(714) 772-6030

Presbyterian

First Presbyterian Church of Anaheim
310 West Broadway
(714) 535-2176
www.angelfire.com/nv/anaheimpres/

New Life Mission Church
101 East Orangethorpe Avenue
(714) 879-9712

Other Denominations

Anaheim First Christian Church
520 West South Street
(714) 635-9330

Ethiopian Christian Church
819 South Harbor Boulevard
(714) 535-6985

Corona

Baptist

Grace Baptist Church of Corona
2781 South Lincoln Avenue
(909) 736-7466

West Grand Baptist Church
709 West Grand Boulevard
(909) 737-2442

Catholic

Saint Matthew's Catholic Church
2140 West Ontario Avenue
(909) 737-1621

Jewish

Temple Beth Sholom
823 South Sheridan Street
(909) 734-4033

Latter-day Saints

Church of Jesus Christ of Latter-day Saints
6313 Archibald Street
(909) 735-0754

Lutheran

Grace Lutheran Church
1811 South Lincoln Avenue
(909) 737-2187

Methodist

Corona United Methodist Church
114 East 10th Street
(909) 737-5225

Presbyterian

First Presbyterian Church
950 West Ontario Avenue
(909) 734-1920

Other Denominations

Inland Vineyard Church/Vineyard Christian Fellowship
268 North Lincoln Avenue, #17
(909) 549-1192

New Hope Worship Center
804 South Lincoln Avenue
(909) 737-4673

Costa Mesa

Baptist

Harbor Trinity Baptist Church
1230 Baker Street
(714) 556-7787

Catholic

Saint John the Baptist Roman Catholic Church
1015 Baker Street
(714) 540-2214

Latter-day Saints

Church of Jesus Christ of Latter-day Saints
333 Merrimac Way
(714) 546-9300

Lutheran

Christ Lutheran Church
760 Victoria Street
(949) 631-1611

Prince of Peace Lutheran Church
2987 Mesa Verde Drive East
(714) 549-0521

Methodist

First United Methodist Church
420 West 19th Street
(949) 548-7727

Mesa Verde United Methodist Church
1701 Baker Street
(714) 979-8234

Presbyterian

Presbyterian Church of the Covenant
2850 Fairview Road
(714) 557-3340

Other Denominations

Arabic Assembly
777 West 19th Street
(949) 642-9673

Vineyard Christian Fellowship
102 Baker Street East
(714) 556-8463

Fullerton

Baptist

Emanuel Baptist Church
601 East Valencia Drive
(714) 738-7761

Catholic

Saint Mary's Church
400 West Commonwealth Avenue
(714) 525-2500

Latter-day Saints

Church of Jesus Christ of Latter-day Saints
801 North Raymond Avenue
(714) 871-6060

Jewish

Temple Beth Tikvah
1600 North Acacia Avenue
(714) 871-3535

Lutheran

Fullerton First Lutheran Church
215 North Lemon Street
(714) 871-7820

Saint Paul's Lutheran Church
111 West Las Palmas Drive
(714) 879-8290

Methodist

Orangethorpe United Methodist Church
2351 West Orangethorpe Avenue
(714) 526-8317

Presbyterian

First Presbyterian Church
838 North Euclid Street
(714) 526-7701

Garden Grove

Buddhist

Won Buddhism Orange County Temple
13091 Brookhurst Street
(714) 638-0404

Latter-day Saints

Church of Jesus Christ of Latter-day Saints
10212 Stanford Avenue
(714) 636-0130

Methodist

Glory Church Korean Methodist Church
9851 Bixby Avenue
(714) 530-1313

Presbyterian

Sansung Presbyterian Church
9596 Garden Grove Boulevard
(714) 537-0537

Other Denominations

Brazilian Evangelical Church/Living Spring Christian Church
9851 Bixby Avenue
(714) 537-4105; (714) 539-1232
www.livingspring.com

Faith United Church of Christ
9621 Bixby Avenue
(714) 539-1131

Huntington Beach

Baptist

Calvary Baptist Church
8281 Garfield Avenue
(714) 962-6860

Central Baptist Church
7661 Warner Avenue
(714) 848-5511

Saint Vincent De Paul Baptist Church
8345 Talbert Avenue
(714) 842-3000

Catholic

Saints Simon & Jude
20444 Magnolia Street
(714) 962-3333

Saint Vincent De Paul Catholic Church
8345 Talbert Avenue
(714) 842-3000

Christian Science

Christian Science Church
18051 Beach Boulevard
(714) 847-6610

Jewish

Chabad of West Orange County
5052 Warner Avenue
(714) 846-2285

Latter-day Saints

Church of Jesus Christ of Latter-day Saints
6531 McFadden Avenue
(714) 891-4568

Church of Jesus Christ of Latter-day Saints
19191 17th Street
(714) 842-7359

Lutheran

Grace Lutheran Church
6931 Edinger Avenue
(714) 897-0361

Methodist

First United Methodist Church
2721 Delaware Street
(714) 536-3537

Presbyterian

Christ Presbyterian Church
20112 Magnolia Street
(714) 968-4940

Other Denominations

Church of Religious Science
7641 Talbert Avenue
(714) 969-1331

Kingdom Hall-Jehovah's Witnesses
7851 Talbert Avenue
(714) 847-4006

Stonebridge Christian Church
5555 McFadden Avenue
(714) 897-3583

Irvine

Baptist

Pacific Church of Irvine
15 Orange Tree
(949) 552-6774

Catholic

Saint John Neumann Catholic Church
5101 Alton Parkway
(949) 559-4006

Christian Science

Christian Science Church
25 Orange Tree
(949) 262-9540

Jewish

University Synagogue
4915 Alton Parkway
(949) 654-2720

Latter-day Saints

Church of Jesus Christ of Latter-day Saints
23 Lake Road
(949) 786-9091

Lutheran

Shepherd of Peace Lutheran Church
18182 Culver Drive
(949) 786-3326

Moslem

Islamic Educational Center
17945 Sky Park Circle
(949) 222-0320

Presbyterian

Irvine Presbyterian Church
4445 Alton Parkway
(949) 786-9627

Other Denominations

Creekside Christian Fellowship
4849 Alton Parkway
(949) 786-4849

Irvine United Church of Christ
4915 Alton Parkway
(949) 733-0220
www.iucc.org

Lake Forest

Baptist

El Toro Baptist Church/ International Baptist Church
23302 El Toro Road
(949) 830-7473; (949) 830-4859

Catholic

Santiago De Compostela Church
21682 Lake Forest Drive
(949) 951-8599

Latter-day Saints

Church of Jesus Christ of Latter-day Saints
24755 Trabuco Road
(949) 380-9944

Lutheran

Abiding Savior Lutheran Church
23262 El Toro Road
(949) 830-1461

www.abidingsavior.com

Other Denominations

Grace Community Church
26052 Trabuco Road
(949) 581-4248

Kingdom Hall–Jehovah's Witnesses
23051 El Toro Road
(949) 951-8034

Orange

Baptist

First Southern Baptist Church
840 North Shattuck Place
(714) 639-2070

Gospel Truth Fellowship
1419 East Collins Avenue
(714) 771-9865

Catholic

Saint Norbert Catholic Church
300 East Taft Avenue
(714) 637-4360

Christian Science

Christian Science Church
1424 East Walnut Avenue
(714) 532-4301

Lutheran

Grace Lutheran Church/Our Saviour's Lutheran Church
800 North Cambridge Street
(714) 639-6658

Methodist

First United Methodist Church
161 South Orange Street
(714) 532-6363

www.fumco.org

Presbyterian

Covenant Presbyterian Church
1855 North Orange Olive Road
(714) 998-6650

Other Denominations

Church of the Living God
826 West Katella Avenue
(714) 532-6525

Cornerstone Bible Church
681 South Tustin Street, #108
(714) 633-8676

Santa Ana

Baptist

Bethel Baptist Church
901 South Euclid Street
(714) 839-3600

Second Baptist Church of Santa Ana
1915 West McFadden Avenue
(714) 541-4155

Catholic

Saint Anne's Church
1344 South Main Street
(714) 835-7434

Saint Barbara's Catholic Church
5304 West McFadden Avenue
(714) 531-5868

Saint Barbara's Catholic Church
730 South Euclid Street
(714) 775-7733

Christian Science

Christian Science Church
920 North Main Street
(714) 542-5521

Jewish

Temple Beth Sholom-Orange County
2625 North Tustin Avenue
(714) 771-9229

Latter-day Saints

Church of Jesus Christ of Latter-day Saints
2500 North Bristol Street
(714) 547-4546

Lutheran

Calvary Lutheran Church
5321 West McFadden Avenue
(714) 775-5758

Methodist

First United Methodist Church
609 North Spurgeon Street
(714) 542-2322

Moslem

Darul-Uloom Falah-E-Darain
720 North Fairview Street
(714) 953-6219

Presbyterian

First Presbyterian Church
600 North Main Street
(714) 542-7253

Sikh

Sikh Temple of Orange County
2514 West Warner Avenue
(714) 641-9034

MOVING TIP

Fill some disposable containers with household cleaners and keep them handy during the move. Your old place will need a once-over, and there's no better time to freshen up the new home than before the furniture arrives.

Other Denominations

Elim Christian Church
2829 West 1st Street
(714) 835-0597

First Apostolic Church
308 North Main Street
(714) 664-0448

First Christian Church
1720 West 17th Street
(714) 547-4173

Tustin

Baptist

Chinese Baptist Church
13841 Red Hill Avenue
(714) 669-1700

Jewish

Congregation B'Nai Israel
2111 Bryan Avenue
(714) 730-9693

Lutheran

Red Hill Lutheran Church
13200 Red Hill Avenue
(714) 544-3131

Latter-day Saints

Church of Jesus Christ of Latter-day Saints
1800 San Juan Street
(714) 838-5112

Presbyterian

Great World Presbyterian Church
655 South Boulevard
(714) 573-1546

Other Denominations

Church of Scientology
1451 Irvine Boulevard
(714) 544-5491

Main Place Christian Fellowship/Serrano Hills Community Church
13841 Red Hill Avenue
(714) 505-1734; (714) 771-0600

www.serranohills.com

Post Offices

LOS ANGELES COUNTY

Burbank
2140 North Hollywood Way
(818) 846-3155

Chino
5375 Walnut Avenue
(909) 627-3631

Downtown
(City of Los Angeles)

505 South Flower Street
(213) 629-3777

300 North Los Angeles Street
(213) 617-4409

760 North Main Street
(213) 617-4641

100 West Olympic Boulevard
(213) 627-2639

1122 East 7th Street
(213) 622-8008

508 South Spring Street
(213) 622-1357

819 West Washington Boulevard
(213) 749-9131

Glendale
313 East Broadway
(818) 502-3202

120 East Chevy Chase Drive
(818) 265-9251

101 North Verdugo Road
(818) 265-9252

840 Sonora Avenue
(818) 265-9254

1009 North Pacific Avenue
(818) 265-9257

339 North Central Avenue
(818) 265-9202

Hollywood
(City of Los Angeles)
1615 Wilcox Avenue
(323) 464-2194

1425 North Cherokee Avenue
(323) 460-4819

6457 Santa Monica Boulevard
(323) 466-7381

1825 North Vermont Avenue
(323) 660-3240

1125 North Fairfax Avenue
(323) 654-6902

Lancaster
2763 West Avenue L
(661) 722-4555

567 West Lancaster Boulevard
(661) 948-4170

1008 West Avenue J2
(661) 948-1691

Long Beach
2300 Redondo Avenue
(562) 494-2300

300 Long Beach Boulevard
(562) 983-3056

Ontario
1555 East Holt Boulevard
(909) 983-1873

Palmdale
38917 20th Street East
(661) 266-2800

846 West Palmdale Boulevard
(661) 947-9716

Pasadena
80 Valley Street
(626) 304-7145

281 East Colorado Boulevard
(626) 304-7125

600 Lincoln Avenue
(626) 304-7122

99 West California Boulevard
(626) 304-7126

1355 North Mentor Avenue
(626) 304-7128

2609 East Colorado Boulevard
(626) 304-7129

967 East Colorado Boulevard
(626) 304-7127

Van Nuys
(City of Los Angeles)
6230 Van Nuys Boulevard
(818) 778-1800

Pomona
2138 North Garey Avenue
(909) 593-6711

580 West Monterey Avenue
(909) 623-4476

Santa Monica
2720 Neilson Way
(310) 576-2620

1217 Wilshire Boulevard
(310) 576-2616

1248 5th Street
(310) 576-2626

1020 Colorado Avenue
(310) 576-2606

1025 Colorado Avenue
(310) 576-2610

Torrance

3856 Sepulveda Boulevard
(310) 373-6751

1433 Marcelina Avenue
(310) 320-0587

18080 Crenshaw Boulevard
(310) 324-8709

2510 Monterey Street
(310) 222-5900

Venice

1601 Main Street
(800) 275-8777

Westlake
(City of Los Angeles)

1525 North Alvarado Street
(213) 413-3838

2462 West Pico Boulevard
(213) 382-7348

1808 West 7th Street
(213) 483-3502

Westwood
(City of Los Angeles)

11000 Wilshire Boulevard
(800) 275-8777

ORANGE COUNTY

Anaheim

701 North Loara Street
(714) 520-2601

Corona

414 West Grand Boulevard
(909) 737-0451

Costa Mesa

1590 Adams Avenue
(714) 546-5330

2230 Fairview Road
(949) 646-3474

Dana Point

24551 Del Prado
(949) 496-5832

Fullerton

202 East Commonwealth Avenue
(714) 879-1827

1920 West Commonwealth
Avenue
(714) 526-3894

1820 Sunnycrest Drive
(714) 871-1102

1350 East Chapman Avenue
(714) 525-2787

Garden Grove

11947 Valley View Street
(714) 897-5211

10441 Stanford Avenue
(714) 537-1301

Huntington Beach
316 Olive Avenue
(714) 536-2563

9151 Atlanta Avenue
(714) 963-0791

6771 Warner Avenue
(714) 847-5665

Irvine
15642 Sand Canyon Avenue
(949) 453-4900

17192 Murphy Avenue
(949) 474-0407

14982 Sand Canyon Avenue
(949) 551-4870

4255 Campus Drive
(949) 854-1122

Lake Forest
24552 Raymond Way
(800) 275-8777

Mission Viejo
28081 Marguerite Parkway
(949) 364-5020

Orange
2683 North Orange Olive Road
(714) 282-1245

3744 East Chapman Avenue
(714) 639-0980

308 West Chapman Avenue
(714) 744-1645

1075 North Tustin Street
(714) 997-1255

Santa Ana
34 Civic Center Plaza
(714) 836-2500

1609 North King Street
(714) 835-3397

1620 West 1st Street
(714) 541-3137

2201 North Grand Avenue
(714) 667-6776

1517 South Greenville Street
(714) 545-7030

2230 South Grand Avenue
(714) 641-0261

3101 West Sunflower Avenue
(714) 662-6200

1415 South Main Street
(714) 836-1369

Tustin
340 East 1st Street
(714) 544-5170

CHAPTER 10

Local Schools and Colleges

Southern California is thick with schools. Their quality varies, from those with falling test scores in parts of the Los Angeles Unified School District to those that deliver outstanding education to Irvine's students.

As with anything else in Southern California, the answers to your educational needs are here if you look for them. The list of schools following is by no means complete—a comprehensive list would fill volumes—but it gives you a strong head start.

For more information, contact the State of California's Department of Education by calling (916) 323-0611 or sending an e-mail to *edsec@ose.ca.gov*. You can also look up the department's Web site at *www.ca.gov/edu_index.shtml*.

Preschools and Day Care Centers

LOS ANGELES COUNTY

Burbank

Kedren Headstart & Preschool
2828 West Magnolia Boulevard
(818) 567-4682

Killgore Kiddie Kamp
2207 West Burbank Boulevard
(818) 842-5437

Partners In Learning Preschool
3821 West Victory Boulevard
(818) 846-5531

Chino

Children's World Learning Center
6010 Riverside Drive
(909) 591-0473

Childtime Children's Center
3656 Riverside Drive
(909) 591-9169

Rainbow Canyon Preschool
4122 Chino Avenue
(909) 591-4476

Glendale

Bonnie Day Nursery School
534 West Glenoaks Boulevard
(818) 244-3241

Glendale Employers Day Care
1015 North Central Avenue
(818) 240-0718

Glendale Preschool & Kindergarten
225 South Verdugo Road
(818) 244-4567

Hollywood (City of Los Angeles)

Hollywood Little Red Schoolhouse
1248 North Highland Avenue
(323) 465-1320

Komitas Day Care Center
1645 North Normandie Avenue
(323) 666-1520

Lancaster

A Child's Place
747 West Avenue J12
(661) 723-6722

Kinder Care Learning Center
43536 22nd Street West
(661) 948-3570

Long Beach

Creative Arts School
1423 Walnut Avenue
(562) 591-2508

Oakwood Pre-School
2650 Pacific Avenue
(562) 424-4994

Ontario

Kinder Care Learning Center
2140 South Euclid Avenue
(909) 983-5007

YMCA
1140 North Corona Avenue
(909) 986-6634

Palmdale

Children's World Learning Center
3035 East Avenue S
(661) 947-0703
www.childrensworld.com

YMCA School Age Child Care
38620 33rd Street East
(661) 538-1025

Pasadena

Children's Center at Caltech
293 South Chester Avenue
(626) 793-7308

Kids Klub Pasadena
380 South Raymond Avenue
(626) 795-2501

Pomona

Peter Piper School
703 North Huntington Boulevard
(909) 629-9304

Phillips Ranch Youth World
4 Village Loop Road, #A1
(909) 622-5798

Santa Monica

Cornerstone Children's Center
1620 26th Street, #1020
(310) 449-0047

Rogers School Age Program
2401 14th Street
(310) 399-6950

MOVING TIP

Keep a phone book from the city you left. No matter how well you planned your relocation, there will be loose ends to tie up. You'll want to share your relocation adventures with old friends, and the last thing you need is a big bill for directory assistance.

Santa Monica Preschool
2615 Santa Monica Boulevard
(310) 315-1982

Torrance

Busy Bee's Preschool
1215 Crenshaw Boulevard
(310) 328-6313

Hickory Tree School
21720 Madrona Avenue
(310) 533-4830

YMCA Torrance South Bay
2900 Sepulveda Boulevard
(310) 329-0824

Van Nuys
(City of Los Angeles)

Serendipity School
14125 Burbank Boulevard
(818) 785-8574

Sherman Oaks Nursery School
5520 Van Nuys Boulevard
(818) 787-6481

Venice
(City of Los Angeles)

Mercado Home Day Care
2428 Walnut Avenue
(310) 574-3239

Westlake
(City of Los Angeles)

Good Beginnings
1839 South Hoover Street
(213) 747-6254

Head Start at Inner City
1322 South New Hampshire
Avenue
(213) 487-9565

Westwood
(City of Los Angeles)

STAR Inc.
1541½ Westwood Boulevard
(310) 445-1428

ORANGE COUNTY

Anaheim

Childtime Children's Center
1000 South State College
Boulevard
(714) 772-7225

Kinder Care Learning Center
2560 East La Palma Avenue
(714) 991-5443

YMCA Children's Station
100 South Atchison Street
(714) 774-5437;
(714) 239-2825

Corona

Kinder Care
1187 Magnolia Avenue
(909) 734-7800

La Petite Academy
1421 Rimpau Avenue
(909) 736-8570

YMCA
1331 River Road
(909) 736-9622

Costa Mesa

Little Star Children's Center
2501 Harbor Boulevard, #33
(949) 645-0365

Step By Step
2525 Fairview Road
(714) 966-5264

Fullerton

Fullerton Child Development
1701 East Chapman Avenue
(714) 526-7855

YMCA
2000 Youth Way
(714) 879-9622

Garden Grove

Garden Grove First Pre-School
8461 Garden Grove Boulevard
(714) 537-8900

World Daycare Center
12345 Euclid Street
(714) 537-8291

Huntington Beach

Kinder Care Learning Center
19342 Beach Boulevard
(714) 964-2569

La Petite Academy
19860 Beach Boulevard
(714) 962-0339

YMCA
19231 Harding Lane
(714) 968-6163

Irvine

Childtime Children's Center
4876 Irvine Center Drive
(949) 551-4533

Kinder Care Learning Center
26 Lake Road
(949) 857-1263

Lake Forest

Years of Discovery Preschool
24442 Muirlands Boulevard
(949) 830-7900

Mission Viejo

La Petite Academy
23421 Madero
(949) 458-7567

Orange

YMCA
2241 East Palmyra Avenue
(714) 633-9622

YWCA ASAP Program
3022 East Vine Avenue, #A
(714) 744-2653

Santa Ana

Katharine Irvine Day School
1002 West 2nd Street
(714) 541-8164

Storybook Pre-School
1032 North Ross Street
(714) 541-9378

Tustin

Aldersgate Children's Center
1201 Irvine Boulevard
(714) 544-5510

Newport Avenue Preschool
13682 Newport Avenue
(714) 730-3424

YMCA
12712 Elizabeth Way
(714) 544-0173

Elementary Schools

LOS ANGELES COUNTY

Burbank

Disney Elementary School
1220 West Orange Grove Avenue
(818) 558-5385

Edison Elementary School
2110 Chestnut Street
(818) 558-4644

Harte Elementary School
3200 West Jeffries Avenue
(818) 558-5533

McKinley Elementary School
349 West Valencia Avenue
(818) 558-5477

Providencia Elementary School
1919 North Ontario Street
(818) 558-5470

Roosevelt Elementary School
850 North Cordova Street
(818) 558-4668

Stevenson Elementary School
3333 West Oak Street
(818) 558-5522

Chino

Countrywood Elementary School
5001 Riverside Drive
(909) 627-8827

Dickson Elementary School
3930 Pamela Drive
(909) 591-2653

El Rancho Elementary School
5862 C Street
(909) 627-9496

Gerald F. Litel Elementary School
3425 Eucalyptus Avenue
(909) 591-1336

Gird Elementary School
4980 Riverside Drive
(909) 627-9638

Newman Elementary School
4150 Walnut Avenue
(909) 627-9758

Walnut Avenue Elementary School
5550 Walnut Avenue
(909) 627-9817

Downtown/Central City (City of Los Angeles)

Castelar Elementary School
840 Yale Street
(213) 626-3674

Esperanza Elementary School
680 Little Street
(213) 484-0326

Ninth Street Elementary School
820 Towne Avenue
(213) 622-0669

San Pedro Street Elementary School
1635 South San Pedro Street
(213) 747-9538

Tenth Street Elementary School
1000 Grattan Street
(213) 380-8990

Glendale

Columbus Elementary School
425 Milford Street
(818) 242-7722

John Marshall Elementary School
1201 East Broadway
(818) 242-6834

Mark Keppel Elementary School
730 Glenwood Road
(818) 244-2113

R. D. White Elementary School
744 East Doran Street
(818) 241-2164

Hollywood (City of Los Angeles)

Cheremoya Avenue Elementary School
6017 Franklin Avenue
(323) 464-1722

CITY FACT

The least expensive homes within Los Angeles County are in such communities as Compton, Pomona, Lancaster, Lynwood, Hawaiian Gardens, East Los Angeles, Paramount, and Palmdale. The cheapest houses in Orange County are for sale in Stanton, Santa Ana, Garden Grove, and La Habra.

Grant Elementary School
1530 North Wilton Place
(323) 469-4046

Santa Monica Boulevard Elementary School
1022 North Van Ness Avenue
(323) 469-0971

Selma Avenue Elementary School
6611 Selma Avenue
(323) 461-9418

Vine Street Elementary School
955 Vine Street
(323) 469-0877

Lancaster

Del Sur Elementary School
9023 West Avenue H
(661) 942-0488

Desert View Elementary School
1555 West Avenue H10
(661) 942-9521

Jack Northrop Elementary School
831 East Avenue K2
(661) 945-9839

Mariposa Elementary School
737 West Avenue H6
(661) 942-0437

Monte Vista Elementary School
1235 West Kettering Street
(661) 942-1477

Sierra Elementary School
747 West Avenue J12
(661) 942-9536

Sundown Elementary School
6151 West Avenue J8
(661) 722-3026

Sunnydale Elementary School
1233 West Avenue J8
(661) 948-2636

Long Beach

Burnett Elementary School
565 East Hill Street
(562) 595-9466

Lafayette Elementary School
2445 Chestnut Avenue
(562) 426-7075

Newcomb Elementary School
3351 Val Verde Avenue
(562) 493-3596

Roosevelt Elementary School
1574 Linden Avenue
(562) 599-1888

Signal Hill Elementary School
2285 Walnut Avenue
(562) 426-8170

Whittier Elementary School
1761 Walnut Avenue
(562) 599-3111

Ontario

Bon View Elementary School
2121 South Bon View Avenue
(909) 947-3932

Central Elementary School
415 East G Street
(909) 983-8522

Del Norte Elementary School
850 North Del Norte Avenue
(909) 986-9515

Euclid Elementary School
1120 South Euclid Avenue
(909) 984-5119

Levi H. Dickey Elementary School
2840 South Parco Avenue
(909) 947-6693

Lincoln Elementary School
440 North Allyn Avenue
(909) 983-9803

Mariposa Elementary School
1605 East D Street
(909) 983-4116

Sultana Elementary School
1845 South Sultana Avenue
(909) 986-1215

Palmdale

Barrel Springs Elementary School
37230 37th Street East
(661) 285-9270

Buena Vista Elementary School
37230 37th Street East
(661) 285-4158

Cactus Elementary School
38060 20th Street East
(661) 273-0847

Chaparral Elementary School
37500 50th Street East
(661) 285-9777

Cimarron Elementary School
36940 45th Street East
(661) 285-9780

Daisy Gibson Elementary School
9650 East Palmdale Boulevard
(661) 944-6590

Desert Rose Elementary School
37730 27th Street East
(661) 272-0584

Manzanita Elementary School
38620 33rd Street East
(661) 947-3128

Mesquite Elementary School
37622 43rd Street East
(661) 285-8376

Quail Valley Elementary School
37500 50th Street East
(661) 533-6215

Wildflower Elementary School
38136 35th Street East
(661) 272-1571

Pasadena

Hamilton Elementary School
2089 Rose Villa Street
(626) 793-0678

Jefferson Elementary School
1500 East Villa Street
(626) 793-0656

Madison Elementary School
515 East Ashtabula Street
(626) 793-1181

Pomona

Decker Elementary School
20 Village Loop Road
(909) 397-4585

Harrison Elementary School
425 East Harrison Avenue
(909) 397-4601

Lexington Elementary School
550 West Lexington Avenue
(909) 397-4616

Madison Elementary School
351 West Phillips Boulevard
(909) 397-4644

Mendoza Elementary School
851 South Hamilton Boulevard
(909) 397-4648

Ranch Hills Elementary School
2 Trabuco Road
(909) 397-4978

Westmont Elementary School
1780 West 9th Street
(909) 397-4680

Santa Monica

P.S. No. 1 Elementary School
1454 Euclid Street
(310) 394-1313

Will Rogers Elementary School
2401 14th Street
(310) 452-2364

Torrance

Edison Elementary School
3800 West 182nd Street
(310) 533-4513

Fern Elementary School
1314 Fern Avenue
(310) 533-4506

Halldale Avenue Elementary School
21514 Halldale Avenue
(310) 328-3100

MOVING TIP

Before Moving Day, master the art of tying a secure, standard, and easily released knot. Take a moment to teach this skill to one another, and stick with it throughout the move. This is especially important if you will be staying at motels along the way. Obscure knots aren't safe, and they take a long time to untie.

Hickory Elementary School
2800 West 227th Street
(310) 533-4470

Lincoln Elementary School
2418 West 166th Street
(310) 533-4464

Torrance Elementary School
2125 Lincoln Avenue
(310) 533-4500

Van Nuys
(City of Los Angeles)

**Bassett Street Elementary
School**
15756 Bassett Street
(818) 782-1340

Chandler Elementary School
14030 Weddington Street
(818) 789-6173

**Sylvan Park Elementary
School**
6238 Noble Avenue
(818) 988-4020

Van Nuys Elementary School
6464 Sylmar Avenue
(818) 785-2195

Venice
(City of Los Angeles)

Broadway Elementary School
1015 Lincoln Boulevard
(310) 392-4944

**Coeur D'Alene Avenue
Elementary School**
810 Coeur D'Alene Avenue
(310) 821-7813

**Westminster Avenue
Elementary School**
1010 Abbot Kinney Boulevard
(310) 392-3041

Westlake
(City of Los Angeles)

**Hobart Boulevard Elementary
School**
980 South Hobart Boulevard
(213) 386-8661

Leo Politi Elementary School
2481 West 11th Street
(213) 480-1244

**Los Angeles New Elementary
School**
1211 South Hobart Boulevard
(323) 734-8233

**Magnolia Avenue Elementary
School**
1626 Orchard Avenue
(213) 748-6281

Westwood
(City of Los Angeles)

**Fairburn Avenue Elementary
School**
1403 Fairburn Avenue
(310) 470-1344

ORANGE COUNTY

Anaheim

Abraham Lincoln Elementary School
1413 East Broadway
(714) 517-9214

Benito Juarez Elementary School
841 South Sunkist Street
(714) 517-9206

Guinn Elementary School
1051 South Sunkist Street
(714) 517-8773

Jefferson Elementary School
504 East South Street
(714) 517-8716

Sunkist Elementary School
500 North Sunkist Street
(714) 517-8744

Theodore Roosevelt Elementary School
1600 East Vermont Avenue
(714) 517-8733

Thomas Edison Elementary School
1526 East Romneya Drive
(714) 517-8760

Thomas Jefferson Elementary School
890 South Olive Street
(714) 517-8777

Corona

Garretson Elementary School
1650 Garretson Avenue
(909) 736-3345

Jefferson Elementary School
1040 South Vicentia Avenue
(909) 736-3226

Parkridge Elementary School
750 Corona Avenue
(909) 736-3236

Vicentia Elementary School
2005 South Vicentia Avenue
(909) 736-3228

Costa Mesa

Adams Elementary School
2850 Clubhouse Road
(714) 424-7935

College Park Elementary School
2380 Notre Dame Road
(714) 424-7960

Davis Elementary School
1050 Arlington Drive
(714) 424-7930

Rea Elementary School
661 Hamilton Street
(949) 515-6905

Wilson Elementary School
801 West Wilson Street
(949) 515-6995

Fullerton

Acacia Elementary School
1200 North Acacia Avenue
(714) 447-7700

MOVING TIP

Before you move into a neighborhood, make sure that you and your kids can speak the language. In the schools of Los Angeles County, for example, about ninety different languages are spoken. There has also been an ongoing, statewide controversy about bilingual education versus "English immersion"—that is, teaching kids temporarily in their immigrant parents' native tongues versus teaching them in English only.

Golden Hill Elementary School
732 Barris Drive
(714) 447-7715

Laguna Road Elementary School
300 Laguna Road
(714) 447-7725

Raymond Elementary School
517 North Raymond Avenue
(714) 447-7740

Richman Elementary School
700 South Richman Avenue
(714) 447-7745

Garden Grove

A. G. Cook Elementary School
9802 Woodbury Avenue
(714) 663-6251

Brookhurst Elementary School
9821 Catherine Avenue
(714) 663-6556

Ethel M. Evans Elementary School
12281 Nelson Street
(714) 663-6558

Excelsior Elementary School
10421 Woodbury Road
(714) 663-6106

Louis G. Zeyen Elementary School
12081 Magnolia Street
(714) 663-6535

Stanford Elementary School
12721 Magnolia Street
(714) 663-6458

Sunnyside Elementary School
9972 Russell Avenue
(714) 663-6158

Huntington Beach

Golden View Elementary School
17251 Golden View Lane
(714) 847-2516

Hope View Elementary School
17622 Flintstone Lane
(714) 847-8571

Joseph R. Perry Elementary School
19231 Harding Lane
(714) 962-3347

Lake View Elementary School
17451 Zeider Lane
(714) 842-2589

Marine View Elementary School
5682 Tilburg Drive
(714) 846-0624

Oak View Elementary School
17241 Oak Lane
(714) 842-4459

Irvine

Culverdale Elementary School
2 Paseo Westpark
(949) 786-3008

Deerfield Elementary School
2 Deerfield Avenue
(949) 559-0100

Eastshore Elementary School
155 Eastshore
(949) 552-7228

El Camino Real Elementary School
4782 Karen Ann Lane
(949) 551-3090

Greentree Elementary School
4200 Manzanita
(949) 551-2301

Springbrook Elementary School
655 Springbrook North
(949) 552-6623

Stone Creek Elementary School
2 Stone Creek South
(949) 551-1201

Lake Forest

La Madera Elementary School
25350 Serrano Road
(949) 770-1415

Lake Forest Elementary School
21801 Pittsford
(949) 830-9945

Rancho Canada Elementary School
21801 Winding Way
(949) 768-5252

Santiago Elementary School
24982 Rivendell Drive
(949) 586-2820

Mission Viejo

De Portola Elementary School
27031 Preciados Drive
(949) 586-5830

Glen Yermo Elementary School
26400 Trabuco Road
(949) 586-6766

Montevido Elementary School
24071 Carrillo
(949) 586-8050

Reilly Elementary School
24171 Pavion
(949) 454-1590

Orange

California Elementary School
1080 North California Street
(714) 997-6104

Cambridge Elementary School
425 North Cambridge Street
(714) 997-6103

Handy Elementary School
860 North Handy Street
(714) 997-6183

Prospect Elementary School
379 North Virage Street
(714) 997-6271

Serrano Elementary School
17741 Serrano Avenue
(714) 997-6275

Taft Elementary School
1829 North Cambridge Street
(714) 997-6254

Villa Park Elementary School
10551 Center Drive
(714) 538-9710

Santa Ana

Edison Elementary School
2063 Orange Avenue
(714) 241-6491

Franklin Elementary School
210 West Cubbon Street
(714) 558-5684

Kennedy Elementary School
1300 East McFadden Avenue
(714) 558-5772

Lowell Elementary School
700 South Flower Street
(714) 558-5841

Madison Elementary School
1124 Hobart Street
(714) 558-5836

Martin Elementary School
939 West Wilshire Avenue
(714) 241-6503

Pio Pico Elementary School
931 Highland Street
(714) 543-3148

Tustin Memorial Elementary School
12712 Browning Avenue
(714) 730-7546

Walker Elementary School
811 East Bishop Street
(714) 547-9830

Tustin

Benson Elementary School
12712 Elizabeth Way
(714) 730-7531

Beswick Elementary School
1362 Mitchell Avenue
(714) 730-7385

Helen Estock Elementary School
14741 North B Street
(714) 730-7390

Lambert Elementary School
1151 San Juan Street
(714) 730-7457

MOVING TIP

Don't pack belongings in grocery store produce boxes, which are often host to spider eggs. You won't want to infest your new home when they hatch. Use boxes that contain canned, bottled, or dry goods. Liquor stores are a good source for boxes.

Marjorie Veeh Elementary School
1701 San Juan Street
(714) 730-7544

W. R. Nelson Elementary School
14392 Browning Avenue
(714) 730-7536

Junior High Schools

LOS ANGELES COUNTY

Burbank

David Starr Jordan Middle School
420 South Mariposa Street
(818) 558-4622

John Muir Middle School
1111 North Kenneth Road
(818) 558-5320

Luther Burbank Middle School
3700 West Jeffries Avenue
(818) 558-4646

Chino

Magnolia Junior High School
13150 Mountain Avenue
(909) 627-9263

Ramona Junior High School
4575 Walnut Avenue
(909) 627-9144

Glendale

Theodore Roosevelt Middle School
1017 South Glendale Avenue
(818) 242-6845

Eleanor J. Toll Middle School
700 Glenwood Road
(818) 244-8414

Woodrow Wilson Middle School
1221 Monterey Road
(818) 244-8145

Hollywood (City of Los Angeles)

Thomas S. King Middle School
4201 Fountain Avenue
(323) 664-1176

Lancaster

Challenger Middle School
41725 170th Street East
(661) 264-1790

New Vista Middle School
753 East Avenue K2
(661) 726-4271

Park View Intermediate School
808 West Avenue J
(661) 942-0496

Piute Intermediate School
425 East Avenue H11
(661) 942-9508

Long Beach

Benjamin Franklin Middle School
540 Cerritos Avenue
(562) 435-4952

Cecil B. De Mille Junior High School
7025 East Parkcrest Street
(562) 421-8424

Charles Evans Hughes Junior High School
3846 California Avenue
(562) 595-0831

Constellation Middle School
501 Pine Avenue
(562) 435-7181

Hamilton Middle School
1060 East 70th Street
(562) 602-0320

Hill Middle School
1100 Iroquois Avenue
(562) 598-7611

Hubert Howe Bancroft Junior High School
5301 East Centralia Street
(562) 425-7461

John Marshall Junior High School
5870 East Wardlow Road
(562) 429-7013

Rogers Middle School
365 Monrovia Avenue
(562) 434-7411

Stanford Middle School
5871 East Los Arcos Street
(562) 594-9793

Thomas Jefferson Junior High School
750 Euclid Avenue
(562) 438-9904

Washington Middle School
1450 Cedar Avenue
(562) 591-2434

William Logan Stephens Junior High School
1830 West Columbia Street
(562) 595-0841

Ontario

De Anza Middle School
1450 South Sultana Avenue
(909) 986-8577

Oaks Middle School
1221 South Oaks Avenue
(909) 988-2050

Vina Danks Middle School
1020 North Vine Avenue
(909) 983-2691

Wiltseyl Middle School
1450 East G Street
(909) 986-5838

Woodcrest Junior High School
2725 South Campus Avenue
(909) 923-3455

Palmdale

Juniper Intermediate School
39066 Palm Tree Way
(661) 947-0181

CITY FACT

According to *The Comparative Guide to U.S. Suburbs*, Corona has had the area's most permits for new housing, followed by Irvine, Temecula, Chino Hills, Fontana, and Murrieta. Areas with the fewest new homes include Cerritos, Cudahy, Maywood, South El Monte, South Gate, and Stanton.

Mesa Intermediate School
3243 East Avenue R8
(661) 947-0188

Shadow Hills Intermediate School
37315 60th Street East
(661) 533-8001

Pasadena

Washington Middle School
1505 North Marengo Avenue
(626) 798-6708

Woodrow Wilson Middle School
300 South Madre Street
(626) 449-7390

Pomona

Emerson Junior High School
635 Lincoln Avenue
(909) 397-4516

Fremont Junior High School
725 West Franklin Avenue
(909) 397-4521

John Marshall Junior High School
1921 Arroyo Avenue
(909) 397-4532

Palomares Middle School
2211 North Orange Grove Avenue
(909) 397-4539

Simons Junior High School
900 East Franklin Avenue
(909) 397-4544

Santa Monica

John Adams Middle School
2425 16th Street
(310) 452-2326

Lincoln Middle School
1501 California Avenue
(310) 393-9227

New Roads Middle School
1238 Lincoln Boulevard
(310) 587-2255

Torrance

Calle Mayor Middle School
4800 Calle Mayor
(310) 533-4548

Casimir Middle School
17220 Casimir Avenue
(310) 533-4498

Hull Middle School
2080 West 231st Street
(310) 533-4516

Jefferson Middle School
21717 Talisman Avenue
(310) 533-4794

Lynn Middle School
5038 Halison Street
(310) 533-4495

Madrona Middle School
21364 Madrona Avenue
(310) 533-4562

Magruder Middle School
4100 West 185th Street
(310) 533-4527

Richardson Middle School
23751 Nancylee Lane
(310) 533-4790

Van Nuys (City of Los Angeles)

Mulholland Middle School
17120 Vanowen Street
(818) 345-5446

Robert Fulton Middle School
7477 Kester Avenue
(818) 785-8624

Van Nuys Middle School
5435 Vesper Avenue
(818) 785-5475

Westlake (City of Los Angeles)

Berendo Middle School
1157 South Berendo Street
(213) 382-1343

Westwood (City of Los Angeles)

Emerson Middle School
1650 Selby Avenue
(310) 475-8417

Paul Revere Middle School
1450 Allenford Avenue
(310) 451-5789

ORANGE COUNTY

Anaheim

Ball Junior High School
1500 West Ball Road
(714) 999-3663

Brookhurst Junior High School
601 North Brookhurst Street
(714) 999-3613

Crescent Intermediate School
5001 East Gerda Drive
(714) 997-6371

Dale Junior High School
900 South Dale Avenue
(714) 220-4210

El Rancho Middle School
181 South Del Giorgio Drive
(714) 281-8791; (714) 997-6238
www.orangeusd.k12.ca.us/
rancho

Mable Street Junior High School
1557 West Mable Street
(714) 563-4088

South Junior High School
2320 East South Street
(714) 999-3667

Sycamore Junior High School
1801 East Sycamore Street
(714) 999-3617

Corona

Raney Intermediate School
1010 West Citron Street
(909) 736-3221

Fullerton

Ladera Vista Junior High School
1700 East Wilshire Avenue
(714) 447-7765

Nicolas Junior High School
1100 Olive Avenue
(714) 447-7775

Parks Junior High School
1710 Rosecrans
(714) 447-7785

Garden Grove

Alamitos Intermediate School
13281 Dale Street
(714) 663-6101

Hilton D. Bell Intermediate School
12345 Springdale Street
(714) 663-6466

James Irvine Intermediate School
10552 Hazard Avenue
(714) 663-6551

Jordan Intermediate School
9821 Woodbury Avenue
(714) 663-6124

Leroy L. Doig Intermediate School
12752 Trask Avenue
(714) 663-6241

Walter C. Ralston Intermediate School
10851 Lampson Avenue
(714) 663-6366

Walton Intermediate School
12181 Buaro Street
(714) 663-6040

Huntington Beach

Ethel Dwyer Middle School
1502 Palm Avenue
(714) 536-7507

Isaac L. Sowers Middle School
9300 Indianapolis Avenue
(714) 962-7738

Mesa View Middle School
17601 Avilla Lane
(714) 842-6608

Spring View Middle School
16662 Trudy Lane
(714) 846-2891

Stacey Intermediate School
6311 Larchwood Drive
(714) 894-7212

Orange

Cerro Villa Junior High School
17852 Serrano Avenue
(714) 997-6251

Emerson High School
4100 East Walnut Avenue
(714) 633-4776

Portola Middle School
270 North Palm Drive
(714) 997-6361
www.orangeusd.k12.ca.us/portola

Santiago Middle School
515 North Rancho Santiago Boulevard
(714) 997-6366
www.orangeusd.k12.ca.us/santiago

Yorba Middle School
935 North Cambridge Street
(714) 997-6161
www.orangeusd.k12.ca.us/yorba

Costa Mesa

Te Winkle Intermediate School
3224 California Street
(714) 424-7965

Irvine

Lakeside Middle School
3 Lemongrass
(949) 559-1601

Rancho San Joaquin Middle School
4861 Michelson Drive
(949) 786-3005

Sierra Vista Middle School
2 Liberty
(949) 797-6601

South Lake Middle School
655 West Yale Loop
(949) 726-8600

Venado Deerfield Middle School
4 Deerfield Avenue
(949) 552-4771

Lake Forest

Serrano Intermediate School
24642 Jeronimo Road
(949) 586-3221

Santa Ana

Carr Intermediate School
2120 West Edinger Avenue
(714) 241-6430

Fitz Intermediate School
4600 West McFadden Avenue
(714) 663-6351

Hewes Middle School
13232 Hewes Avenue
(714) 730-7348

Lathrop Intermediate School
1111 South Broadway
(714) 542-2097

MacArthur Intermediate School
600 West Alton Avenue
(714) 513-9800

McFadden Intermediate School
2701 South Raitt Street
(714) 435-3710

Sierra Intermediate School
1901 North McClay Street
(714) 835-9581

Spurgeon Intermediate School
2701 West 5th Street
(714) 480-2200

Willard Intermediate School
1342 North Ross Street
(714) 480-4800

Tustin

A. G. Currie Middle School
1402 Sycamore Avenue
(714) 730-7360

C. E. Utt Middle School
13601 Browning Avenue
(714) 730-7573

Columbus Tustin Middle School
17952 Beneta Way
(714) 730-7352

Mission Viejo

La Paz Intermediate School
25151 Pradera Drive
(949) 830-1720

Los Alisos Intermediate School
25171 Moor Avenue
(949) 830-9700

MOVING TIP

Confirm that your subscriptions, credit/ charge card statements, and outstanding bills will be forwarded to your new address. You'll miss your favorite magazines and might inadvertently harm your credit rating if you overlook this detail.

High Schools

LOS ANGELES COUNTY

Lancaster

Antelope Valley High School
44900 Division Street
(661) 948-8552

Desert Winds High School
45030 3rd Street East
(661) 948-7555

Palmdale

Highland High School
39055 25th Street West
(661) 538-0304

Palmdale High School
2137 East Avenue R
(661) 273-3181

Burbank

Bellarmine-Jefferson High School
465 East Olive Avenue
(818) 972-1400

Burbank High School
902 North 3rd Street
(818) 558-4700

John Burroughs High School
1920 Clark Avenue
(818) 558-4777

Monterey High School
1915 West Monterey Avenue
(818) 558-5455

Providence High School
511 South Buena Vista Street
(818) 846-8141

Chino

Buena Vista High School
13509 Ramona Avenue
(909) 628-9903

Chino High School
5472 Park Place
(909) 627-7351

Don Antonio Lugo High School
13400 Pipeline Avenue
(909) 591-3902

Downtown/Central City (City of Los Angeles)

Cathedral High School
1253 Bishop Road
(323) 225-2438

Metropolitan High School
727 Wilson Street
(213) 623-4272

Glendale

Allan F. Daily High School
220 North Kenwood Street
(818) 247-4805

Glendale Senior High School
1440 East Broadway
(818) 242-3161

Herbert Hoover Senior High School
651 Glenwood Road
(818) 242-6801

Hollywood (City of Los Angeles)

Fairfax Senior High School
7850 Melrose Avenue
(323) 651-5200

Hollywood High School
1521 North Highland Avenue
(323) 467-6191

John Marshall High School
3939 Tracy Street
(323) 660-1440

Long Beach

David Starr Jordan Senior High School
6500 Atlantic Avenue
(562) 423-1471

Polytechnic Senior High School
1600 Atlantic Avenue
(562) 591-0581

Reid High School
235 East 8th Street
(562) 997-8000

Robert A. Millikan High School
2800 Snowden Avenue
(562) 425-7441

Wilson High School
4400 East 10th Street
(562) 433-0481

Ontario

Chaffey High School
1245 North Euclid Avenue
(909) 988-5560

Italo M. Bernt High School
2230 East 4th Street
(909) 988-7451

Ontario High School
901 West Francis Street
(909) 988-7411

Valley View High School
1801 East 6th Street
(909) 985-0966

Pasadena

Blair High School
1201 South Marengo Avenue
(626) 441-2201

John Muir High School
1905 North Lincoln Avenue
(626) 798-7881

Pasadena High School
2925 East Sierra Madre Boulevard
(626) 798-8901

Rose City High School
325 South Oak Knoll Avenue
(626) 795-9541

Pomona

Ganesha Senior High School
1151 Fairplex Drive
(909) 397-4406

Santa Monica

Concord High School
1831 Wilshire Boulevard
(310) 828-9443

New Roads High School
1900 Pico Boulevard
(310) 396-6249

Olympic High School
721 Ocean Park Boulevard
(310) 392-2494

MOVING TIP

Talk to your veterinarian about your pet's special needs well in advance of Moving Day. Most moving companies will not assume responsibility for pets or plants. Your pet may require a portable kennel or even sedatives.

Santa Monica High School
601 Pico Boulevard
(310) 395-3204

Torrance

North High School
3620 West 182nd Street
(310) 533-4412

Shery High School
2600 Vine Avenue
(310) 533-4440

South High School
4801 Pacific Coast Highway
(310) 533-4352

Torrance High School
2200 West Carson Street
(310) 533-4395

West High School
20401 Victor Street
(310) 533-4299

Van Nuys
(City of Los Angeles)

Birmingham Senior High School
17000 Haynes Street
(818) 881-1580

Independence High School
6501 Balboa Boulevard
(818) 881-7737

Ulysses S. Grant Senior High School
13000 Oxnard Street
(818) 781-1400

Van Nuys High School
6535 Cedros Avenue
(818) 785-5427

Venice
(City of Los Angeles)

Del Rey Senior High School
8801 Park Hill Drive
(310) 641-3858

Venice High School
13000 Venice Boulevard
(310) 306-7981

Westlake
(City of Los Angeles)

Belmont High School
1575 West 2nd Street
(213) 250-0244

Harold McAllister High School
2808 Glassell Street
(213) 381-2823

Harris Newmark High School
134 Witmer Street
(213) 250-9675

Loyola High School
1901 Venice Boulevard
(213) 381-5121

Riley High School
1139 West 6th Street
(213) 625-6748

Westwood
(City of Los Angeles)

Brentwood School
100 South Barrington Place
(310) 476-9633

ORANGE COUNTY

Anaheim

Anaheim High School
811 West Lincoln Avenue
(714) 999-3717

Canyon High School
220 South Imperial Highway
(714) 532-8000
www.orangeusd.k12.ca.us/
canyon

Esperanza High School
1830 North Kellogg Drive
(714) 779-7870

Fairmont High School
2200 West Sequoia Avenue
(714) 999-5055

Gilbert High School
501 North Crescent Way
(714) 999-3605

Horizon High School
1720 West Glenoaks Avenue
(714) 956-9411

Katella High School
2200 East Wagner Avenue
(714) 999-3621

Loara High School
1765 West Cerritos Avenue
(714) 999-3677

Magnolia High School
2450 West Ball Road
(714) 220-4221

Polaris High School
830 South Dale Avenue
(714) 220-4004

Savanna High School
301 North Gilbert Street
(714) 220-4262

Servite High School
1952 West La Palma Avenue
(714) 774-7575

Corona

Buena Vista High School
300 South Buena Vista Avenue
(909) 736-3367

Centennial High School
1820 Rimpau Avenue
(909) 736-6523

Corona High School
1150 West 10th Street
(909) 736-3211

Horizon High School
13031 Orange Street
(909) 736-3339

Rio Rancho High School
8120 Grapewin Street, #A
(909) 272-9774

Santiago High School
3211 South Main Street
(909) 736-4600

Costa Mesa

Costa Mesa High School
2650 Fairview Road
(714) 424-8700

Estancia High School
2323 Placentia Avenue
(949) 515-6500

Fullerton

Fullerton High School
201 East Chapman Avenue
(714) 870-3720

Horizon High School
698 East Commonwealth Avenue
(714) 447-1880

La Fierra High School
201 West Amerige Avenue
(714) 446-7602

La Vista High School
*909 North State College
Boulevard*
(714) 870-6551

Rosary High School
1340 North Acacia Avenue
(714) 879-6302

Sunny Hills High School
1801 Warburton Way
(714) 870-3406

Troy High School
2200 Dorothy Lane
(714) 870-3604

Garden Grove

Bolsa Grande High School
9401 Westminster Avenue
(714) 663-6246

Garden Grove High School
11271 Stanford Avenue
(714) 663-6115

Pacifica High School
6851 Lampson Avenue
(714) 663-6515

Rancho Alamitos High School
11351 Dale Street
(714) 663-6415

Santiago High School
12342 Trask Avenue
(714) 663-6215

Huntington Beach

Coast High School
16666 Tunstall Lane
(714) 847-2873

Marina High School
15871 Springdale Street
(714) 893-6571

Ocean View High School
17071 Gothard Street
(714) 848-0656

Irvine

Irvine High School
4321 Walnut Avenue
(949) 552-4211

San Joaquin High School
311 West Yale Loop
(949) 857-2682

University High School
4771 Campus Drive
(949) 854-7500

Woodbridge High School
2 Meadowbrook
(949) 786-1104

Lake Forest

El Toro High School
25255 Toledo Way
(949) 586-6333

Mission Viejo

Capistrano Valley High School
26301 Via Escolar
(949) 364-6100

Mira Monte High School
25632 Diseno Drive
(949) 830-8857

Silverado High School
25632 Diseno Drive
(949) 586-8800

Trabuco Hills High School
27501 Cordova Road
(949) 768-1934

Orange

El Modena High School
3920 East Spring Street
(714) 997-6331

Emerson High School
4100 East Walnut Avenue
(714) 633-4776
www.orangeusd.k12.ca.us/emhs

Orange High School
525 North Shaffer Street
(714) 997-6211
www.orangeusd.k12.ca.us/ohs

Richland High School
615 North Lemon Street
(714) 997-6167

Villa Park High School
18042 Taft Avenue
(714) 532-8020

Santa Ana

Century High School
1401 South Grand Avenue
(714) 568-7000

Foothill High School
19251 Dodge Avenue
(714) 730-7464

Hillview High School
19061 Foothill Boulevard
(714) 730-7356

Horizon High School
515 West 17th Street
(714) 558-8287

Mountain View High School
3002 West Centennial Road
(714) 241-6470

Saddleback High School
2802 South Flower Street
(714) 513-2900

Santa Ana High School
520 West Walnut Street
(714) 567-4900

Santa Ana Valley High School
1801 South Greenville Street
(714) 241-6410

Tustin

Sycamore High School
13780 Orange Street
(714) 730-7395; (714) 999-3617

Tustin High School
1171 El Camino Real
(714) 730-7414

Colleges and Universities

LOS ANGELES COUNTY

Community Colleges

Antelope Valley College
3041 West Avenue K
Lancaster, CA 93536
(661) 943-3241
Tuition: $390/year

Compton Community College
1111 East Artesia Boulevard
Compton, CA 90221
(213) 637-2660
Tuition: $390/year

East Los Angeles College
1301 Avenida Cesar Chavez
Monterey Park, CA 91754-6099
(323) 265-8650
Tuition: $327/year

El Camino Community College
16007 Crenshaw Boulevard
Torrance, CA 90506
(310) 532-3670
Tuition: $205/year

Long Beach City College
4901 East Carson Street
Long Beach, CA 90808
(310) 420-4111
Tuition: $410/year

Los Angeles City College
855 North Vermont Avenue
Los Angeles, CA 90029
(213) 953-4000
Tuition: $300/year

Los Angeles Pierce College
6201 Winnetka Avenue
Woodland Hills, CA 91371
(818) 347-0551
Tuition: $300/year

Los Angeles Valley College
5800 Fulton Avenue
Van Nuys, CA 91401
(818) 781-1200
Tuition: $300/year

Los Angeles Trade-Technical College
400 West Washington Boulevard
Los Angeles, CA 90015
(213) 744-9058
Tuition: $390/year

Pasadena City College
1570 East Colorado Boulevard
Pasadena, CA 91106
(818) 585-7123
Tuition: $312/year

Four-Year Universities

California Institute of Technology
1201 East California Boulevard
Pasadena, CA 91125
(818) 395-6811
Tuition: $15,900/year

California State Polytechnic University Pomona
3801 West Temple Avenue
Pomona, CA 91768
(909) 869-5659
Tuition: $1,384/year

California State University Dominguez Hills
1000 East Victoria Street
Carson, CA 90747
(310) 516-3300
Tuition: $1,611/year

California State University Long Beach
1250 Bellflower Boulevard
Long Beach, CA 90840
(310) 985-4111
Tuition: $1,567/year

California State University Los Angeles
5151 State University Drive
Los Angeles, CA 90032
(213) 343-3000
Tuition: $1,433/year

California State University Northridge
18111 Nordhoff Street
Northridge, CA 91330
(818) 885-1200
Tuition: $1,546/year

University of California Los Angeles
405 Hilgard Avenue
Los Angeles, CA 90024
(310) 825-4321
Tuition: $3,549/year

University of Southern California
University Park
Los Angeles, CA 90089
(213) 740-2311
Tuition: $16,810/year

Specialty Schools

Art Center College of Design
1700 Lida Street
Pasadena, CA 91103
(818) 584-5000
Tuition: $13,205/year

DeVry Institute of Technology
901 Corporate Center Drive
University Center
Pomona, CA 91768-2642
(909) 622-8866
Tuition: $5,609/year

Emperor's College of Traditional Oriental Medicine

1807-B Wilshire Boulevard
Santa Monica, CA 90403
(310) 453-8300

Tuition: $7,000/year

Fashion Institute of Design and Merchandising

Los Angeles Campus
919 South Grand Avenue
Los Angeles, CA 90015
(213) 624-1200

Tuition: $10,350/year

Fuller Theological Seminary

135 North Oakland
Pasadena, CA 91182
(818) 584-5200

Tuition: $8,000/year

Los Angeles College of Chiropractic

16200 Amber Valley Drive, B1166
Whittier, CA 90604
(310) 947-8755

Tuition: $13,114/year

CITY FACT

The area's lowest unemployment rates, says *The Comparative Guide to U.S. Suburbs,* are in Yorba Linda, Laguna Niguel, Mission Viejo, Seal Beach, Newport Beach, and Rancho Palos Verdes. The highest rates are in Compton, Bell Gardens, Huntington Park, Lynwood, Bell, and Maywood.

ORANGE COUNTY

Community Colleges

Fullerton College

321 East Chapman Avenue
Fullerton, CA 92632
(714) 992-7000

Tuition: $312/year

Golden West College

15744 Golden West
Huntington Beach, CA 92647
(714) 892-7711

Tuition: $312/year

MOVING TIP

If you are intending to transfer to another college, university, or graduate school, you must send your old school written permission to release your sealed transcript to the new registrar.

Four-Year Universities

California State University Fullerton

800 North State College Boulevard
Fullerton, CA 92634
(714) 773-2011
Tuition: $1,820/year

University of California Irvine

Campus Drive
Irvine, CA 92717
(714) 856-5011
Tuition: $3,705/year

Orange Coast College

2701 Fairview Road
Costa Mesa, CA 92628
(714) 432-0202
Tuition: $264/year

Saddleback College

28000 Maguerite Parkway
Mission Viejo, CA 92692
(714) 582-4500
Tuition: $312/year

Santa Ana College

1530 West 17th Street
Santa Ana, CA 92706-9979
(714) 564-6000
Tuition: $327/year

Specialty Schools

Art Institute of Southern California

2222 Laguna Canyon Road
Laguna Beach, CA 92651
(714) 497-3309
Tuition: $8,850/year

Western State University College of Law of Orange County

State College Boulevard and Dorothy Lane
Fullerton, CA 92631
(714) 738-1000
Tuition: $12,159/year

Finding a Job

CHAPTER 11

Working in the City

Southern California has always been known for its boomtown economy. Plenty of people have arrived here and become quick millionaires, and plenty of people have arrived and gone broke—sometimes the same people.

But no place survives for as long as Southern California on boomtown industries alone. Measured by numbers of employees, the 2000 State Profile by Woods & Poole Economics declares that the largest sector of the economy is, by far, services—about 2 million employees in Los Angeles County (out of a total of 5.5 million) and about 600,000 in Orange County (out of 1.8 million). That's a lot of waiters and cashiers.

Beyond the service sector, the two regions differ. The second biggest sector in L.A. County is manufacturing (675,000 workers), but Orange County's runner-up is retail trade (284,000). The smallest sector in L.A. County is farming (6,000 workers), while Orange County's smallest is mining (2,500).

Though Orange County offers fewer jobs than L.A. County, it also has a lower unemployment rate. In fact, Orange County has in recent years been better off at its worst than L.A. County at its best. Since 1996, unemployment in Orange County has fluctuated between 2.5 percent and 4.1 percent of the workforce, while L.A. County peaked at 8.2 percent and fell to only 5.4 percent.

Even in Orange County, though, money doesn't stretch far enough. The Economic Research Institute's Geographic Reference Report 2000 notes that in both counties, the cost of living outstrips wages and salaries. The gap is particularly wide in the city of Los Angeles, where wages are high—about 11 percent above the national average—but the cost of living is higher (28 percent to 36 percent higher than the national rate). Anaheim, on the other hand, has wages comparable to L.A. but a more bearable cost of living (17 percent to 20 percent higher than the national rate).

For the future, the State of California's Employment Development Department expects Los Angeles County to offer job growth in the garment industry, while Orange County will see growth in transportation (especially flight attendants and reservation and ticket agents). Both counties will offer plenty of jobs for retail salespeople, cashiers, and waiters and waitresses. If you're interested in life at higher echelons, the state predicts a boom in openings for general managers and top executives.

Job Hunting

If you're going to hunt for a job in L.A., you need to remember the basic principles of job hunting and the basic principles of living here.

Every job-hunting expert recommends networking: getting in touch with people who work in your chosen field, asking them to refer you to employers, and meeting face to face with employers whether they have openings at the moment or not. (If they don't have an opening now, they may have one soon, and you want them to know you when they do.) Networking is as important in Southern California as it is anywhere else, but the region's lengthy distances between areas make it hard to bump into someone who can help you.

So join a group. Your chosen field almost certainly has a professional organization with a chapter or branch in Southern California. Attend the meetings, participate in the activities, make friends with the other members, and build connections.

Also: Pay attention to entrepreneurs. Remember that one of the region's biggest areas for job growth is in general managers and top executives. A company can have only a very few executives of that rank, so the high number of jobs for those executives suggests a high number of companies, rather than a few huge monoliths like Exxon or AT&T. "Since 1970, firms with 100 employees or fewer have created two out of every three jobs," writes employment expert Marc Dorio in his book *The Complete Idiot's Guide to Getting the Job You Want*. "The easiest way to contact a person with the power to hire you is to call a company with fewer than fifty employees and ask for the name of the boss." These principles hold very true in Southern California. The movie business, for example, is filled with relatively small companies founded by former employees of big companies.

When you get the chance to apply for a job, consider the commute you'll have. On a map, Glendale isn't far from downtown Los Angeles. But a trip from Glendale Community College to a job interview at Los Angeles City Hall may mean taking the Glendale Freeway to the Golden State Freeway to the Pasadena Freeway to the Hollywood Freeway—any or all of which can be jammed—plus a bewildering slew of surface streets. And that's the easy way: by car. Public transit can be even tougher. So give yourself plenty of time to get wherever you need to go, and always ask for directions.

Finally, remember: Southern California is, more than many other places, a land of newcomers and immigrants. Even the natives can feel like immigrants: Someone who grew up in northwest Los Angeles County's Canyon Country can seem pretty rough-and-tumble—and feel very out of place—in the ritzy world of Orange County's Newport Beach. Lots of people in a position to hire you are as new to the area as you are.

After all, Southern Cal's oldest surviving tradition is that of coming here from somewhere else.

Job Resources

Wherever you land, there will be work. And thanks to the Internet, anyone in the world can find out about jobs in Southern California. Plenty of Web sites list job fairs, classified ads, employment agencies, and other organizations devoted to helping people build careers.

Good luck.

About.com

www.about.com

Acadame This Week

chronicle.merit.edu/.ads/
.links.html

**Academic Employment
Network**

www.academploy.com

**Academic Physician &
Scientist**

www.acphysic.com/aps.htm

Access Staffing Home Page

520 El Camino Real, Suite 624
San Mateo, CA 94402
(650) 227-9000

www.accstaff.com/index.html

Accountants Northwest

jobsearch.about.com/business/
jobsearch/msubtemp.htm?iam=
ask

Accountants West

1641 North First Street,
Suite #240
San Jose, CA 95118
(408) 452-0390
(408) 452-8397 (fax)

Accounting.com

www.accounting.com/

Accountingjobs.com

www.accountingjobs.com/

Account Temps

(800) 803-8367

www.accountemps.com/jobsat/
profile_search.html

Adquest3d

Poweradz.Com L.L.C.
96 Thompson Hill Road
Rensselaer, NY 12144
(800) 373-3547

www.adquest3d.com/search/
search.asp?brd=1&pag=87

Allied Health Opportunities

www.gvpub.com

Altavista Careers

www.careeraltavista.com

**American Association Of
Finance & Accounting**

www.aafa.com/

American Banker Careerzone

www.americanbanker.com/

**American Medical
Association**

www.ama-assn.org

**American Physical Therapy
Association**

www.apta.edoc.com

American Preferred Jobs
www.preferredjobs.com/altsearch/jobseekers_resources.asp

American Society for Mechanical Engineers
www.asme.org/jobs

America's Employers
www.americaemployers.com/

America's Employers Resume Book
www.americasemployers.com/resume.html

America's Healthcare Source
www.healthcaresource.com

America's Job Bank
www.ajb.dni.us/

America's Online Help-Wanted
www2.ohw.com/

Aquent Partners—Los Angeles
6100 Wilshire Boulevard, Suite 410
Los Angeles, CA 90048
(877) PARTNER
(323) 634-7696 (fax)
www.aquent.com/

Association of Online Professionals
www.aop.com/

Best Bets from the Net
www.lib.umich.edu/chdocs/employment

Bilingual Jobs
www.bilingual-jobs.com/

Boldface Jobs
www.boldfacejobs.com/help.htm

California Federation of Legal Secretaries
2250 East 73rd Street,
Suite 550
Tulsa, OK 7416
(918) 493-3540

California Jobs
www.abag.ca.gov/buyarea/commerce/globe/globe.htm

Caljobs
www.caljobs.ca.gov/

Careerbabe
www.careerbabe.com/

Careerbuilder
www.careerbuilder.com

Careercast, Inc.
5963 La Place Court,
Suite 309
Carlsbad, CA 92008
(760) 602-9502

www.careercast.com/

Career City
www.careercity.com

Careerexchange
www.careerexchange.com/

Career Lab
www.careerlab.com/

Career Links
www.careers.org

Careermagazine
www.careermag.com/
employers/index.html

Careermosaic
(888) 339-8989

www.careermosaic.com/
cm/home.html

Careernet.com
(305) 665-8219

www.careernet.com/

Career Paradise
www.service.emory.edu/career/
main/links.html

Careerpath
webmaster@careerpath.com

www.careerpath.com/

Careerscape.com
(800) 992-0313;
(978) 531-6722

www.careerscape.com/
about.html

Careershop.com
www.careershop.com

Careers in Business
www.careers-in-business.com/

Careerspan.com
www.careerspan.com/

Careertips
www.careertips.com/

Career USA
6400 Congress Avenue,
Suite 1050
Boca Raton, Florida 33487
(561) 995-7000;
(888) CAREERS
(561) 995-7001 (fax)

cusabhq@flinet.com

www.careersusa.com/

Careerweb
info@cweb.com

www.careerweb.com

Careerworld.com/

www.resunet.com/cgi-bin/
gate2?resunet|/cw/search.html

Check Your References

www.myreferences.com/

Chronicle of Higher Education

www.chronicle.com

Classifieds2000.com

www.classifieds2000.com

Collegehire.com
6034 West Courtyard Drive
Austin, TX 78730
(512) 685-3901
www.collegehire.com

Community Career Center

www.nonprofitjobs.org

Companies Online

www.companiesonline.com/

The Computer Jobs Store

www.computerjobs.com

Computer Professionals

www.A1acomputerpros.net

Computerworld's Online IT Careers

www.computerworld.com

Contract Employment Connection

www.ntes.com/

Contract Executives

www.imcor.com/

Conyea Online Career Center

www.aol.com/career

Cool Works

www.coolworks.com/

Corptech
12 Alfred Street, Suite 200
Woburn, MA 01801

www.corptech.com/
researchareas/researchareas.cfm

CTS International
11100 NE 8th Street,
Suite 510
Bellevue, WA 98004-4441
www.ctsinternational.com/

Dice Hi-Tech Jobs Online

www.dice.com

Direct Hire
(949) 653-2638
direct-hire.com/
direct_hires_content_page.html

Diversity

www.eop.com/

Diversitylink

www.diversitylink.com/

The Education Jobsite

www.edjobsite.com/

Educators Network

www.school-jobs.com/

CITY FACT

Anaheim contains more than 18,000 hotel rooms—nearly half of them within walking distance of Disneyland.

Elaine & Associates, INC

2029 Century Park East,
Suite 1080
Los Angeles, CA 90067
(310) 785-0560

Electronic Engineering Times

www.eet.com

E-Math

www.ams.org/employment

Employersonline.com

(877) 543-2031

admin@employersonline.com

www.employersonline.com/

Employmax.com

c/o Searchforce, Inc.
2907 West Bay Drive
Belleair Bluffs, FL 33770
(727) 588-4400

employmax.com/

Employment Spot

www.employmentspot.com

Engineering Jobs

www.engineeringjbos.com

E-Span

www.espan.com

Executive Jobs

www.jobreports.net

Exec.U.Net

www.execunet.com/

Federal Jobs

U.S. Department of Commerce
Springfield, VA 22161
(703) 605-6000

www.fedworld.gov/jobs/
jobsearch.html

Federal Jobs Central
370 Maple Avenue West, Suite 5
P.O. Box 1059
Vienna VA 22183-1059

www.fedjobs.com/

Fedworld
webmaster@fedworld.gov
www.fedworld.gov

Fedworld Federal Job Announcements
www.fedworld.gov

Geoweb Interactive
www.ggrweb.com

Getting a Job
lwww.americanexpress.com/
student

Go.com
Infoseek Corporation
1399 Moffett Park Drive
Sunnyvale, CA 94089-1134

www.go.com/center/
careers?svx=gopher_careers

Good Works
www.essential.org/goodworks/

Go Jobs
www.gojobs.com/

Govworks
81 Franklin Street
New York, NY 10013
(800) 597-0549

www.jobsingovernment.com/

Great Summer Jobs
www.gsj.petersons.com/

Headhunter.Net
www.headhunter.com

Healthcare Careerweb
www.healthcarecareerweb.com

Healthcare Jobs Online
www.hcjobsonline.com

Healthcare Recruitment Online
www.healthcarerecruitment.com

Health Opps
www.healthopps.com

Help Wanted USA
www.iccweb.com/

Hiring Network
www.817jobs.com/

Hospital Web
www.neuro-www.mgh.
harvard.edu/hospitalweb.shtml

Hotjobs.com

hotjobs.about.com/cgi-bin/
job-search?template=/
htdocs/about-job-search.
html&keywords=job+technical

HR Advisors, Inc.

954 Katella Street
Laguna Beach, CA, 92651

www.hradvisors.com/
job_seekers.html

IEEE

www.ieee.com

Iminorities.Com, Inc.

140 Carondelet Street
New Orleans, LA 70130
(504) 523-0154

www.minorities-jb.com/

Incpad

4701 Patrick Henry Drive,
Suite 1901
Santa Clara, CA 95054
(408) 970-8800;
(888) 999-6505
(408) 970-4938 (fax)

www.vjf.com/emdirtxt.html

Industry Insite

www.industryinsite.com/

Inroads Inc.

www.inroadsinc.org

Interbiznet

www.interbiznet.com

International Jobs

www.internationaljobs.com/

Internet Career Center

www.iccnc.com/

Internet Job Source

www.statejobs.com/

The Internet Job Source

P.O. Box 45
Guilderland, NY 12084
(518) 869-9279

Internetsourcebook

www.internetsourcebook.com

Internet World

www.internet.com

Itinfo.Net

111 Mission Street
Santa Cruz, CA 95060
(831) 460-4300

info@itinfo.net
www.itinfo.net/

Jaegers' Interactive

www.jaegerinc.com/

Job & Career Site Links

www.usbol.com/wjmackey/
weblinks.html

Jobbank USA, Inc.
3232 Cobb Parkway, Suite 611
Atlanta, GA 30339
(404) 266-9330

www.jobbankusa.com/

The Job Center
(800) 562-2368

www.jobcenter.com

Jobcue
www.employeefind.com/

Jobdirect.com
www.jobdirect.com/

The Job Doctor
www.thejobdr.com

The Job Resource
www.thejobresource.com/

Job Resources by U.S. Region
www.wm.edu/carv/career/
stualum/region.html

Jobsamerica
www.jobsamerica.com/

Jobs & Career Links
www.gordonworks.com

Jobs at USC
(800) 735-2922

www.usc.edu/dept/personnel/
employment/

Jobs-Career
ww2.itoday.com/jobs-careers/
career2.html

Jobs.com
www.jobs.com/

Jobs-Connect
oxfordnt@cyberusa.com

webusers.anet-stl.com/~cheng/
jobmenu.htm

Job Searching at About.com
jobsearch.about.com/business/
jobsearch/

Job Search Right Here
jobsearchtech.about.com/
business/jobsearchtech/library/
bljobsearch.htm

Jobs for Bankers
www.bankjobs.com

Jobs for IT
info@jobs4it.com
or info@corecompsys.com

www.jobs4it.com/

Jobs.Internet.com
501 Fifth Avenue,
3rd Floor
New York, NY 10017
(212) 547-7900
(212) 953-1733 (fax)

jobs.internet.com/

Jobsmart

jobsmart.org/socal/index.htm

Jobs Online

954 West Washington Street,
Suite 7W
Chicago, IL 60607
(312) 432-1665

www.jobs-online.net/

Jobtrak

(800) 999-8725

static.jobtrak.com/careerfair/
index.html

Jobwarehouse

28 West Central Boulevard, Suite
210
Orlando, FL 32801-2466

www.jobwarehouse.com/
jobwarehouse/seeker.html

Jobweb

webmaster@jobweb.org
www.jobweb.org

Kelly Services

www.kellyservices.com/

Los Angeles County Job
Listings

www.co.la.ca.us/

Los Angeles Times

www.latimes.com/class/employ/
search.htm

Manpower

www.manpower.com/

Med Search America

www.medsearch.com/

Minorities Job Bank

www.minoritiesjobbank.com/

Monster.com

www.monster.com/

National Diversity Newspaper
Job Bank

www.newsjobs.com/splash.html

Nationjob

www.nationjob.com/

Nation Job Network

601 SW 9th Street, Suites J&K
Des Moines, IA 50309
(800) 292-7731

www.nationjob.com/

Nerd World

www.nerdworld.com/

Netshare

www.netshare.com/

Net-Temps

www.net-temps.com/

Top Echelon
Top Echelon Network, Inc.
P.O. Box 21390
Canton, OH 44701
(330) 455-1433
www.topechelon.com/

Non-Profit Jobs
www.philanthropy-journal.org

Norell
4751 Wilshire Boulevard,
Suite 301
Los Angeles, CA 90010
(323) 243-8566

Nursing Spectrum
www.nursingspectrum.com

Office-Team
www.officeteam.com/jobsot/
future/index.html

100 Careers in Cyberspace
www.globalvillager.com/
villager/scs.html

1-Jobs.com
(972) 221-8800
(972) 221-8700;
(800) 593-0101 (fax)
www.1-jobs.com/

Online Jobs
(954) 341-2291
www.online-jobs.com/

Online Sports Career Center
(800) 856-2638
www.onlinesports.com/pages/
careercenter.html

Orange County Register
www.ocregister.com/employ-
ment/

The Origin Group
124 North York Road
Elmhurst, IL 60126
(630) 782-0900
www.theorigingroup.com

CITY FACT

The October 1999 issue of *Entrepreneur* magazine named Orange County one of America's twenty-five best places for entrepreneurs to do business, and the third best place in the West. The magazine should know. One company based in Orange County—specifically, in Irvine—is *Entrepreneur* itself.

Outstanding Job Resources
www.job-hunt.org

Penton Publishing
www.penton.com/

Planet Resume
www.planetresume.com/
planetresume/pr_search_jobs.ht
ml

Powerjobs
www.powerjobs.com/

PR Newswire Job Bank
865 South Figueroa, Suite 2310
Los Angeles, CA 90017
(213) 626-5500; (800) 321-8169

Project Connect
www.careers.soemadison.
wisc.edu/projcon.htm

PTS Staffing
24102 Brookfield Circle
Lake Forest, CA 92630-3718
(949) 457-9035

www.ptsstaffing.com/

Recruiters Online Network
www.ipa.com/

Recruiting-Links.com
3354 Perimeter Hill Drive,
Suite 235
Nashville, TN 37211
(615) 843-2630; (800) 252-5665

www.recruiting-
links.com/job_search.asp

Relistaff
10351 Santa Monica Boulevard,
Suite 302
Los Angeles, CA 90025
(310) 201-2171

Resume Express
www.resumeexpress.com/

Resumenetwork
www.resumenetwork.com

Resumes on the Web
sdas@ifu.net

www.resweb.com/

Retail Jobs
www.retailjobnet.com/

The Riley Guide
www.dbm.com/jobguide

Robert Half International
(800) 474 4253

www.roberthalf.com/

Robsjobs
www.robsjobs.com/

Search.com
search.cnet.com/single/
0,7,0-150181,0200.html

Select Jobs
www.selectjobs.com

Shawn's Internet Resume Center
www.inpursuit.com/sirc

6figurejobs.com
6figurejobs.com/jobseekers/index.html

Snelling.com
www.snelling.com/cgi-bin/job-search.new.pl

Socratescareers
www.socratescareers.com/

Teacher Jobs
www.teacherjobs.com

Tech Specialists
1485 Response Road, Suite 200
Sacramento, CA 95815
(916) 648-9380
(916) 648-9325 (fax)
www.techspec.com/

Techjobbank
www.techjobbank.com/

Techjobs.com
techjobs.supersites.net/

Technet Staffing Service
www.technet-inc.com/
searchframe2.html

Telecommuting Jobs
www.tjobs.com/

Temping.com
255 Old New Brunswick Road,
Suite S220
Piscataway, NJ 08854
(732) 235-2600
www.temping.com/

Temp 24-7
www.temp24-7.com/live/issue/current/home_frames.html

Thomas Staffing
Corporate Service Center
P.O. Box 19578
Irvine, CA 92623
(949) 261-5400
www.thomas-staffing.com/ocjobs.htm

Topjobsusa
www.topjobsusa.com/

UCLA Resources
www.ucla.edu/home/jobs.html

Vault.com
(888) 562-VAULT
209.10.50.150/jobboard/
searchjobs.cfm

Wall Street Journal
www.localcareers.com/
enter.html

Webjobs USA
www.webjobsusa.com/

West Coast Recruiting
200 Pacific Coast Highway, #342
Huntington Beach, CA 92648
(714) 960-9673 (fax)
www.intimedesign.com/
westcoast/index.html

Work Now
www.worknow.com/

Www.Career.Com
www.career.com

Yahoo Resume Bank
www.yahoo.com/

**Yahoo! Internet Life:
Employment Resources**
www3.zdnet.yil/content/profit/
profess/empl1.html

Sources

Knock 'Em Dead 2000, by Martin Yate (Adams Media Corporation)

www.about.com/
www.ask.com/
www.excite.com/
www.infoseek.com/
www.webcrawler.com

INDEX

items for storage kept together
on truck, 333
keeping children away from
movers' work, 331
keeping household cleaners
handy for old and new
home, 388
keeping phone book from old
neighborhood, 355
knots for moving, practicing,
363
labeling boxes by room, 295
languages in schools, checking
for compatibility of, 121
liquor stores as good sources
of boxes, 369
loading children's TV, VCR,
and videos last for play
during move, 141
Local Talk information about
Orange County services,
80
measuring and recording
spaces in old and new
homes, 148, 163
money-saving, 141–143
movers regulated by California
Public Utilities
Commission, 117
packing nonessentials early,
150
pet needs for moving, 380
practicing parking rental
truck, 310
retirement community needs,
282
right turn on red as legal, 109
taking valuables by car, 231
tipping movers, 196
transcript transfers, 348
truck rental, 143

volunteers for self-move,
number of, 303
Moving to Los Angeles, 137–200
day of, events in, 183–200
organizing for, 145–146, 157
planning for, 139–182
quickly, 144–145
scheduling, 144–145
Museums
Los Angeles area, 208–212,
225–226, 239–240, 271–272
outside of Los Angeles,
281–285, 289, 293, 295
Musical organizations, Los
Angeles area, 216–217

N
"Necessary Box," 160
checklist for, 171–172
Neighborhood, exploring new,
192, 201–304
Neighborhoods in Los Angeles
descriptions of, 3–75
list of, 5–6
Networking for job sources,
392–393
New Home Safety Checklist,
173–174
Normalcy during and following
move, tips for maintaining,
191–192

O
Oceanside attractions, 290–291
Ontario, 6, 71
neighborhood statistical
profile of, 71–72
Opera companies, Los Angeles
area, 216–217
Orange, 6, 54
map of, 53

About

 monstermoving.com

Because moving affects almost *every aspect* of a person's life, Monstermoving.com is committed to improving the way people move. Focusing on an individual's needs, timing, and dreams, the site provides everything for the entire lifestyle transition and every stage of the move. Free service provider content, interactive products, and resources give consumers more control, saving them time and money, and reducing stress. Site features include cost-of-living comparisons, home and apartment searches, mortgage calculators and services, an interactive move-planning application, an address change service, relocation tax advice, and virtual city tours. Monstermoving.com is committed to remaining the most effective, comprehensive, and lifestyle-centric point of service for everyone involved in moving.

Monstermoving.com is part of the Interactive Division of TMP Worldwide (NASDAQ: "TMPW;" ASX: "TMP"). For information, visit *www.monstermoving.com* or call (800) 567-7952.

$10 Off an Avis Weekend Rental

Rent an Avis car for a minimum of two consecutive weekend days and you can save $10 off your rental.

For reservations and information, call your travel consultant or Avis toll free at: 1-800-831-8000.

- Rental must begin by December 31, 2001.
- Valid on an Intermediate through Full Size four-door car.
  - Valid at participating locations in the contiguous U.S.
  - Subject to complete Terms and Conditions on reverse side.
  - An advance reservation is required
  - Visit Avis Online at www.avis.com

Coupon # **MUWA014**

BEKINS Bekins is pleased to offer you the following extra value services and cost savings on your next out of state move.

You will receive:

- A minimum discount of 52% off a move between 5,000–7,999 lbs., or a minimum discount of 55% off a move 8,000 lbs. and over.
- Free First Day Service – Bekins will unpack up to 5 cartons of essential items that you will need upon arriving at your new home.
- The FAS-Hotline – Instant access to a powerful collection of relocation assistance services such as a preferred mortgage program, cost of living reports and much more.
- Firm Pick-Up and Delivery Dates on shipments greater than 5,000 lbs.

To find the participating agent nearest you, please use our agent locator at www.bekinsagent.com, or look in the yellow pages under the "movers" heading.

Terms & Conditions

You must have a minimum weight of 5,000 lbs. within the continental U.S. to qualify for the discounts. The rules and restrictions of all programs are described in and governed by HGB 400-M tariff and section 13 of the HGB 104-F tariff, or as amended or reissued.

Coupon must be presented at the time of the estimate, must accompany your moving documents, has no cash value, is void where prohibited, may not be combined with any other discount and is subject to service availability. Coupon sets forth minimum discount level; final discount offer may be affected by prevailing market conditions. Offer is valid at participating Bekins agents only and cannot be used if estimate has already been performed. Offer is not valid for local or intrastate moves. DOT52793. Shipment must be registered using corporate code number 31402.

Coupon valid on an Intermediate (Group C) through a Full Size four-door (Group E) car. Minimum two day weekend rental required. Coupon must be surrendered at time of rental; one per rental. May not be used in conjunction with any other coupon, promotion or offer. Coupon valid at participating Avis locations in the contiguous United States. Weekend rental period begins Thursday noon and car must be returned by Monday 11:59 p.m. or a higher rate may apply. Offer may not be available during holiday and other blackout periods. Offer may not be available on all rates at all times. **An advance reservation is required.** Cars subject to availability. Taxes, local government surcharges vehicle licensing fee no higher than $1.93/day in CA, $.35/day in FL, $.55/day in UT, $1.42/day in Montana, and $1.65/day in Texas, airport recoupment fee up to 15% and optional items, such as LDW ($19.99/day or less), additional driver fee and fuel service, are extra. Renter must meet Avis age, driver and credit requirements. Minimum age is 25, but may vary by location. Rental must begin by 12/31/01.

Rental Sales Agent Instructions

At checkout:
• In CPN, enter **MUWA014**
• Complete this information:

RA # _____

Rental location_____
* Attach to coupon tape.

✂

Bekins is pleased to offer you the following extra value services and cost savings on your next out of state move.

You will receive:

· A minimum discount of 52% off a move between 5,000–7,999 lbs., or a minimum discount of 55% off a move 8,000 lbs. and over.
· Free First Day Service – Bekins will unpack up to 5 cartons of essential items that you will need upon arriving at your new home.
· The FAS-Hotline – Instant access to a powerful collection of relocation assistance services such as a preferred mortgage program, cost of living reports and much more.
· Firm Pick-Up and Delivery Dates on shipments greater than 5,000 lbs.

To find the participating agent nearest you, please use our agent locator at www.bekins agent.com, or look in the yellow pages under the "movers" heading.

Terms & Conditions

You must have a minimum weight of 5,000 lbs. within the continental U.S. to qualify for the discounts. The rules and restrictions of all programs are described in and governed by HGB 400-M tariff and section 13 of the HGB 104-F tariff, or as amended or reissued.

Coupon must be presented at the time of the estimate, must accompany your moving documents, has no cash value, is void where prohibited, may not be combined with any other discount and is subject to service availability. Coupon sets forth minimum discount level; final discount offer may be affected by prevailing market conditions. Offer is valid at participating Bekins agents only and cannot be used if estimate has already been performed. Offer is not valid for local or intrastate moves. DOT52793. Shipment must be registered using corporate code number 31402.

Call 1-800-252-9141 to save more than $98

Yes! **Please start everyday L.A. Times home delivery at the special savings rate of $2.25 per week for a total savings of up to $98.28 for 52 weeks.** I understand I have to prepay 26 weeks of service to receive this special savings rate. (SP#1458, Sales Origin CPB)

❏ I've enclosed a check or money order for **$58.50** made payable to the **Los Angeles Times** as a prepayment.

❏ I'll prepay via the credit card checked here: ❏ AMEX ❏ VISA ❏ MasterCard ❏ Discover

Credit Card #: _/_/_/_/   _/_/_/_/   _/_/_/_/   _/_/_/_/   Exp. Date: _/_/ _/_/
                                                                         Month   Year

Signature

Name

Address   Unit

                                                        ( )
City   ZIP   Telephone

Mail to: Los Angeles Times, Consumer Marketing, #410, 202 West First Street, Los Angeles, CA 90012. Offer valid to new subscribers only in areas where subscribers are billed directly by the L.A. Times. May not be combined with any other offer. Orange County residents should call 1-800-252-9141 to receive their special savings rate. All weekly rates include applicable CA sales taxes.